Women's
studies
Ams

ALSO BY SUSAN GRIFFIN

Pornography and Silence: Culture's Revenge Against Nature

Rape: The Power of Consciousness

Woman and Nature: The Roaring Inside Her

Unremembered Country

Made from This Earth

Like the Iris of an Eye

Voices

A CHORUS OF STONES

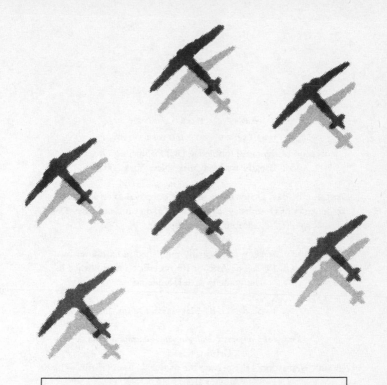

A CHORUS
OF STONES

THE PRIVATE LIFE OF WAR

SUSAN GRIFFIN

ANCHOR BOOKS
DOUBLEDAY
New York   London   Toronto   Sydney   Auckland

An Anchor Book

PUBLISHED BY DOUBLEDAY

a division of Bantam Doubleday Dell Publishing Group, Inc.
1540 Broadway, New York, New York 10036

ANCHOR BOOKS, DOUBLEDAY, and the portrayal of an anchor are
trademarks of Doubleday, a division of Bantam Doubleday Dell
Publishing Group, Inc.

A Chorus of Stones was originally published in hardcover by
Doubleday in 1992. The Anchor Books edition is published by
arrangement with Doubleday.

Book design by Marysarah Quinn

Library of Congress Cataloging-in-Publication Data
Griffin, Susan.
A chorus of stones : the private life of war / Susan Griffin.—1st
Anchor Books ed.
p.   cm.
1. War—Psychological aspects. 2. Violence—Psychological
aspects. 3. Denial (Psychology) 4. Secrecy—Psychological
aspects. I. Title.
[U22.3.G75   1993]
355'.001'9—dc20   93-17492
                                                         CIP

10   9   8   7   6   5

Dedicated to the memory of Elissa Melamed,
who devoted the last years of her life to peace

and to all our children

ACKNOWLEDGMENTS

A great many people helped me with the creation of this book. The late Elissa Melamed was my companion in this effort in numerous ways. She read the first chapters of the book, encouraged me, inspired me, and pointed me toward crucial issues. Fran McCullough, who has been my editor in the past, was the first editor at Doubleday. Her early belief in the book as well as her critical insights were very important. Loretta Barrett as an interim editor was sensitive and supportive. In an editorial capacity for a brief period, Susan Moldow gave the manuscript an enthusiastic reception. But the book's principal editor has been Sallye Leventhal, who has given the book the kind of close, intelligent, and creative attention which all authors wish for but which is extremely rare. I am very grateful for her work. In addition, Diane Cleaver has faithfully and brilliantly represented this work. Jackie Stevens and Chris Stapleton both assisted me with retrieving volumes from the library; Kimn Neilson and Anna Lewis helped with proofreading and copy editing; Kacy Tebbel copy edited the final draft. And I was fortunate to work with two very able and helpful typists, Rosalyn Heimburg and Sari Broner. A number of people read parts of the manuscript and offered critical feedback and encouragement; others helped with interviews and research. Among these are Mioko Fujieda, Becky Jennison, Keiko Ogura, Betsy

ACKNOWLEDGMENTS

viii

Blakeslee, Mary Felstiner, Wendy Roberts, Benina Gould, Joanna Macy, Edith Sorel, Odette Meyers, Alice Miller, Don Johnson, Suzanne Kahn-Ackermann, Carolyn Kizer, Lee Howard, the late R. D. Laing, Emilie Conrad Da'Oud, Chellis Glendinning, Lenke Rothman, Linda Tumulty and Dorien Ross. My partner, Nan Fink, read, reread, and offered insightful editorial comments, proofread the manuscript, and gave me invaluable emotional support throughout the last years of writing. My daughter, Chloe Levy, was supportive and encouraging. A great many friends and acquaintances, together with those I have never met, came to my aid during the severe crisis in my health which occurred during the writing of this book. They are too numerous to name here, except for a very few without whom I would not have survived this period. They are Nancy Bardacke, Joanna Macy, Marilyn Sewell, Nancy Snow, Ingrid May, Lenore Friedman, Mimi Sternberg, Barbara Hazard, Ruth Zaporah, Cornelia Schultz, Abigail Van Alyn, Naomi Newman, David Shaddock, Paul Berman, Annie Prutzman, Clare Greensfelder, Joan Sutherland, Martha Boesing, Emilie Conrad Da'Oud, the late Elle Maret Gaup-Dunfjeld, Gloria Orenstein, Burt Jacobson, Bob Baldach, Diane Di Prima, Guenther Wieland and Rhiannon. I would especially like to thank Marya Grambs and Jan Montgomery for their support during this time, and others who have given me important material support for this project. Among those who contributed privately to the support of this book, let me first mention Alice Walker and Sallie Bingham for their generous kindness. In addition, Sidney and Jean Lanier, Barbara Austin, Margy Adams, Robert Haas, Ty Cashman, Roger Keyes, Donna Korones, Ronnie Gilbert, Ellen Bass, Bettina Aptheker, Margaret Brennan-Gibson, Pat and Dan Ellsberg, Kate Coleman, Kenneth Cloke, Terry Ryan, Elizabeth Janeway, Anna Douglas, Morton and Gerry Dimondstein, Cornelia Schultz, Barbara Hazard, Tracy Gary, Kirsten Grimstad, Diana Gould, Deena Metzger, Nancy Bacall, Naomi Newman, Lois Sasson, Leslie Gore, Adrienne Rich, Lily Engler, Miriam Levy and the late Irving Levy, Milton Taubman, James Oglivy, Joan

Drury, Wendy Lichtman and Jeff Mandel, Sally Belfrage, Janet Kranzberg, Liz Luster, Joshua Mailman, Irene Diamond and Suzanna Dakin all contributed. In addition, during the eight years that I spent writing this book I received support and grants from the Threshold Foundation, the Levinson Foundation, the Kentucky Foundation for Women and the Arts, the Barbara Deming Memorial Fund, and the MacArthur Foundation for Peace and International Cooperation. I also wish to thank the MacDowell Colony and the Djerassi Foundation.

Portions of the first draft of this book in progress were published by *City Lights Review, Whole Earth Review, Hurricane Alice, The American Voice, Creation,* and *Open Places.*

CONTENTS

A CHORUS OF STONES

When someone lifts us
He lifts in his hand millions of memories
Which do not dissolve in blood
Like evening.
      —NELLY SACHS. *Chorus of the Stones*

For every atom belonging to me as good belongs to you.
      —WALT WHITMAN. *Song of Myself*

DENIAL

The cells of our bodies and the bodies of all mammals first appeared on this earth billions of years ago as plankton. Now, we can only speculate at the cause of this birth. Something changed at its core. Elements which had before been divided came together for the first time. A new thought perhaps took form. And the progeny of these plankton still float in the sea, not too close to the surface, nor too far from the light.

I am not free of the condition I describe here. I cannot be certain how far back in human history the habit of denial can be traced. But it is at least as old as I am. In our common history, I have found it in the legends surrounding the battle of Troy, and in my own family I have traced it three generations back, to that recent time past when there had been no world wars and my grandparents were young. All that I was taught at home or in school was colored by denial, and thus it became so familiar to me that I did not see it. Only now have I begun to recognize that there were many closely guarded family secrets that I kept, and many that were kept from me.

When my father was still a small boy, his mother did something unforgivable. It was a source of shame as many secrets are, and hence kept hidden from my father and, eventually, from me. My great-aunt would have told me this secret before she died, but by that time she could not remember it. I have always sensed that my grandmother's transgression was sexual. Whatever she did was taken as cause by my grandfather and his mother to abandon her. They left her in Canada and moved to California, taking her two sons, my father and his brother, with them.

My father was not allowed to cry over his lost mother. Nor to speak her name. He could not give in to his grief but instead was taught to practice the military virtue of forbearance and to set an example in his manhood for his younger brother, Roland. In this way I suppose my grandfather hoped to erase the memory of my grandmother from all of our minds. But her loss has haunted us.

How old is the habit of denial? We keep secrets from ourselves that all along we know. The public was told that old Dresden was bombed to destroy strategic railway lines. There were no railway lines in that part of the city. But it would be years before that story came to the surface.

I do not see my life as separate from history. In my mind my family secrets mingle with the secrets of statesmen and bombers. Nor is my life divided from the lives of others. I, who am a woman, have my father's face. And he, I suspect, had his mother's face.

There is a characteristic way my father's eyelids fold, and you can see this in my face and in a photograph I have of him as a little boy. In the same photograph there is a silent sorrow mapped on his face, and this sorrow is mine too.

I place this photograph next to two others which are on my desk. Tracing the genesis of the bombing of civilians, I have come across a photograph of Dresden taken in 1945. A few dark figures hunch over a sea of corpses. There are ruined buildings in the background and smoke from a fire. The other photograph was sent to me by my cousin, after I asked her if she knew the name of my paternal grandmother, or if she might have a picture of her.

The photograph my cousin did send me has a haunted quality, though it was taken in Canada before the erasure of my grandmother. It is not a picture of my grandmother. It is a picture of my grandfather with my father. It was taken a few years before masses of soldiers died on the battlefields of World War I, and over three decades before the bombing of Dresden, the concentration camps, Hiroshima. And yet, my grandfather's face bears an expression of grief just as if he were looking over a scene of senseless destruction, a field of bodies. What was his sorrow?

Whatever it is, I recognize it. There are times when I have said the words *I want to die* to sound an alarm through my own tissues. And yet, just as readily, I have avoided knowing this pain.

If I tell here all the secrets that I know, public and private, perhaps I will begin to see the way the old sometimes see, Monet, recording light and spirit in his paintings, or the way those see who have been trapped by circumstances—a death, a loss, a cataclysm of history—grasping the essential.

I was surprised to feel a kinship with my grandfather. I had never liked him. By the time I was born, he was a different man than the one whom this photograph captured. He rarely spoke. His face showed no emotion at all. He sat for long hours staring at, apparently, nothing. I remember thinking about him as if he were inanimate substance. Some feeling which surrounded him made my natural curiosity about people and things recede in his presence.

It was just this year, at the age of forty, that I learned for the first time my grandfather was an alcoholic. When my mother called to ask me what I was writing about, I described the photograph of Grandpa Hal I had received. Then she told me a story I had never heard.

Grandpa Hal was a quiet drinker. He was one of those men who could be past feeling, past knowing, wrapped in a blurred, numbed cloud, and yet walk and talk as if he were sober. Once, when my mother and father had quarreled, my mother tried to speak to him about her feelings. She went to the edge of the garden where he worked. But he would not respond. I might describe him as being like stone except that stones record history. The hard surface of the stone is impervious to nothing in the end. The heat of the sun leaves evidence of daylight. Each drop of rain changes the form; even the wind and the air itself, invisible to our eyes, etches its presence.

On my desk close to the photograph of my grandfather and father is a round triangle of black granite polished to a shine. At its center is the impression of a centipede, long segmented creature which left this ancient self-portrait, image of an ancestor from millions of years into our past. All history is taken in by stones. And perhaps it is this knowledge which made them weep when Orpheus sang. But what my grandfather suffered and witnessed was never to be told. His very manner discouraged questions.

He did have a life, one which the adult women of his household knew about, but what he did when he was away from the house existed in the category of scandal and thus, like my grandmother, was never mentioned. He had lovers. Women unworthy of being brought home, because they were considered *whores*. (And what he did with them was called *whoring*.) He spent time with these lovers in bars. My mother's father had had the same double life, and he never breathed a word of it to me but, like all scandals, it was whispered.

Grandpa Hal's mother was a very strong-willed woman whose disapproval hardly needed to be spoken. So different was she from her son that for her even silence itself was a kind of speech. One said about her, *She has eyes in the back of her head.* I could have sequestered myself carefully in the garden, safe from all scrutiny, when suddenly her voice would penetrate the tall grass and bend around the trunk of a lemon tree to warn me to be careful of the kitten I had captured since it had a habit of scratching. There was such a divide between my grandfather and my great-grandmother, in my mind, that I seldom thought of them as mother and son.

In the same way, until I looked upon that photograph, I did not claim this man as my grandfather. In my mind, I had only one grandfather, whose name was Ernest, and he was my mother's father. In a strange unspoken manner, this made my father seem orphaned to me, as if his parentage were remote and shadowy, and he had been handed on, a foundling, to my very definite, palpable great-grandmother. That he had a brother was even harder for me to comprehend. Roland had died before I was born. Thus I had no physical evidence, except for one old photograph, that he had ever lived. And my father seldom spoke of him.

My father, who was named Walden, did not get along with his brother. Walden was the good, well-behaved son. But his younger brother Roland was wild. I never knew that he too was alcoholic until that recent conversation with my mother. Roland took after his father. He would go out on the town; he would *whore;* the family would be called late at night from some police station, to come and retrieve him after he had been arrested for brawling or causing a disturbance.

But one day my uncle's life changed. It was as if by a miracle. He fell in love, deeply so, with a woman who loved him deeply. And, as in numinous fables of transformation, this love redeemed him. He stopped drinking. He stopped all his misbehavior. He married, got a steady job as a lumberjack, and settled with his young wife in the redwood forests of Oregon. They had a child, my cousin David. And then, just as suddenly, and by an accident of his trade, before he had reached the age of thirty he died.

I learned about this death as a child. But a recent story my mother told me places my grandfather in a different dimension. For Roland's death had a historical shadow. My grandfather had apparently hidden the serious extent of his dependency on alcohol from the family, until the day when, pruning the apple tree in the garden, he fell and broke his ankle. It was not the fall itself that alerted the family. They learned of this dependency only when, after a few hours in the hospital, deprived of alcohol, Hal began to have tremors and then he went into delirium. Finally the truth was laid bare. But soon after he returned home, this truth, like the cast on his ankle, was forgotten in the way that people forget what they do not want to know, and things went on the way they were before.

My uncle Roland had died when he fell from a tree.

Did anyone else think of this coincidence, I wonder? A bond between father and son, trailing back in time to a bitterness unknown to the son, unexpressed by the father. The fall of one, the fall of the other. Or did all thought of it too exist like a back alley —unrecognized, consigned to each heart as if it were a solitary secret? Somehow, I have always known this story, its essence, without ever having been told. For, on hearing it, I felt like the penitent must have felt after rendering a confession. Suddenly the light itself by which I see was purified. A nameless grief now named hence lifted.

I am beginning to believe that we know everything, that all history, including the history of each family, is part of us, such that, when we hear any secret revealed, a secret about a grandfather, or an uncle, or a secret about the battle of Dresden in 1945, our lives are made suddenly clearer to us, as the unnatural heaviness of unspoken truth is dispersed. For perhaps we are like stones; our own history and the history of the world embedded in us, we hold a sorrow deep within and cannot weep until that history is sung.

Long before the firebombing of Dresden, the German government knew about the terrible effect of firestorms. Late on the night of July 27, 1943, and in the early morning hours of July 28, the first firestorm was created. It was a new phenomenon, even to its makers, who dropped 7,931 tons of bombs, almost half of these incendiary, over the city of Hamburg. Several conditions conspired to cause it: a heat wave, the concentration of high buildings, so many fires started simultaneously, a fire feeding itself, transforming space into a chamber of combustion. The whole of the city became so hot that even the atmosphere above was heated and began thus to draw the flames out explosively. The air literally roared as it rushed upward, like a tornado, tearing trees, people, animals alike into the flames with its force. Walls of flame raced across the city at thirty, forty, one hundred miles an hour.

It is said that the close study of stone will reveal traces from fires suffered thousands of years ago. These would have been natural conflagrations, waves of flame burning through forests. This fire was not anomalous but part of the cycle of life. In Inverness, a peninsula which juts out into the Pacific Ocean, not far from where I live, a kind of tree grows, the bishop pine, which requires fire for regeneration. Only the intense heat of flames will open the seed pods. So much a part of the evolution of the planet, fire has come to symbolize the force of life itself. And in our shared imagination fire also stands for the power of the human mind to create. The glowing motion of flame seems to flow from hard substance by a miracle of transubstantiation which makes evident the heart of existence. Yet, by another turn, there is no death that is as devastating as a death by fire. And this twinned identity, as giver and taker of life, lends this element the air of divinity in action, a force that purges gross reality of its impurities and transforms mortals into gods. No wonder that the Third Reich chose the swastika, a symbol for fire, to emblazon its flags.

The phenomenon of the firestorm should have changed the entire civil defense procedure for incendiary bombs. Under the most usual conditions for air raids during World War II, it was wise to stay hidden underground, in shelters, for at least forty minutes, after all planes, or sounds of planes, had passed, in the case that a second attack was planned. But during a firestorm a shelter becomes an oven, an inferno with temperatures as high as 1,000 degrees Fahrenheit. And thus, when such an effect is likely to be created, it is best to escape the shelter and run through the fires in an attempt to reach an area that is not being bombed.

But Goebbels decided to keep the truth about firestorms secret. Were it possible, he said, he would have silenced any news of attacks by air on German cities. *Not a word,* he declared. Because of his policy, in Dresden citizens stayed in their shelters after the first bombing, believing that they were safe underground.

I spoke with a woman in London who had been in one of those shelters when the firestorms began. Gurda was a refugee from Lithuania. By the winter of 1945 she had already traveled with her family all over Europe, alternately hiding or running for several years. She was alert by now for even the subtlest of signs which might point her toward survival. As they settled in the shelter she noticed two men in trench coats near the door. These men barred the exit, not allowing anyone to leave. Then, after the first round of attacks, she saw them run out through the same doors they had guarded.

Feeling these men must know something she did not, she convinced her husband and her mother-in-law that they should take the children and run out of the shelter. They ran through walls of flame and powerful winds which carried flying timbers as big as trees. But, miraculously, they all lived. The only one who died was her father-in-law, who refused to leave the shelter.

Many soldiers from other armies, who were being held prisoner, were commandeered to clear away the bodies and help with the procedure of identifying the many who died in that city. There were 135,000 who perished and thus the task was enormous, and horrifying.

One group of Romanian prisoners refused to enter a certain cellar, and the director of these operations had to be called. Now, writing this, I feel like one of those prisoners, or like the director who finally went into the cellar himself, alone, to set an example. I do not want to tell you what he found there, or, in setting down the words, to make it a part of my own consciousness.

And yet, does not my own private sorrow contain and mirror, no matter how subtle, small traces of this horror, this violent death? In some way I knew of the effects of this bombing, and of the terrors of the concentration camps and Hiroshima, before I read about them in history books. Am I trying to write off the sufferings of my own mind and of my family as historical phenomena? Yes and no. We forget that we are history. We have kept the left hand from knowing the right. I was born and brought up in a nation that participated in the bombing of Dresden, and in the civilization that planned the extermination of a whole people. We are not used to associating our private lives with public events. Yet the histories of families cannot be separated from the histories of nations. To divide them is part of our denial.

What did he find in the cellar? A lake of flesh and blood and bone, twelve feet high.

We can speak about the airplanes and the kinds of bombs. We can even number the dead. But the actual dismemberment of bodies must only be hinted. Needless to say, the contents of that cellar were kept secret. And everywhere in the old city, as much as possible, those faced with the prodigious effort of burial tried to carry this out in secrecy too. The bodies could not be taken to the burial grounds outside Dresden, for to take them there necessitated the transport of wagons filled with corpses through a part of Dresden that had not been bombed. The authorities did not wish to confront those citizens with the sight of the dead. Finally bodies were dumped unidentified into mass graves. Like plutonium waste which we would like to forget, these bodies had become poisonous. They were contaminated with typhus.

But even the work of placing the bodies in mass graves went too slowly. It was turning spring. The weather was warm. Thus, in secret, wagonloads of bodies were driven by peasants to Altmarkt Square. In 1349, this same square was the site where Frederick the Great ordered the burning of Jews because he had accused them of having brought the plague to Dresden. Now the peasants arranged the bodies of the dead into great pyres, and they were burned.

I am looking at a photograph of British Air Marshal Arthur Harris. During the Second World War he was known as "Bomber Harris." He was the man who commanded the bombing of Dresden. The photograph is on the cover of an old copy of *Life* magazine. It is dated April 10, 1944, ten months before that famous air raid took place. The air marshal is wearing his uniform in the photograph. There are many uniformed figures in this issue of *Life,* General Stilwell in Burma, several New Zealand infantrymen in Cassino, Sergeant Berkley Willis at a canteen in Hollywood, Chili Williams in a helmet and boots exposing her legs, an unknown model dressed in a naval officer's uniform, recommending Colgate toothpaste. A uniform would have been a ubiquitous sight that year.

The air marshal simultaneously holds a telephone and takes notes while he sits at his desk. He wears half-rimmed reading glasses, peering out over the top of them at the photographer. Now, as I look back through time and into his eyes, I am not convinced. Is this really a moment from history? The photograph seems posed. It has a flat and arranged feeling. I know the marshal would have had no time for any elaborate staging; still, the lighting is too perfect, the angle straight on, and his gaze is so clearly directed at the camera.

He is of course very well cast for the role. A broad and manly chest, graying hair and mustache, and a stern fatherly expression. One imagines his voice will be gruff, not corrugated like Bogart's voice, but somehow eroded, as if exposed to harsh elements over time. If he plays his role well, it is after all one he has prepared for, in one way or another, since the earliest days of his childhood.

Opening the pages of *Life,* the drama begins to seem more real. There is the map showing cities targeted in Germany, the figures totaling Allied losses in January, February and March, the photograph of an aero-engine factory at Limoges before and after bombing, a section of Berlin reduced to rubble by the Royal Air Force.

In still another photograph, the air marshal himself is looking at pictures. He is studying portraits, taken from the air, of cities that have been bombed. He looks at these images through a small aperture in a wooden box called a stereopticon, a device which adds a third dimension to what he sees. Through this instrument, a two-dimensional, gray landscape suddenly reveals *gaping craters, heaps of rubble, burned out buildings with the walls still standing, acres and acres of roofless buildings.*

On the opposing page, the air marshal leafs through his famous *Blue Book,* a huge document he has prepared to impress the leaders of the Allied effort with the efficacy of strategic bombing. It contains maps of several German sites which he has marked, according to *Life,* for *emasculation.*

I am, of course, stopped by this last word. The author has placed it in quotations, as if it were Harris's language, or the choice of the RAF. What is meant by this word? Is it the implicit unmanning of the vanquished by conquering armies? Or is it that emasculation which occurs when one man's women and children are harmed by another man? Or both of these. And of course there is the obvious meaning, the loss of a part of the body, the sexual body by which a man is defined. But even this literal reading moves to a larger implication, the loss of identity itself. That stripping away of every extraneous layer, of every role we play in life, which one suffers when faced with unmitigated terror.

The concept began earlier in the century during the First World War: the suggestion then that a war might be won by destroying the economic stability of the enemy, and by terrorizing its civilian population. In the discussion that ensued the issue of masculinity was implicit. Various groups considered less stalwart than well-bred Englishmen—the English working class, women, the civilian population of France as a whole—would, it was believed, crumble quickly under the strain of an enemy attack.

And then there was the other emasculation. The nations which fought in the First World War were literally unmanned; a whole generation of young men had died on the battlefields. With a change in planning, death might be spread more evenly among the people: women as well as men, old as well as young, weak as well as strong.

The air marshal's famous mentor, Sir Hugh Trenchard, the man known as the father of the RAF, began as a critic of strategic bombing. German planes had bombed London and the public cried out for retaliation in kind. Trenchard wanted airplanes to be used on the battlefield. But this brief opposition ended in 1917 when, near the end of the First World War, he was put in charge of strategic bombing for the Allied forces. Then he began to imagine the gradual destruction from the air of the inner strength of the enemy. He wanted as many new four-engine Handley Page bombers as factories could produce. With these he planned to destroy Berlin. After this destruction, he reasoned, there would be many refugees who would flee to neighboring cities. It was then he argued that Allied bombers should destroy those cities too. And as the ranks of refugees grew, every city to which they might escape should be destroyed until they had no place to hide. Trenchard asserted that it was by this means alone that the war could be won. But the war ended by other means. Stalemate, exhaustion, the introduction of fresh troops from America. There was an armistice. He would have to wait nearly three decades to see his plan put into action over Dresden, a city designated as a free port, and into which refugees were evacuating from all over Europe.

I am imagining Air Marshal Harris now a year after he appeared on the cover of *Life*. He has in his hands photographs of Dresden after the bombing. He is passing them through the instrument by which he can see the true dimensionality of the destruction. But despite this technology, there is a depth in the field of his vision that is missing. There are details too small to be caught in the lens. Stains. Discarded clothing. The smell of fires unseen. And perhaps, if he were there, in the place itself, he might feel something from the fragments of stone which must have absorbed the atmosphere of this event, strangely quiet as they are. Though still, a certain kind of silence is a common effect of catastrophe.

I saw it in Gurda. She could recite all the events that had happened to her and her family since they left their home. But there was a quality of flatness in her voice. It was the Russian advance they feared first. History had taught them this. So, after the Stalin-Hitler pact, when the German armies arrived in 1939, they were welcome. But Gurda had given birth recently, and the strain of events reached her. She was hospitalized for the stress of it. Then, out the hospital window, she saw truckloads of children leaving the city. And this sight gave her an inexplicable fear. *I pulled myself together,* she told me, *because I knew we had to leave.*

She stayed pulled together in that way for the duration of the war, as a refugee without papers, hunting for castoff food, stealing from the fields at night, teaching her children not to cry out or scream lest this reveal them to their hunters. And in the same way, even before she reached Dresden, she herself learned not to cry, or to fall apart, to dull the full dimension of her feeling.

Thinking again now of the air marshal as he gazes at the ruins he has commanded into creation, I find myself wondering if perhaps the brief portrait I have drawn of him is also lacking in depth. The training he has received, not to respond in any way except as a soldier, has become so habitual, he hardly has to remind himself now to stay calm. No hand goes over his mouth to silence him. He is steady. Unblinking. But still, despite the success of years, some trace of descent into a less ordered region of himself must exist.

How many small decisions accumulate to form a habit? What a multitude of decisions, made by others, in other times, must shape our lives now. A grandmother's name is erased. A mother decides to pretend that her son does not drink too much. A nation refuses to permit Jewish immigrants to pass its borders, knowing, and yet pretending not to know, that this will mean certain death. The decision is made to bomb a civilian population. The decision is made to keep the number of the dead and the manner of their death a secret.

But wherever there is a secret there is a rumor. After the bombing of Dresden, the Propaganda Ministry of the Third Reich purposely produced a leak, sending out whispers of a government document which exaggerated the numbers of the dead. It was not to save lives that Goebbels created this rumor, but rather to cause fear of a monstrous death-dealing enemy so that this fear might inspire resistance against the Allied invasion. Yet I am certain there was another reason for the creation of this rumor, a reason seated deeper in the mind than ordinary consciousness lets us see. For deep in the mind we know everything. And wish to have everything be told, to have our images and our words reflect the truth. Goebbels must have known that the end was near. And just like polite society which pretends not to know about indiscretion, and yet gossips, Goebbels could see his own divided consciousness reflected in declaration and in rumor. He could have the right hand, and the left, and keep them divided.

I go to look at my face in the mirror. I have my mother's jaw but my father's eyes, those lids with a double fold. My father died at the age of forty-nine; crossing a street, he was struck by a car. It was just at sunset and the light was blinding. I do not honestly think he meant to die that way. But the event has haunted me with the knowledge of a despair he always carried within him, a despair covered over with a smile, an outward cheer.

Before his funeral friends told me not to look at the open casket, and so I waited at the back of the church while everyone else filed by him. A funeral director, proud of his work, urged me to join the other mourners, saying that they had repaired his body and made him *as good as new*. Though I would not look, inadvertently he had brought home to me the violence of my father's death. Even today, my body tenses with fear every time I cross a street. What at one time one refuses to see never vanishes but returns, again and again, in many forms.

Now that I have heard these stories from my family history, the past and this present moment seem more alive to me. What was blurred in both is now clearer, and a sorrow that was in the background has come forward to claim my attention.

It is December 24, 1968. A spacecraft, set in orbit by a rocket, hovers near the moon. It carries three men who pilot the vehicle as it makes a slow circle around the lunar surface. From an entirely new perspective, these men watch the moon and the earth bright against a dark space.

CLYTEMNESTRA'S
MEMORY

11

The first forms of life, simple single-celled creatures, develop in water. These cells have the same fundamental form as will human cells which come into being after several billion years.

It is a hot summer day in Tennessee in the midst of the sixth decade of this century. The girl has climbed the fence to get to the swimming hole she has visited so many summers of her life in the time before this part of the land was enclosed. She stands now at the edge of it. Her body is sticky with heat. The surface of the water moves slightly. Sunlight shimmers and dances in a green reflection that seems as she stares at it to pull her in even before her skin is wet with it. Drops of water on the infant's head. All the body immersed for baptism. Do these images come to her as she sinks into the coolness? The washing of hands before Sunday's midday meal. *All our sins washed away.* Water was once the element for purification. But at the bottom of this pool, *There is no telling what is there now.* This is what the girl's father will say to her finally: corroded cans of chemical waste, some radioactive substances. *That was why they put the fence there.* She is not thinking of that now. The words have not yet been said, and so for her no trouble exists here. The water holds up her body. She is weightless in this fulsome element, the waves her body makes embracing her with their own benediction. Beneath her in the shadowy green, she feels the depth of the pond. In this coolness as the heat mercifully abates, her mind is set free, to dream as the water dreams.

It is in the first century A.D. that a ballista is used as a weapon in the Greco-Roman Empire. By pulling down and then suddenly releasing a long wooden arm, the ballista hurls a stone toward city walls.

It is after nightfall, April 6, 1945. Following instructions from Wernher von Braun, his assistant, Dieter Huzel, drives the first of many trucks to an abandoned mine shaft, twelve kilometers north of Dörnten in the Harz Mountains. The trucks are filled with cartons of documents, green for design and development, blue for manufacturing, red for testing, which detail the production of rockets in Germany. Each carton will be carried into a vaulted room in the mine. And the next day an explosion will seal the shaft so that even the most curious will not ask what is inside.

Four or five billion years ago, when the earth first came into being, the temperature and the atmosphere could not sustain life.

Does anyone in his hurried plans stop to contemplate the subtler meanings of this geography? The drama of the current moment perhaps supersedes such speculation. Just now American and Russian troops cross over German borders from two directions. As part of his scorched earth policy, Hitler has ordered that all records of rocket research be destroyed. Can Von Braun, who has dreamed for so long of reaching the moon, have time to consider the polarity that history requires? All his knowledge of flight through space hidden deep in the recesses of the earth?

A medieval siege weapon, the trebuchet, uses a heavy counterweight that falls to provide the power to hurl stones for great distances.

It is the first week in May. The Americans have reached Garmisch-Partenkirchen. They race against time. Since the Allies are partitioning Germany, rockets, designs, scientists must be assembled quickly. The research facilities at Peenemünde and the missile factories at Nordhausen will soon belong to the Soviets. The first of many interrogations have begun. To show his cooperation with his captors, Dr. von Braun begins to write a paper. It is entitled *Übersicht, Survey of Previous Liquid Rocket Development in Germany and Future Projects.* He is looking to the future. His paper contains two prophecies. One that men will soon reach the moon. And the other that a mastery of rockets will change the world as much as the invention of airplanes.

Slowly an atmosphere of hydrogen, methane and ammonia was transmuted into oxygen, carbon dioxide and nitrogen which would be able to nourish a living organism.

Waiting for his American captors to reach a decision, does the scientist turn his head and gaze out his window into the night sky? Is he staring at the moon? Despite all the chaos of shifting borders, mingling languages, troops in different uniforms, lost husbands, wives, children, and all the secrets, questions, revelations so urgently hunted here, there is a certain aimlessness. The scientists exist in a shadowy world, belonging to no nation in particular, suspended as if outside time, outside history. For hours on end they play Monopoly, making the game more complex with their own rules. Von Braun's brother Magnus, also a scientist, directs a production of *The Importance of Being Earnest.* Do the male scientists play female roles? Everything seems to be fluctuating. Is this what Von Braun thinks as he looks out his window? How everything on earth and in heaven is in a state of flux? Perhaps it can never be measured, this moon whose face constantly changes. Glowing through the clouds and then darkened, then shining again, this is all that remains to be charted. Every other place, Africa, Asia, jungles of South America, North and South Poles are part of the known, except this body, explored, unknown, just out of reach, floating between sun and earth, luminous, belonging to no one yet.

It is in the late fourteenth century that a breech-loading cannon which fires steel balls first appears. It is the first weapon which has enough power to destroy the walls of fortifications and render cities vulnerable.

Was there a time in his earlier years when he gazed at the moon from the famous observatory of the University of Berlin? This is located not far from Berlin in a city called Potsdam, the city where Frederick the Great built a famous château, and the same city the Allies have chosen for their meeting now. They are assembled to discuss the map of Europe: who shall occupy Germany, what will be the fate of Central Europe, who will invade Japan. It is July 16, 1945, in the early evening when President Harry Truman, in Potsdam for just over twenty-four hours, receives a coded message. *Operated on this morning,* the message reads. *Diagnosis not yet complete but results seem satisfactory and already exceed expectations.* He knows immediately what this means. He had postponed the meeting at Potsdam so that now it coincided with the experimental deployment of a secret weapon at Alamogordo. *If it explodes,* he reasoned, . . . *I'll certainly have a hammer on those boys.* Stalin has been a formidable negotiator. Two days later, in the midst of the first plenary session, he receives another coded message. The blast of the weapon could be heard fifty miles away and was seen from a distance of two hundred and fifty miles. Now he returns to the negotiations with a new fortitude.

Over millions of years molecules of oxygen, carbon dioxide and nitrogen were transformed by the sun's heat into amino acids, fats and proteins, and the essential nucleic acids of the cell came into being.

There are those who think a story is told only to reveal what is known in this world. But a good story also reveals the unknown.

Of its nature, of course, the unknown cannot be fully depicted. It is there perhaps just in the tone of voice, or a style that is loosely knit, and admits thus of other possibilities. If, when a character and a situation meet, the outcome is already determined, the story lacks dimension. For it is the unpredictable outcome, the transformation of expectations, that points us in the direction of deeper insights. It is perhaps then possible that a weapon, so powerful as to be unimaginable, will not be used, except as a demonstration, an inducement to peace, and that, in the future, as some of the scientists who invented the weapon suggest, the knowledge of this power be shared. Or the story need not follow this unpredictable course, but only indicate that it existed as a possibility, as in a tragedy, when the hero or heroine, so set on a path that we in the audience can see leads to doom, cannot or does not turn to see the opening, the patch of spontaneous space, just behind, just over the shoulder, and beautiful even in memory.

It is in the sixteenth century that Niccolò Tartaglia, studying the pathways of flying shots, determines that such trajectories are curved.

It is August 6, 1945. Does he hear it over the radio? Is an announcement made at the plant that day? So much of his life will be part of the life of this event. There is no fence yet around the swimming hole. His daughter Iris is not yet born. Is he proud? He was part of what made it possible. And the war is over.

On the same day, in his statement accompanying the news of the bombing of Hiroshima, President Truman announces that the technical processes of the production of the bomb will not be revealed. *We must count ourselves trustees of this new force,* he declares, three days later. In just one week, as the Second World War is formally ended, the Department of War orders that all scientific and technical knowledge about nuclear energy be kept secret.

Within the cell, proteins create the building materials, and carbohydrates and fats supply energy.

The word *secret* has an erotic edge, as if in hiding anything, a story, a weapon, a piece of candy still wet from the mouth, clinging to the flannel lining of a pocket, one moves closer to a sequestered sexual body at the core of being. During my childhood the absence left by all the secrets my parents and the other adults kept from children was numinous and hot. There was the war that had just occurred and, beneath those images of heroism, unspeakable whispered horrors. There was my mother's drinking, just like her father's before her, the flashing sight of her wild laughter and then rage, before my father pulled her out of the hallway and into the privacy of their bedroom. The secret process of atomic fission, the secret mechanisms of missiles. All these secrets migrated into one space in my imagination, a geography of lost and missing pieces.

It is in the eighteenth century, during the War of the Spanish Succession, that a cannon invented for use on the battlefield is deployed. Its brass or sometimes iron gun barrel is elaborately decorated. It sits on wheels, which allow it to be transported by horse.

Does it appear to him like a moonscape, this flat expanse of desert, so stripped of anything familiar, dry, full of sand and dust? Nothing like Germany. In the moonlight he might easily imagine that the moon herself had been severed from this place before being flung out into the void. This is all of the moon he will see now. His vision is circumscribed by a more modest experimentation. The slow reassembling of parts. The careful explanation of old designs. On May 10, 1946, almost exactly a year after the end of the war in Germany, the first American V-2 rocket is launched from this strip of desert, located midway between El Paso, Texas, and the Trinity site in New Mexico, where the first atomic weapon was detonated. The rocket rises to an altitude of seventy-one miles. To commemorate the occasion, the lieutenant colonel in charge gives each of the participants a wooden model of the rocket.

It is not what he had hoped for. Just now the moon recedes farther and farther from him. So many obstacles impede his journey. Is it far-fetched to liken him to the lover whose ardor shines brighter as his beloved recedes from his grasp? The moon of course says nothing, being silent, mysterious, aloof as a maiden in a castle. But as I enter the field of his passion, it is not a desire for intimacy I sense so much as the will to possess whatever exists as part of an empire of knowledge. Meanwhile he must raise an army to assault her bastion. And to do this, it is other men he must woo.

Is his tone seductive? Certainly he is aware of the value of what he knows. Knowledge is the only currency of his power. Does he let it drop at a dinner party? Or is he standing at a bar, in a hallway, in the lobby of a theatre? A hint, almost casually mentioned, that another weapon was designed at Peenemünde. Someone else is building rockets. The moon may even have another suitor. Helmut Gottrum, who worked with him at Peenemünde, is there now in the land of rivals looming large and phantasmagorical at the borders of imagination. When a more formal meeting is arranged, he cautions his listeners that of course he cannot know for certain. This is just an educated guess, a scientist's conjecture. It would perhaps be three years before the Soviets would be able to produce this rocket.

No words need pass precisely delineating the terms. A deal is struck but it is not written. They are called gentlemen's agreements. The negotiators know and they do not know what they do.

There are those who wish to deport Dr. von Braun. Members of the Nazi Party are forbidden entrance to the United States. And there is a suggestion that he is a war criminal. According to the official procedures, which are followed to the letter, Dr. von Braun is interrogated. Yes, he was a member of the Nazi Party, and a major in the SS, but all this was simply a part of his winding path to the moon. Memos are written. Remarks passed in the same hallways, at clubs, in certain familiar gathering places. There is the Soviet threat. The interballistic missile just now being born from the old V-2 designs. Finally the President issues a new interpretation of the standing policy. Those who joined the Nazi Party for opportunistic reasons will be exempted from the rule. Though Dr. von Braun's name is never mentioned, a certain understanding has been reached.

It is speculated that the first single-celled organisms were created from the union of less complicated structures.

It is June 26, 1948. Following Stalin's orders, all traffic into the western sector of Berlin is being stopped at the eastern border. The city has been without access to food or coal for two days. Now, just as plans for a massive airlift of supplies are being set in motion, the President orders two squadrons of B-29s into Berlin. These airplanes will carry nothing to meet the needs of those who are garrisoned. They serve another purpose. As they fly over the eastern territory to their destination, the silhouettes of wings, engines, tails, carry another message mimed for those who watch. Even unspoken, all participants quickly grasp the meaning. These are the only airplanes capable of delivering atomic bombs.

This is the way diplomacy has always been conducted. The covert suggestion of possibilities not so much threatened as displayed. Does the President take pleasure in this gesture? He knows that he possesses the most powerful weapon in the world. Is it possible that he feels this new strength even in his body? Short in stature, now no one can argue with his power. It is a virility superhuman in its proportions. And the power is more than physical. It is also mental. He is the only one who knows if the weapon will be used. It is through this uncertainty that he makes an assault on his enemy. And can it also be said that, in the wake of his rival's ignorance, he feels, at this moment, in command of all knowledge?

———

I was just three years old in the year of the Berlin airlift. I was the youngest in the family. And everyone knew more of the world than I. Just mastering language, I made my family laugh as certain words eluded my still undeveloped skill for speech. It was that innocent laughter reserved for the small and young, those not yet on sturdy legs, stumbling and vulnerable, staying near their mothers for protection. I had seen images of mushroom clouds but this was vastly diminished in my child's mind by the height of the back steps to our house which I had just mastered.

It is September 1949. In the beginning the President will not believe the report. The response is a common one. We have all experienced this. By denying the truth of an event, one gains the illusion of control. But it is true. Air force intelligence has found radioactivity in air samples gathered near Siberia. Later reports will all confirm: a plutonium bomb has been detonated in the Soviet Union. The period of exclusive knowledge has ended.

It is June 25, 1950. Massive forces from the north have crossed the South Korean border. General MacArthur delays sending word to Washington. For several hours the battlefield will be his alone. Without seeking permission from the President, he orders the dispatch of munitions to South Korea. Is it perhaps a giddy feeling he has now? This is, he says, *Mars's last gift to an old warrior.* As he goes just to the edge, and then just over the edge, of his legal powers, he is something like an acrobat, leaning over an abyss of space. Our sense of perspective would argue that he should fall; but nevertheless he seems to defy gravity.

Imagining myself in the general's place, I can just begin to perceive the outlines of his reasoning. His character after all has been carefully constructed for such challenges. Whatever fears accompanied him, the nausea before he took his examinations at West Point, the abiding nightmare of failure and public shame that still haunts him, are diminished again and again by his victories. And who should know better how to proceed in this war? He has spent over half his life in this region. He was a young man, traveling with his father, then a general, when he first encountered Asia. Through this first impression, this region gained what he called a *mystic hold* on him. He had discovered, he would say later, *Western civilization's last frontier*. Where was it in his mind that this frontier existed? At the edge of a bamboo forest, elegantly quiet? On a warm beach surrounded with the scent of tropical flowers? In a city filled with exotic sounds, strange clothing, new tastes, unpredictable movements? In his mind now he is the commander of the Far East, and it falls to him to seize and restore order in his suzerainty.

History rarely moves in a single direction. While the notion of empire expands in one place, it diminishes in another. Nineteen hundred and fifty is also the year in which the state of India finally becomes a sovereign republic. The European colonies of Asia and Africa are breaking away. But at the same time another frontier is opening. This is also the year that Wernher von Braun and his rocket team move to Huntsville, Alabama, to begin work on a missile with a range of five hundred miles. In Dr. von Braun's mind is this five hundred miles closer to the moon? The work proceeds more slowly, and by a more circuitous route, than he would wish, the moon remaining elusive, so near and yet so far.

Strange as it seems, when I think of General MacArthur stretching as far as possible the limits of legal authority over Asia, the image of an astronaut, making giant steps with an elated buoyancy, enters the territory of my imagination. It is as if, in my mind, all the events of history take place simultaneously. As I sit in a darkened theater watching film taken of the first lunar landing in 1968, one astronaut plants a flag, while another, almost floating across the strangely beautiful moonscape, tells us he has recently discovered something essential about human nature: *man's need to explore*.

Breaking natural law, sailing into unknown space, is it only here in this territory free of the familiar that the voyager tastes the true meaning of life? But free though he is, the journey is not limitless. The flag must be saluted; the airship turned home again. And there is always the possibility of a fatal error in calculation by which one will be planted forever in the void.

It is 1951. If the general has held a precarious balance it is only momentary. He sends a cable to Washington. Can he use atomic bombs to cut off the supply routes from Vladivostok and Manchuria? Can he surround the north with a band of radioactive waste? He disobeys orders and crosses the 38th parallel. And when the Chinese enter the war, he boasts to Japanese diplomats that China will be crushed with a nuclear attack.

It is in the early spring then that the President relieves him of his command. There is a procedure which must be followed. If the President has made his own innuendos about nuclear weapons, words were placed artfully. The balance of power is intricate, the rules infinitely complex. The balance tips first this way and then that. And at either end of an incline perhaps too steep are consequences whose proportions are still stunning the world.

For those who have never seen it, the sight is spectacular. *A white chimney of fire, a light with an intensity many times brighter than the midday sun, golden, purple, violet, gray and blue, lighting every peak and crevasse of the mountain, the beauty great poets dream about, followed by an awesome roar which warns of doomsday.* Tourists, busloads of schoolchildren, whole families travel to Mount Charleston in the hours before dawn to watch the explosions. The travel section of the *New York Times* promises the likelihood of an attenuated cloud passing right over the observer's head.

It is still 1951. Moved from the Marshall Islands because of the proximity of the Korean War, the test site has been a feature of the Nevada landscape since the beginning of the year. Now, late in the same year, the army constructs a bivouac, temporary buildings, tents, offices, a canteen. Thousands of troops are arriving to witness the explosion and to conduct field exercises under the extending clouds. Pigs and rabbits dressed in military uniform will be placed closer to the blast. This is how it is explained to the Atomic Energy Commission. The soldiers will be taught protective measures. And the army will study the effects of the explosion on their emotions.

A three-inch mortar used by the Union in the Civil War during sieges was known to have a devastating effect on advancing troops.

Of course the military study of emotions does not go beyond what is necessary to an army. So much in the range of human emotions is forbidden to the well-trained soldier. Even if stoicism fails him momentarily, he is quick to regain his composure. Does the blast reverberate into heretofore unknown territories in his mind? Might it unlock secret traumas, a child's terrified weeping, a small and delicate body prey to the overwhelming force of others more powerful than he is?

The military mind shies clear of a certain kind of knowledge. Just as in our imagination of public events, we banish what we call private life to the background of our telling, the soldier excludes particular feelings and memories from his idea of who he is. I am thinking now of my father. How well he learned neither to speak of nor to think about his mother. Yet the thought must have been perpetually at the back of his mind, in that place that escapes apprehension. He had a sorrow that he himself could not explain.

There are events in our lives that we cannot understand because we keep a part of what we know away from understanding. War is one of those events. And there are other, private events which mystify us, as if there were no explanation for them except nature itself. That we are mystified becomes a habit passed from one generation to the next. My father suffered from the silence of his father, and I suffered from his.

In the steady continuum of history we meet a divide between

public and private events. Shifting from one to another, the discourse changes. Even the tone of voice, when entering the world we call private, slows down, drops a scale, and perhaps softens. This is partly why we seldom associate military repression with the unnatural silences of childhood.

The troubling nature of censorship is clearer when it falls on the very young. A certain kind of silence, that which comes from holding back the truth, is abusive in itself to a child. The soul has a natural movement toward knowledge, so that not to know can be to despair. In the paucity of explanation for a mood, a look, a gesture, the child takes on the blame, and carries thus a guilt for circumstances beyond childish influence.

I was told a story by a woman whose name I cannot tell, for she must protect her family and her livelihood. It is a story filled with silences. She grew up in a poor family in Appalachia, and what happened to her, both at work and in her home, is not uncommon in that region. So emblematic is her story of the lives of men and women in that part of the country (and I suppose of any poor part of this country) that, where I have changed details of her life to conceal her identity, I have simply substituted details true in another life from that place.

She did not tell her mother. But her mother knew. And she was certain of this because after that day she was never again allowed to be in the house alone with her father.

From those few details I begin to have a sense of her mother. The sociologists give us a picture of the mother of the girl who is sexually abused by her father. This woman was perhaps abused herself. And in a way becomes complicit in the rape of her daughter. If the girl tells her, the mother chastises the girl, and may even testify against the child in court. She is a passive, frightened woman, who will not believe the truth.

But the mother of the woman who told me this story was not like this. She was not passive. She had the characteristic strength of the people of this geography, who year after year survive against great odds. They are courageous and they adapt, and this is due not to any exotic mixture of genes but to the lessons of poverty, taught to generation after generation.

To this day, no one in the family has ever spoken a word of it, but all the female children were abused by their father. And yet with each, this happened only once. And that one time was like a signal to the children's mother, who thereafter kept them separate from the father. She did not leave her husband. She no doubt could not conceive of this as an alternative. The first time that it happened, she already had four children. With both parents working, the family was still in serious debt, barely eating, barely keeping one car running.

I can see her coming into the house, recognizing a look on her child's face, setting her jaw one more time. *From now on,* she says, *from now on, you go over to Grace's house, and don't come home before I do. You hear?* And the child hears, and does as she is told because she knows why she must.

No doubt Grace knew too, why this child would wait at her house before she could return to her home after school. And she lent her support willingly, without mentioning the reason. Or even saying it to herself.

The child's father was often home, and thus she was often at Grace's house. Her father was not a well man. She was six years old and her father forty-seven when one of his lungs collapsed. It was the coal dust. The particles enter and settle and over the years do a damage that turns into emphysema, or pneumonia, or tuberculosis. It is called black lung disease. And it goes with the work. The men in the mines expect this illness. Just as they expect the explosions that occasionally occur, or the poison gases that can kill a laborer more quickly than a fire. Like the other men of the area, her father would often work without his mask. To do so was a sign of manhood, whereas to be concerned with safety meant being called "sissy," too much like a woman.

It was because his lungs were damaged that he was not accepted for the army and had to keep working in the mines when

America entered the Second World War. He knew little of the meaning of the conflicts in Europe, but he was a patriotic man and wanted to prove his worth on the battlefield. And so in the midst of the war, when he and the other miners went on strike and Roosevelt sent down the National Guard to break up that strike, something in him was proud. The President had declared that the Guard was sent in because the work in those coal mines was essential to the national war effort.

I can sense the posture of his pride, though I have never met the man. In my mind's eye, it makes him dogged. I wonder if he gave up everything for this pride, or if, at an early age, it seemed that everything was taken from him, so that pride was his only recourse.

Men, the way they have been shaped from childhood, and because of this pride, do not suffer well the loss of a livelihood. They will risk a great deal to keep it. In 1957, before a unit of Marines was ordered into trenches three miles away from the experimental explosion of a nuclear weapon, they were told, *What you are about to do is very special and for the benefit of all mankind. . . . Your country will be proud of you.*

Afterward these men crouched down in trenches. They were told to cover their faces with their hands and wait. There was a long slow countdown. And when it stopped a very bright light, brighter than the sun. Though their eyelids were shut, they could see the bones in their hands. It was as if the world had turned inside out and nothing could be relied upon to be as it had been before. The sound of the explosion was shattering. And then the ground began to shake violently. Several more miles away, a woman thought she felt an earthquake. Some men were quickly buried in earth. And all this instilled a particular terror, so that even men who had been close to death in combat were frightened and lost control. Some were weeping. The light was still blinding when a powerful wind, a wind which threw even men half buried in the earth on their backs, began to blow. A mush-room cloud formed over the sky. And a thick dust began to fill the air so that no one could see more than a few feet in any direction.

Moments before this bomb went off, one man who had gone through another explosion wanted to stand up and shout, *Stop! Stop! We don't deserve to die this way!* This explosion was to be more powerful than the first he had experienced, but he did not know the danger he was in. He was told his body was in no danger from the radiation, and he could not see it or taste it himself. Yet I believe there was something he felt, not palpable to the senses as we know them, but there.

He had been through four years of a military academy in the South. He had had the ambition of becoming a Marine Corps officer and now he was one. One of his teachers in the basic officers' training had told him that the greatest honor he could achieve would be to die on the battlefield.

His body shook uncontrollably but still he did not speak, and only feared, along with his body's terror, that this shaking might be seen by the men he was commanding.

Shall I call her Nelle, the woman whose name I cannot tell you? I name her after my great-aunt, who was born in southern Illinois, which is almost like the South. When I imagine her father forcing himself up a hill and into the mines, I imagine his hands trem-bling, as my own hands have trembled when I am overtired. And I can imagine Nelle trembling too, after her father had forced him-self upon her, trembling, and not knowing where to take this trembling.

The men who emerged from the trenches were deeply impressed by the devastation they saw. Tanks were melted. Heavy equip-ment had become cinders. There was a kind of confusion. No one seemed to know quite what to do. Men appeared in clothing designed to protect them from radiation, clothing the Marines did not wear. Some men were directed away from areas which had been called contaminated. On a mountain range several miles north, yucca trees were burning. The men could not find equipment they had been ordered to operate. But still, they formed columns of twos and marched in time over this landscape.

I can imagine these men standing at attention the morning after this explosion. They have on clean, pressed uniforms. They are washed and shaven. It is before breakfast and they are hungry. Each man is relieved to pass inspection. As they wait for their next orders, do they hope against hope that it will not happen again?

When I ask this I think right away of Nelle's mother. When her first daughter was raped, two others had already been born. I try to become her and immediately I have a feeling for the event. I find myself gripping the edge of my desk as if the ground were shaking violently.

And as the violence of my imagination stops, there is a kind of numbness, and a kind of confusion. *Things somehow have got to go on,* I say to myself. And over time, I begin to forget why I do not let my oldest daughter come home until I am home. *That's just how things are,* I say to myself. Mercifully, like a nightmare whose images give me only a vague feeling of discomfort in the daytime, this violent event recedes from my consciousness. But nightmares recur. There are other daughters.

Iphigenia was not the first child whom Clytemnestra saw Agamemnon murder. The great general had abducted Clytemnestra when she was already married. He had slain her husband and then torn her child from her (the text as set down by Euripides reads *from her breast)* and smashed it to the ground before her eyes. This is as violent an image as I can imagine, yet Clytemnestra all but erased it from her memory. She said she grew to love this man. And thus, when he sent for his daughter to be brought to his military camp, telling the queen that the girl was to be married to his greatest warrior, Achilles, Clytemnestra believed him. She remembered the death of her first child only when she learned that her daughter was not intended for marriage but was instead to be immolated as a sacrifice to Artemis, because Agamemnon needed wind for his sails, so that he could wage his war.

Pleading for her daughter's life, Clytemnestra warned Agamemnon that he would not be able to kiss any of his living children, for they would be afraid of him in the future. But this did not happen. His other children, Orestes and Electra, remained loyal to him.

Orestes was only an infant when his sister was murdered by his father. And thus one can argue that it was in ignorance that he killed Clytemnestra for murdering his father. Yet he could not have been entirely ignorant. He knew, and his knowledge haunted him. He was pursued afterward by the furies.

No detail that enters the mind, nor the smallest instance of memory, ever really leaves it, and things we had thought forgotten will arise suddenly to consciousness years later, or, undetected, shape the course of our lives. And this is also true of the effect of radiation on the body. The body does not rid itself of radiation, and thus exposure is cumulative. Years and years can pass between the exposure to one X ray and another, but the effects of the first X ray are still in the body, which can take fifteen to thirty years to exhibit damage. And if radiation has damaged a chromosome, the damage may not show up until the next generation or, in cases where the inherited damage itself is genetic, the next generation after that. Paul Cooper was twenty-one years old when he was exposed to radiation from the explosion of a nuclear bomb in 1957. It was not until 1976 that he learned he had leukemia. He died two years later, in 1978, at the age of forty-four. William Drechin was nineteen when he witnessed a nuclear explosion at Bikini from the deck of the U.S.S. *Ottawa,* in 1946. Eight years later his wife gave birth to a son with cerebral palsy. And the next year she gave birth to a second son with the same disease. Nine years later the younger son had died. And eleven years after that death, the oldest son died too.

Israel Torres was half buried in a trench by the explosion of a bomb in 1957, and he began to vomit immediately. When he came out of the trench he was still nauseous and his vision was blurred. These symptoms did not go away but instead they worsened. He began to suffer from severe headaches, dizziness and muscle spasms. But his illness was not taken as a warning sign of things to come in the lives of the other men who had been exposed. Instead the doctors denied that the radiation to which he had been exposed could have caused his illness.

For years the connection between coal dust and black lung disease was officially denied. And there are still doctors today who work for insurance compensation companies or the mines who deny that coal dust does damage to the human body. Israel Torres was ridiculed and even warned by one doctor that, were he to continue returning for sick call, he might endanger his career in the marines. But the marines meant his life to him. The same way his work, his ability to do his work, meant life to Nelle's father. He had to feel the illness in him, feel even the coal dust entering his lungs. I can feel what he felt, sitting there on the edge of the bed, pausing to catch his breath before he pulled on his shoes, standing to pull up his pants with a certain amount of pride that he could keep going, a pride in his manhood.

Despite his illness, Israel Torres joined his brigade in a march for a hundred miles with a forty-pound weight on his back. He wanted to prove his loyalty, and that he was physically fit. The day after the hike he could not walk; his whole body was numb, and he was sent into surgery.

There was a joke in our family, never openly laughed at, but still a subject of ridicule, whose cruelty astonishes me now. It was about Nelle, not the Nelle of this story, but my great-aunt. She was never married. She was thus a spinster. And somehow the implication was that therefore she had failed as a woman. Is there a worse shame to carry than to be failed as a man or a woman? The father of the other Nelle, the Nelle of this story, did not fail as a man. And the same masculinity that pushed him toward his own death in the mines somehow brought him to commit a rape against his own daughters. But this masculinity was not in his body. He had to torture his body at times, to make it conform to what he called male.

There are those who say that rape is part of male nature. Human error is often blamed on nature or the gods. Orestes blamed his fate on Apollo. And, in the first play Euripides wrote about Iphigenia, it was only when Orestes could recognize that his own father had sinned against him that he could be freed from the torment of the furies.

I don't remember my father ever speaking in love or in hate about his father. Someone else in the family told me how they used to work together in my grandfather's business, delivering ice. Did they ever speak to each other about anything of consequence? I have no evidence for that. I think whatever feelings existed between them were as silent and invisible as radiation.

Once, years ago, when I was eleven years old, my father and I went in search of radiation. He had rented a Geiger counter, hoping to locate a uranium mine and make us rich. My father was a workingman, but in an unambitious, oddly innocent way he had dreams of clever inventions that might win him a fortune. What a strange pair we made, father and daughter, wandering aimlessly among the rocks of a California canyon, straining to hear if the strange machine my father held might make a clicking sound, and not really knowing, either of us, why we were there.

He knew little of the history of the atom bomb, or of the other uses to which uranium might be put. He did not know what the effects of radiation were on the body. He did not know that Marie Curie herself had died of radiation poisoning. That the women who painted radium dials on clocks, and moistened their brushes with their tongues, died of cancer of the mouth. That the air around us was contaminated with fallout from atomic tests which might make either of us fatally ill in twenty years. He had a naive belief in the wonders of science, an appreciation, and a trust. And I trusted him, and trusted what he trusted, and his knowledge of it, which seemed like a kind of magic to me. The night he fixed the radio, when I was five, I hunkered by him, watching his efforts, certain I would soon see tiny people emerge from the set, and then mystified that somehow he could make those wires produce human sounds. And I remember our trips to the Sears, Roebuck down the block to buy shoes. That was my favorite store. I always asked to go back there, because they had a machine which let you see the bones in your feet through a green light. And I looked at my feet again and again, amazed and awed.

In my circle of friends, in the last three years, five have developed cancer. And Zoe has died.

1957. We were not thinking about radiation. This was an eventful year. The year of Sputnik. I remember it well. I was fourteen years old. The papers were full of drawings, a round object perpetually made a concentric circle around the earth. I was just entering high school. Studying my second year of Latin. *Gallia est omnis divisa in partes tres.* All of Gaul is divided into three parts, in the mind of the Roman emperor. We memorized his words. In another class on current events we debated the emerging movements for African independence. Kenya. Nigeria. Strange places on a map.

This is the year in which the United States begins to take space seriously. Is Von Braun hopeful now? It is only a matter of time. The best way to conquer space, he tells Congress, is to establish a national agency for its exploration.

In the films of the first moon landing the flag looks as if it is blowing proudly in a strong wind. But there is no wind on the moon. Later I learned the flag was made permanently erect with some plastic material. For some reason this reminds me of the crinolines we wore in the decade before the moon's capture.

These starched flounces gave our skirts at one and the same time a lip of excitement and a barrier of stiffness. This style, an invitation and an impediment to intimacy, was not an aesthetic born of girlhood so much as it belonged to the larger system by which girlhood was determined. Can it be true that a hidden aspect, the dark face of a father's abuse of his daughter, or of the exploration of the moon, is an ambivalence toward closeness?

Leaping over a gray lunar surface, an astronaut declares that, despite all strangeness, there is something overwhelmingly familiar about the moon. Perhaps what is feared in intimacy is far less what is strange than what is somehow familiar yet still not entirely known in ourselves.

After Israel Torres was given a medical discharge from the military, it became a question of vital importance to him to establish that his illness had been caused by radiation. The Marine Corps denied that this could be possible, explaining that the level of gamma radiation was too low to cause any harm. Just after the blast, a machine that was passed over Israel Torres's body began to tick wildly. He was not told the measurement the machine registered, but the man who held the machine said to him, *Marine, you have had it . . .* and this he did not forget. When he wrote to the military asking for the reading on the green badge he wore to record his exposure to radiation, he was told that they had lost his particular badge. In 1982 a man who had been a medic in the army at the same test site in 1957 suddenly decided that he would tell the truth, if not about Torres, about the readings on the badges. He had been ordered, he said, to lie about the amount of radiation registered on each badge. He had kept two sets of books, one with the true figures and another with lower, false figures.

But there is more to this story. Even low levels of radiation are harmful to the body. It is a common form of reasoning in this century to reassure those who are wary that the amount of radiation given off by a nuclear power plant, or a nuclear waste site, or a missile, is less than one is exposed to during a medical X ray.

But the work of medical statisticians has revealed that X rays cause a great deal of harm to the body. One X ray of the whole body can lower immunity, so that the age at which we are more susceptible to leukemia or heart disease occurs roughly one year earlier. In fact, the rate of leukemia and heart disease has risen consonant with the years of atomic testing, and the average age for those conditions has lowered.

And there is another part of the story, still. The bomb that exploded and lit up the bones in Israel Torres's hands was designed at Livermore laboratory. In those years that laboratory was developing thermonuclear weapons. And they were trying to design what they called a *clean bomb* because it would give off more intense radiation on the ground, near the impact, but less radiation would rise in a cloud to cause fallout. It has now been established, through a letter written by a lieutenant colonel to one of the men exposed to that bomb, that it was a thermonuclear bomb. And there is some evidence that it was in fact a neutron bomb. In either case, the most intense and harmful rays from that bomb are neutron rays, but the badge that Torres and the other men wore measured only gamma rays.

Just a few months ago camera crews went to the neighborhood of Livermore laboratory and took photographs of water wells, streams and springs that had been contaminated with some kind of chemical. The laboratory denied having any responsibility for this contamination until the poison was traced to its source and then the denial had to be retracted. In the period of time before this denial was retracted I must have carried about a feeling of suspension in my lungs that I hardly knew about, because when I heard over the news that the laboratory had admitted culpability, I took in a deep breath.

From this small moment I can imagine how Israel Torres must have felt as again and again the military denied that his illness, which finally became leukemia, had been caused by that bomb. There was a period when he wanted to give up, when he felt an apathy. Before the laboratory announces its mistake I felt a moment of rage, and then a certain exhaustion seemed to penetrate even my heart. The task of garnering proof seemed too large. I gave up, and in my giving up, everything around me seemed to dull. You can see this look of dullness in the eyes of certain children, and it does not come simply from too little food or from fatigue.

Children who have been abused will turn inward, but there is something that will wake them, bring them back into a circle of humanity. And that is if the abuse to which they have been submitted is named and admitted to be true. And they long especially to have this abuse admitted by the one who abused them. Yet it is most common for a man who has raped a child to deny that the rape occurred. And to imply that the child made the story up, or, if evidence is presented, to claim the child initiated the rape by seducing him. And these claims cause a second suffering as terrible as the first.

But there is another phenomenon among these children. A child beaten to within an inch of her life will reach out longingly for the parent who is separated from her. She will attempt to protect this parent from the scrutiny of the world. And she will mimic her father's logic by blaming herself for his abuse of her.

A psychologist studied the men who were exposed to these bombs and later became ill, and found in them an obsession to establish the truth. But he also discovered that, when they became enraged at the government for denying the truth, they felt guilty for their rage.

What did she feel, Nelle, on the first day she could not return home after school? This is not impossible to imagine. She did not tell her friends and therefore she had a secret of which she was ashamed. Girls learn shame very early and in many different ways. Once I was in a dressing room with a group of girls who were just adolescent. They were whispering among themselves, plotting to trap one of their group while she dressed because they had guessed that this girl did not wear a bra. Girls do not display themselves but try to hide.

Once when I was a girl myself a boy my own age tried to push me down and take off my underpants. He was behaving in a violent way, and his voice commanding me as he pushed me sounded insane. I yelled and he ran off, and later, when I told on him, the whole event was handled discreetly. Except for a long time I associated the clear madness in his voice with the part of my body he had wanted to see.

When Nelle went home that day, if she had forgotten, she then had to remember. The feeling at the dinner table was stiff and uncomfortable and she knew that her mother knew and that her sisters knew because she was the youngest. But no one said a word about it. And she felt nauseous. It was not only her father who was not the same to her, no one was the same. Not herself, not the world. It could never be the same again.

Nor could the world ever be the same for Israel Torres. He never regained his normal sight. He started to go blind. But he was troubled at night with another kind of vision. By things he had seen on the day of the test. Two of the men he commanded had disappeared. He never saw them again after that day, and yet they were not listed as dead. And he had seen something else, a vision that pressed in on him and weighed him down as much as the symptoms of his own illness. In the hospital he told the nurse what he had seen. The next day he was wheeled into a private room and questioned by two doctors and another man who was not identified. These men told him that he had been hallucinating. The next morning a doctor attempted to hypnotize him, but the attempt failed. And the morning after that he was flown to a hospital in San Diego, strapped in and wheeled to another private room where he was questioned by four men. This time the men called him a liar. And a large pill was forced down his throat. When he left that hospital he was warned never again to tell the story about what he had seen.

Two years before, another man, who had never met Israel Torres, had seen a similar vision in the same desert. When he told what he had seen he was given drugs which were supposed to make him calm. And afterward he was sent to a psychiatrist who, whenever he tried to tell the story of what he saw, would show the young man films which were made up of a strange juxtaposition of images: Mickey Mouse and then Hitler, Donald Duck and then the bombing of Hiroshima.

There are many things that we know but we are not supposed to know. Sometimes there is a conspiracy to silence us. But at other times it may be that what we have to tell is something no one wants to know because what we say does not fit into the scheme of things as they are understood to be. A child tells a doctor she has been raped by her father. She may even have signs on her body of this rape, a tear or a fissure. But the doctor refuses to see. A young woman remembers that she was raped, but the doctor hearing this story tells himself he hears only her fantasy.

Recently a woman who grew up in Germany during the Second World War told me this story. She and a friend went to the American base to get some papers signed, and there they saw a display of photographs of people who were in concentration camps. *This is a lie,* she said out loud, not wanting to believe what she saw. So an American soldier, who overheard her, offered to take her to the camps so she could see for herself. She went and afterward suffered great trouble in her mind, for everything she had believed in had been transformed by what she saw. And I could tell that the woman who told me this story felt it was somehow wrong for the soldier to show her friend what he knew.

What Israel Torres and another soldier at another time saw in the desert could have been an image from a concentration camp, from the laboratories of Dr. Mengele where medical experiments were carried out on human beings. Or it could have been an image from Hiroshima, somehow detached from its proper place in time and moved forward, to remind the soldiers what the meaning of their test was. Or, perhaps more frightening to us now, an image from the future traveled backward through time, with the same message.

Torres was in a truck traveling over the desert when one of the men in his platoon cried out and pointed. Israel turned to see a group of people, ten or twelve, in a stockade formed by a chain link fence and barbed wire. Their faces and their hands were deformed. Their hair was falling out. And he thought he saw that their skin was peeling off. He said that they tried to cover their faces with their hands and that they looked more dead than alive.

Two years earlier the second young man, whose name was Jim O'Connor, saw a group of people ushered into a bunker that was closer to the explosion than he would soon be. After the explosion, he moved closer to ground zero and tried to approach the bunker. Then he began to smell flesh burning, and finally he saw a man, on the ground, in agony, blood running from his mouth and his ears and his nose, trying to tear away wires that had been attached to his head.

O'Connor could not forget what he saw. For several years he tried to make his knowledge public. He wrote the Pentagon asking for an investigation. In the response he received there was this sentence: *We can neither confirm nor deny what you saw.*

It is a strange feeling. No doubt Nelle had it too. A memory over the years takes on an air of unreality, hidden as it is in a private unacknowledged world. And yet it persists. Even undefined it retains a vividness; it nags, and will not disappear.

I could feel it in myself. Since I read the story in another history of the atomic testing, I too was haunted. It was on a bright day in late winter that I drove up the coast to a town just north of Santa Barbara, where Israel Torres lived. I wanted to hear the story from him directly.

It was a small home I entered, one of a kind that has come into existence since the end of the last World War. Flat, stucco, small rooms, usually built as part of a tract. I lived in a similar house once myself, and my mother is still in that house. This was the first and only house Israel owned. He paid for it in two years. *I used to love to work for a living,* he told me. But now illness had made him unable to do that.

I asked him about his family. His great-grandfather, he told me, had come from Spain. One could hear traces of Spanish in his English. His mother died before he left home. He remembered his father used to sit with him and his brothers and talk to them about life. How they should be kind to others less able or fortunate than themselves. And how they should stand up for the truth, especially if there was an injustice.

His father had been a marine. He fought in Belgium in World War I. He told stories about how gas was used on those battlefields, but he was not gassed himself. After the war he worked for the border patrol. Was this a natural transition, I wondered, to trade one uniform for another? After this his father owned land and raised cattle, and eventually a couple of bars. All his sons enlisted in the marines. Israel's brothers both fought in Korea. One lost his right ear; the other lost three fingers when a grenade exploded in his hand. Israel enlisted when he was only sixteen. He lied about his age, he told me, because he wanted to follow his brothers.

He was a thick, barrel-chested man, powerful in his appearance despite the illness which had made him frail. Yet there was a softness about him, not in his body so much as in his manner and the atmosphere of his speech. This was perhaps because of the continual presence of his family in his life, in the household with him, and in his memory. His mother and father, both no longer living, his sons, his daughters, his brothers, his wife, his grandchildren. It gave him a different feel than another kind of man, one who does not think of himself as connected to past and future generations.

He was ill immediately after the blast. Nausea. Double vision. Exhaustion. Numbness. A debilitating pain in his bones and muscles. He had been married just months before. Now he suggested to his wife that she was free to leave. But she did not leave.

What gave him the most pain, besides his guilt over the two missing men and the unnamed men he saw in the compound, was fear for the health of his children. Over the years since that time, his wife had had five miscarriages. Twice, he told me, he thought of taking his own life. Once was when his son was ill. The symptoms were so much like his own: hair loss, skin turning yellow, and his blood was abnormal. But his son recovered. The second time was when his grandchild began to pass blood in his stool and urine and Israel said to himself, *That's me again.* He had bled this way intermittently since the test.

The effects of the experiment also continued in his mind. In one dream, he tried to run from the blast while his superior officer shouted, *You're supposed to stay here. You're a leader of men.* That was not the way it happened. *I did stay,* he told me. But the dream still troubled him. Many times he dreamed that the wind returned, the same wind that came with the blast and tore the helmet and gloves right off his body. In these dreams the wind tried to pull him up and out of the earth. In still other returning dreams he tried to find his missing men, and of course he would see the men in the compound again, burned, monstrous, covering their faces with their hands.

Do you know what it is, he asked me, *for a grown man to break down and cry?* I could imagine what it was for him. Not only the pain of all he had endured becoming in one moment no longer endurable, but the shattering, at the same moment, of a sheltering, encircling notion of who he was, a strong man, a protector, responsible to care for those more tender than he, those given to tears, but not the one who breaks down, never breaking down himself.

Many nights he would wake screaming and be unable to sleep again. At two or three in the morning he would come into the living room alone and turn on the television. Once at four in the afternoon he found himself reliving the atomic experiment. He was seeing melted tanks, the mushroom, the medical trucks, dirt flying, the smoke. *The whole thing,* he told me. His sons had to hold him down on the bed until it was over.

I have been in the house with my mother when she, unable to sleep past three or four in the morning, would go into the living room. I would know she was there from the sound of the television, loud through the thin walls of her postwar house. At those times it has seemed to me as if the illness that woke her disturbed the surrounding air, and the television was just another part of this strange cacophonous world, purgatorial, at the fringe of a consciousness belonging to our age.

Israel had been diagnosed with leukemia. He asked me to place my hand over the lumps on his back. They were scattered all over his body. Small and hard like stones. He wanted me to witness their presence in his body. And it was crucial to him that I believe his story. Almost since the day of the blast he had been engaged in a terrible struggle to be believed.

He told me he was afraid to go to the veterans' hospital. They wanted to remove cancer from his prostate gland. But he did not trust them, he said, while he was under anesthesia. There had been that trip to the hospital at Camp Pendleton. The curious holes in his memory. And the dreamlike quality of what he did remember. White pills shoved down his throat in the middle of the night. Waking at Balboa Hospital, six hundred miles away, with no memory of traveling. And the weird, fat, red-faced little captain who had held up a coin, swaying it before his eyes, and had been so angry because he *would not cooperate.*

And there was more. The doctor from the Veterans Administration who told him his radiation count had been low but would not put this in writing. And the other VA doctor who told him that if he wanted his own medical records he would have to hire an attorney. When he returned with a lawyer, this doctor claimed Israel had never been treated by him or anyone at that hospital.

There was the private doctor in Lompoc who had spent hours with him, and began to write letters to the Veterans Administration on Israel's behalf, trying to get his radiation count and his record of treatment. One day when Israel showed up for his regular appointment with this doctor, he found the man had disappeared, with no prior notice, and leaving no forwarding address. Had the Veterans Administration approached him? Had someone threatened him? It was like a nightmare with no resolution, or one of those eerie films, made in the decade after the war's end, in which crimes are committed with no clear reason by no clear perpetrator.

And then there was the newspaper article. At the time of the tests Israel was not allowed to tell his young wife where he was or why, but she read the newspapers. And she saw a picture of him in a local paper with a caption that connected him to the tests. Years later, when Israel began to make inquiries about his own case, and his missing men and the men in the compound, the Veterans Administration claimed they had no record of his participation in these tests and that, as far as they were concerned, officially, he had not been there. It was then that his wife remembered the newspaper.

He wrote a friend in the area where it had been published, who went for him into the newspaper's storage room, what is called the *morgue*, where they keep back issues. Israel's wife was right. The friend sent three copies. Immediately Israel sent one to the VA. What ensued was a travesty of bureaucratic correspondence, worthy of the travails of Joseph K. in Kafka's *The Trial*. Would he send another copy? Would he send the original? He sent another copy. But he could not send the original, since he did not have it. Could he send the name of the newspaper and the date of publication? And still another copy? Yes, he said. He could tell them the name and date, and he did, and did he send another copy? He cannot remember now. Because, when they asked in still another letter for still another copy, he could not find it. So he wrote his friend again. Would he make more copies from the original? Yes, he said he would. And then the next day he received a call. His friend had tried to do this for him, but the original was no longer there. It had vanished.

It is odd how the character of a century should be captured by a novel written at its inception. As I write in the last decade of this century, the word *Kafkaesque* has earned a place in the dictionary; it is defined as nightmarishly strange, mystifying and bizarre. There is, though, to my mind, something lacking in this definition: the particular historical circumstances of the strangeness. Franz Kafka was employed by the Workers Accident Insurance Company for the kingdom of Bohemia from 1908 until near the end of his life, in 1922. He was working there when he wrote *The Trial,* which were also the years of World War I, when Israel's father was fighting in Belgium. Photographs taken of the stairwell and a corridor of the insurance company resemble the airless and dim upper corridors of the court which Joseph K. visited.

In an annual report for the company, a passage written by Kafka concerning accident insurance for wood-planing machine operators is illustrated by a grotesque drawing of seven hands, one whole, one missing the top of the index finger and thumb, another missing all the index finger and part of the thumb, another missing the top of the middle finger and the baby finger, and so on. Apparently Kafka, trained as a lawyer, would go into the tenements where injured workers lived, to interview and take testimony from them. And he must have followed these cases, as requests and responses made on pieces of paper and various forms accumulated to make increasingly voluminous files.

Kafka was frail. He suffered from terrible headaches. Did this make him compassionate toward the wounded wage earners whom he met? On December 15, in the first year of the First World War, he records in his journal, *the joy of lying on the sofa in the silent room without a headache, calmly breathing in a manner befitting a human being.*

One must have the experience of illness over a long period of time to grasp the significance of these words, *in a manner befitting a human being*. One's body, shivering, exhausted, or feverish, wet, becomes alien to one's own existence, and even to all existence. If at one time there was a self who felt as if human, that self has been shaken loose and, as the shaking continues, is ebbing away, disappearing as certainly as a vanished document, spirited by some strange and nightmarish wind.

One does not remember what it is to be well. But something more than absence remains. The finger lost in an accident feels pain, nerves as if extended into a ghostly appendage. Events forgotten reappear in dreams. And fragments of memory left in the mind cry out as if for the connecting knowledge. Unless of course another false order of events has been created from the fragments so that even the scent of memory is threatening.

Just before his death my father wrote a letter to his mother. Though she had written him many times before, he always disdained to answer. What made him respond this time? She sent him a photograph. He showed it to me. A woman standing alone. Middle-aged, rounded, wearing a dark somber skirt and sweater. I did not think of her as my grandmother. Her image in black and white irritated me. What was she doing on my father's bureau? Why did I have to look at her now, and why did I have to remember the image of this stout body printed on a little frayed piece of paper?

In 1922 Franz Kafka left the Workers Accident Insurance Company. He was ill, and he would die just two years later. Was he aware that in this same year the physicist Niels Bohr had conjectured a new model of atomic structure, one that explained the irregularities of the periodic table of the elements? One would not, immediately, link the imaginings of these two men together. Yet history has linked them, in an odd, unpredictable way. For the clarifying perceptions of nuclear history soon entered the obfuscating history of bureaucracies, courts that would not respond to petition, a privileged knowledge denied to those most affected, secret corridors, and conversations bending toward absurdity with nameless judges. In this way meaning was wedded with meaninglessness.

What, then, did they feel, those who answered Israel's letters? Did the answer come from one person or many? Were the letters composed according to the dictates of a policy as mysterious and unaccountable to the authors of the letters as to Israel himself? What passed through the mind of the VA doctor the day that Israel returned to confront him, and began to shout, so that, in order to continue with his schedule, he had to have the man who had been his patient ushered out of the hospital by the military police?

It was in another winter, two years before I met Israel, that I was approached by a woman who wanted to tell me how she had reluctantly participated in a series of anonymous falsehoods. She had been working for the Department of Energy. It was soon after the accident at Three Mile Island. Congress had mandated that the safety of nuclear power plants be studied. The department put her in charge of determining what kind of training the operators at plants were receiving.

Like a runner from the battle of Troy, she told me her story in great gulps of speech. Yet, despite her urgency, her approach was careful. I listened carefully too, sensing she might be struck dumb at any instant, not from any outside force so much as her own fear.

She had written not one but two reports, she told me. The first report showed serious, even dangerous inadequacies in training programs for those who daily operate the control boards of nuclear power plants. But Congress never received this report. It was buried from the public eye. It was only the second report, done at the request of her supervisors, and omitting several very revealing questions, that Congress ever saw.

After she did the second study, she quit her job. Now she wanted to give the first report to someone. Would I take it? She did not have it with her. We met in Kentucky, but the report was in Tennessee where she still lived. I would have to return to the South and visit her there.

It was over a year before I could come again, and circumstances had changed. She had searched for work for several months, until the money she saved was almost gone. Her old job was still there, and she took it. She could not give me the report now. At least not for publication. Did I understand? It would mean the loss of her livelihood. But still she wanted me to visit her. She would tell me her story in greater detail, and show me the inner workings of the place.

The ground was cold and the grass turned brown, the way it does in winter east of the Rockies. I had been to Appalachia before, but never in this season. Still there was a beauty that surprised me. The doe-brown hills were soft like the soft speech of the region. Lee's rented house, though it was in a working-class neighborhood of Knoxville, was surrounded with an expanse of grass and trees. It was made of wood, white, with a sitting porch all along the front.

It was because she loved the Appalachia that she first accepted the offer of a job at Oak Ridge. The research facility that produced fissionable material for the first atomic bomb is situated just outside Knoxville in what was once farm country. It is not too far from the mountains and it shares the culture of the whole region, a culture laid close to the land, familiar with poverty, rebelling against authority yet submitting to seemingly anonymous powers, a culture rich unto itself, with its own vocabulary, its own style of guitar playing, woodcarving, dance, storytelling and wit.

Now writing, I find some irony in this, that her desire to work in the nuclear industry came from a sense of integrity, the wish to live and work in the place where she was born. Though she knew weapons were made there, the original purpose for which she was hired was innocent enough. A private contractor for the Department of Energy, was studying the effects of weatherizing the houses of the poor, and she would assist in that study.

A few days after I arrived she drove me into and around this community. Before she moved to Knoxville she had settled in Oak Ridge itself, the community that was planned around various nuclear plants and research facilities. The first sign to her that something was wrong here was the absence of that soft, musical Appalachian speech so familiar to her.

I recognized a look to the place; it was the same look that had come over the San Fernando Valley where I grew up in the middle fifties. Old farms, orchards, fields, replaced by low concrete buildings, thrown up almost overnight, shopping malls housing *chains,* with a manufactured look, as if life itself were the prefabricated product of an assembly line and lacking any history, or at least missing all memory of the past.

How did it happen? There was some planning. It took place quickly, in the heat of war, under the aegis of the military. Iris, who lived with Lee and was her lover, had seen some of the plans. Her father was a machinist at Oak Ridge and she had grown up there. She described these plans as we sat in their kitchen one night. A separate sector for African-Americans was engineered into the ground plans. And another sector for plant workers, machinists, secretaries, support people, in undistinguished rectangular buildings with thin walls fronted by asphalt parking lots. This was where Iris's parents still lived and it was where Lee lived before she moved to Knoxville. The nicest sector, wooded and comfortable, with front lawns and backyards, and shaded drives ending in circles, was reserved for the scientists and the administrators.

Yet, though there was a hierarchy from the beginning, the look of the place pointed to no seat of power. There was no domed capitol, no ceremonial arch, no wide boulevard leading to an impressive set of marble steps. One sensed instead a hidden power, inaccessible both to the eye and, in some cases, even to reason. There were the omnipresent yet never declared *plans,* unassailable for reasons of national security, dictating that chain link should be thrown around a field, or that access to an old country road be suddenly forbidden. Who ordered this and why was never known.

The place looked amazingly peaceful, even placid, for the site of the manufacture of terrible weapons. But this placidity was like the calm of someone given to hysteria or violence who has been tranquilized. There is a dull calmness that is too still, and then the stories that every once in a while migrate to the surface. The animal laboratory, a nondescript building surrounded by green, looking for all the world like a dentist's office, housing, according to Lee, strange creatures such as six-legged pigs who still survived after years of experiments to determine the genetic effects of radiation. The results of those experiments were labeled top secret. And no one was allowed into that building without a permit. But for what purpose did they still keep the animals?

And then there was the story Lee told me about a truck carrying spent fuel rods that had turned over on the pike. The Department of Energy sent a friend of hers, a photographer, out to document the accident, but in the middle of taking pictures he found himself pinned down by two guards, a pistol pointing at his head. They tore the film from his camera and threatened to arrest him. When finally he convinced them to look at his credentials, they said he did not have the right authorization.

This village belongs to the castle, Kafka wrote earlier in the century, *and whoever lives here or passes the night does so, in a manner of speaking, in the castle itself. Nobody may do that without the Count's permission.*

But who is the Count? And how does one get to the castle? Who gives the proper authorization? Who can tell us why things are the way they are? There was in Oak Ridge no single Count, no single castle, but instead many shadowy Counts, like strange magnets acting at a distance, known only by the indecipherable patterns of what lay within their purview.

As if she were describing this vacuum of identifiable power, pointing out an enclosed piece of the landscape to me, Lee said, *These are called orphan lands*. The phrase had originated among local people to name those parts of what had been public ground, now mysteriously sealed off by some agency at Oak Ridge. The sense of humor is not new. There is a history of absent power in this part of the country. Near the end of the nineteenth century British and Northern capital combined to buy up tracts of land in Kentucky and Tennessee for mineral rights. Hence came the big mines and company towns, and governments within governments whose real power issued from far away.

There were of course small rebellions as well as sly remarks, and for this too the region had a history. It was settled by mountain people, men and women who had forged their way farther and farther into lands ungoverned by white men, people who preferred as little governance as possible. Now there were the burials, for instance, headstones you might encounter anywhere along the turnpike. According to an old Tennessee law, all public lands can be used for private burial, and Lee took these burials to be a mute protest against the seizing of public ground. Of course I read another irony into this image of the dead lying all about these offices from which issued instruments of death.

Lee was born in the coal mining mountains of Tennessee and she had an aching love of the region. Her family was poor but her father had had some education. He was a preacher. One summer she told me she had had to spend every night, seven days a week, sitting in a tent hearing another preacher deliver his sermons, with that unremitting harshness of purpose and predictable repetition which characterize evangelical rhetoric.

The world of fundamental religion does not recognize even

the slightest variation in meaning should this meaning fall outside its own definition of truth. It is only now as I write that I wonder if such a tightly circumscribed structure of thought makes up for early, painful and unaccountable losses. Even the loss, for instance, of all the daylight hours, of one's life force, taken year after year by an obscure and distant ownership, the loss of dignity which comes from poverty and need, by which one is reduced to fear, or begging, or doing what does not seem entirely right, the loss of selfhood when nameless others have so much power over one's life. Just like silence, this loss is repeated from one generation to the next so that its occurrence too seems inevitable.

But all systems of thought, especially if they are rigid, are bound to fail at one moment or another. This happened to Lee's father just after the Second World War. Every explanation for existence he had memorized stood mute before what he witnessed. He had been sent to the South Pacific. And then, six months after the bomb was dropped, he found himself in the ruins of Hiroshima. He would describe it to his children, the spectacular dimensions of the damage. But the crumbling of something inside him could hardly be described. Lee's mother said it more simply, *Nothing before or since had so destroyed him,* she said. *He returned shattered.*

Was it then, shaken and stunned, in the paucity of anything else that might help him survive or even understand what he had seen, that, though all he believed in before had failed this test, still he drew the old beliefs more tightly around him, the same way an abused child clings more desperately to the abusing parent? Certainly it was that way with his idea of manhood. And his sons suffered from this. *The boys were smacked down,* Lee said, *for not being men, on the one hand, and then for being too much men.*

Both sons ended up in various kinds of trouble. The older one started to pull himself together after the younger son was found dead in a drainage ditch. He had been taking drugs and then walked home through an icy countryside in just his shirtsleeves.

When he fell asleep he must have tried to warm himself by lying in this cradle in the earth.

The requirements of gender are like the omnipresent yet partly hidden plans of a secret bureaucracy. I am thinking of Franz Kafka, how he was a small man, in some way unmanned by the terrifying figure of his father, whose standards he could never achieve. It was the critic Walter Benjamin who noticed that the last sentence of *The Trial* speaks of shame: *It was as if the shame of it must outlive him*. Certainly a soldier, judged on the battlefield by his manhood, is compelled by a fear of shame and the desire for a glory that will survive him. Does the shadow of a soldier's life fall over every man?

And is there not shame at the core of all one learns as one learns propriety? The body a terrain of forbidden acts. Hungers, expressions, evidences of flesh permeating an atmosphere of denial. Shame commingling with skin, cells, bone, even breath.

If the shame is intense enough it outlives anyone it touches, whether man or woman. I am still thinking of gender. How shame drives this unbending structure to which we must mold ourselves. In the true logic of this system, if one does not conform, one ceases to exist at all. And any continued evidence of existence is the subject of shame. It is this feeling, that one ought to be invisible, hardly heard, barely making any impression on the whole, that wraps itself inconspicuously through every paradoxical turning, transforming even anger over compromise and loss and discomfort into an energy that sustains the monolithic judgment.

That Lee was a lesbian was a fact only half disclosed where she worked. Though there were those who knew, the truth of her life was never openly discussed. We are all, even the most orthodox among us, used to such little lies of being. We make subtle changes in posture, or dress or speech, to match an occasion at which convention is required, becoming more manly, more lady-like for a period, until, returning home, we feel more ourselves. Moving from home to work, Lee suffered a daily transformation.

Was this part of what allowed her to continue to participate in what she did not condone?

She told me this story. One of her colleagues was a gay man. She was the only one where they worked who knew. Was it the need to keep his private life hidden that made him seem so closed? It is an effective way to keep a secret, to reveal nothing at all of oneself. This strategy need not be planned. Silence over any subject tends to grow. One thought, one moment multiplies until everything is buried and not speaking is a habit. But one day he opened up to her. He had been sent across the country to speak before assemblies of high school students and tell them that the manufacture of nuclear weapons and nuclear power was entirely safe. He knew this was not the truth. But he did it. *How do you live with something like that?* he asked her, and then sank back into his habitual silence.

We sat in the kitchen together eating food familiar to me from my grandmother's southern Illinois childhood, while Lee and Iris spoke of the discomfort they had with this work. Iris had been in love with science and particularly the subatomic world of nuclear physics ever since she could remember. Physicists and engineers had been the heroes of the world she knew. They were the heroes of my world too, growing up in the decades after the war. One felt as if these scientists held a key to an arcane world of meaning once open only to mystics or the most sensitive of theologians. In Iris's world they must have seemed to have the power of God to make and destroy worlds.

But in order to enter the world of meaning, Iris would have to work at cross-purposes with her sense of what was right. The only available employment in the field of nuclear engineering was in the weapons industry. Would she then, over time, sink like Lee's friend at work into a silence that erases all meaning?

The process is like a kind of erosion, diminishing the capacity to see as well as speak. Iris knew now that she had been swimming as a child in polluted waters. Had it affected her health? I asked her. *No,* she told me. But later I learned she had serious arthritis in her hip, requiring surgery, causing her continual pain. A co-worker of Lee's, an industrial safety engineer, had also never made the connection between her own breast cancer and her frequent presence at the Y-Plant until Lee interviewed her for me.

Lee never intended to work in the nuclear industry. After a while the weatherizing contract was completed. And then she found herself presented with contracts of another kind. The transition was smooth, barely perceptible. When she did leave, her résumé showed that she had the greatest experience in the nuclear field. The sense of wrongdoing she felt simply leadened her speech, her gait. She felt as trapped as the *orphan lands,* enclosed in an exclusive world, with its own ethics, its own standards, even its own language.

It is language of disguises that has evolved over four decades, so that it is no longer so strange to speak of a nuclear accident as an *event,* or the explosion at Three Mile Island as a *normal aberration.* All bureaucracies contain such obfuscating terms. It was part of Kafka's brilliance to capture what he called *officialese,* the language of the military and the government that was introduced to Central Europe by Frederick the Great in an attempt to make his armies uniform and obedient. It is an impersonal language, purged of feeling, disembodied, uttered as if by no one with an earthly existence.

One must lie low, Kafka wrote in *The Trial, no matter how much it went against the grain, and try to understand that this great organization remained, so to speak, in a state of delicate balance, and that if someone took it upon himself to alter the disposition of things around him, he ran the risk of losing his footing and falling to destruction, while the organization would simply right itself by some compensating reaction in another part of its machinery—since everything interlocked—and remain unchanged, unless, indeed, which was very probable, it became still more rigid, more vigilant, severer and more ruthless.*

As she spread the two reports she had written before us on the kitchen table, Lee warned me again not to reveal her name or the contents of the first report. Not unless she succeeded in leaving, one day, and in finding other work. Together we read the figures and graphs, Lee translating them into the actual circumstances they represented until gradually I began to see that the boundary separating her world from mine was illusory, as I too, and all I loved, was swept toward the same catastrophe.

When nothing is going wrong, she told me, it is a very easy task to run the control board for a power plant. But if a crisis is brewing, as many as twenty-seven gauges might need to be read, while the same number of lights are flashing, together with buzzers sounding. The effect is pandemonium. The wrong decision can make matters much worse. A crisis can accelerate rapidly, even in a matter of minutes or seconds, becoming irreversible. But the right decision cannot be reached without a thorough knowledge of how nuclear plants function, both theoretically and practically.

The board is shaped in a horseshoe and contains literally dozens of gauges, meters, knobs and switches, many of which look alike. To make matters worse, new technology has required additional gauges and switches, but instead of redesigning existing boards, manufacturers have simply made panels to be added. Often these are placed in back of the operator and in some cases across the room. Even for a well-educated operator the task is difficult.

But at the time she did her study, not even the senior licensed operators who supervised other operators were required to have an undergraduate degree in any field of science. The nonlicensed operators were not even required to have a high school diploma. This placed a heavy burden on the training programs.

By far the most neglected area of training was in general knowledge. Few training programs taught their future operators the principles of thermodynamics. Few of those who operated the boards daily would be required to know what really causes an explosion and why, or even how nuclear energy is generated.

One would hope that at least the future operators, lacking the education they needed to make intelligent decisions in a crisis, would be called upon to repeat certain procedures until they became habit. But very few of the training programs provided drills or simulated trials even for emergency procedures. Most practical experience was acquired on the job while using an activated board with all the attendant risks of failure.

What then was being taught and how? Answers to specific questions, those the industry knew would be on the licensing examination, were fed to the candidates in classrooms or on the job. Certain procedures were memorized but never practiced. Further, the examinations were half oral and that half was graded subjectively by the examiner, who was hardly qualified to judge. (This particular job was not popular, and so examiners had to be chosen from those who had been rejected for other jobs.) Finally, the industry was self-regulating, meaning that the examiners were hired by the industry, and the industry, always short of operators, wanted candidates to pass the test.

I imagined then a new employee, perhaps just licensed, sitting at a control board. As his or perhaps her hand reaches for a particular lever, does she know what process she sets in motion, can she follow the consequences of what she does all the way down the line, or does she make this motion through a fog of reassuring language, any sense of danger or her own ignorance dulled by the seeming normalcy of all her surroundings?

Perhaps this is why in one plant a worker could decide to use a microwave oven, which was provided for employees to heat their lunches, to dry out a piece of radioactive equipment. Or why, in another plant, workers attempted to mend a hole in a pipe with a basketball.

It was chilling now to think of the power plant near my home in Diablo Canyon. Never mind that it is built on an earthquake fault. Was that the plant in the study that offered only four hours' training in radiological protection and control? Or was it one of the twenty-one out of forty-seven plants that offered no training in this field? Was it among the sixteen plants that did put their operators through drills? Was it among the seventeen plants that did not train senior licensed operators in systems design features and operating responsibilities? Was it the plant that offered its supervisors less than an hour of instruction in fuel handling? Or was it among the eighteen that did not train their supervisors how to handle fuel at all?

To protect the city against siege a high wall is built around it.

One likes to believe that somehow there is someone or something safe and infallible standing between oneself and cataclysm. I remember watching a public service film at my grammar school that showed firemen being trained to put out fires. Was that my father standing in the tower? He wore a blue uniform just like my father and jumped as my father was taught to jump from a high place into a net. Even as children, we understood the purpose of this, just as we understood our own fire drills. In case of emergency, you need to be ready. And practice makes perfect.

How then could those who made these decisions fail to provide drills for the operators of nuclear power plants when the flames there would be so much fiercer, so much more difficult to put out, spreading toxic fumes over an unimaginable expanse of space and time? And how could anyone, once the evidence was clear, choose to bury the document that sounded the alarm?

Yet perhaps it is the very extremity of the danger, bordering as it does on the continuity of life itself, the desire for safety as an ultimate state that seals away all fear as if into a foreign country, the wish for a miraculous, mysterious security won not so much by practical effort, or even through theoretical understanding, but by the determination to keep on in one direction despite every indication of trouble, hence vanquishing not only this danger but all catastrophe and every mortal mistake by a sheer act of will, a terrible fear of danger that causes this denial of danger.

But illusion has its own costs. There is also the fear that the unspoken will be spoken. I was intimate once with a woman who told small lies as a matter of habit. She would forget the telling of them, but still they seemed to accumulate, encircling her inner world with a hostile environment. Many old friends and acquaintances were shunned and feared, as if their very presence might endanger an existence based on falsehood. Knowledge that is denied at the core is often pushed to the periphery. Is it not then predictable that one day the periphery will be observed making an assault on even the most carefully built fortifications?

Before the development of the first cell it is speculated that by accident a protein spiroid engulfed nucleic acids and enzymes.

Is it in defense of illusion that violence has come to surround the nuclear industry. The death of Karen Silkwood is one of several mysterious deaths that have occurred in many different locations. Who were the murderers? No one knows exactly. This contributes to the strangeness of the events. Lee and I talked to a doctor whose life had been threatened after he began organizing protests in his community. Many of his patients worked in the plants, and they continually told him about small accidents, emissions of radioactivity into the air, and so he was concerned about the health of his children. But the danger to his family became greater when bullets were fired into his home. He quit his practice and moved to another town.

Lee and I speculated about the report. The data were old. The industry could claim that everything had changed in the years since the study, though Lee doubted that it had. There was the scandal of the burial. The fact that the report never reached Congress. The lies implicated in this concealment. But was this enough to inspire violence? We assured ourselves it was not. Still, when I left, I wrapped the two reports in green shiny paper tied with a red ribbon to make them look like a Christmas present.

The Aurelian wall built around Rome in the third century is nineteen kilometers long and strengthened at thirty-meter intervals with 381 square towers.

What was I to do with what Lee had told me? Even if I never mentioned her name, she would be easily traced. I had promised to keep silent. And I did. What we both knew existed for a while in a kind of limbo, a borderland of disquiet and irresolution, that same silence into which so much had already fallen.

While I was visiting her in Oak Ridge, Lee told me one other story in passing. Oak Ridge Associated Universities had participated in radiation experiments in the late sixties. They used terminally ill cancer patients. Lee thought some of them were the children of military personnel. The story stayed with me. It reminded me of what Israel Torres had seen, the men in the compound. And, of course, I could not help but think of the medical experiments performed in concentration camps that occurred in a distant geography during the first years of my life.

It is probable that the next great advance took place when larger cells engulfed smaller cells.

It was only several years later that I was able to verify Lee's story about the experiments. Neither the patients nor, in the case of children, their parents, were fully informed about the nature of the treatments offered. The study was funded by NASA. They wanted to know precisely what amount of radiation would produce nausea. Men were soon to be sent to the moon. If an astronaut, breathing through an oxygen mask, were to vomit, he would not survive.

I am thinking now of the mother of one of the irradiated children. When she looked on her son's small body, struggling to live, she was thinking neither of astronauts nor of the moon. He weighed less than thirty pounds now. There was so much that he had endured in his six years of life. When was it that she grasped that something more than a simple process of dying was taking place? Was there a slow widening arc to her discomfort, a sense that would not be still, of wrongness? Or was the injustice of it revealed to her suddenly, even if unnamed and obscure in its reasons, in a stunning moment of clarity?

In the 13th century changes in classical Roman fortification are imported from the East by Crusaders. At Carcassonne, a second fortification encircles the first. A large round barbican joins the flank. The towers are hollow from the base, and galleries projecting outward are built of stone.

This knowledge of course does not quiet the mind. One wonders then how such a thing came to pass, a child suffering in this way to bring men to the moon. The mind travels backward in time, tracing first this thread and then that, hoping to unwind the tangle and reach some clear place of origin.

But of course a solitary understanding is not enough. One wants others to know. How grateful was Israel Torres that I heard his story and believed him. And Nelle's story too sought a listener. Or a land of listeners, where all that had happened might come to rest, in the intelligent and curious mind of a shared grief.

For each solitary story belongs to a larger story. Now what took place cannot be told by the witnesses alone. So many of those who might remember—Von Braun, Truman, MacArthur—have died. Yet the story is still told if only as a mute legacy of deeds endured and enacted by the living.

All plants and animals are made from cells.

Lee finally left Oak Ridge in the summer of 1985. *We are talking about/ leaving where we aren't seen/ to go where we are more visible,* she had written in a poem. It was just nine months before the explosion at Chernobyl. History repeated itself. Once again there was denial. The evacuations were too slow. Many children suffered. Many are still ill and will fall ill in the future, unto many generations.

The ideal city of the Renaissance is conceived as radial in plan since this connects the defensive resources at the center of the city to the protective outer walls at the periphery.

Nowhere is there a record of all that has happened in human history, except in living consciousness. And does the truth each of us knows die along with us unless we speak it? This we cannot know. Only we know that the consequences of every act continue and themselves cause other consequences until a later generation will accept the circumstances created of these acts as inevitable. Unless instead this generation tries to unravel the mystery. And if they penetrate the secret whose scent persists in all eventualities, will they say, finally, this death, this wound, this suffering, was not necessary?

The cells of the human body are differentiated according to function. There are cells which make up bone, muscle, blood. Cells which create immunity, send messages from one part of the body to another, cells which remember, understand, see.

The last part of the story Nelle told me is not as dramatic as the vision of Israel Torres. Yet it has weight as consequence and cause. The nuclear power industry and the factories that produce parts of nuclear bombs are situated not too far from the coal mining area of the Appalachia near the Kentucky-Virginia border. Thus it is not uncommon for the unskilled children of coal miners to migrate sixty miles and take up jobs in which, like their fathers, they are exposed to substances dangerous to their health. Nelle wears her protective clothing. She is mindful of the regulations. And yet accidents happen. This is one she told me about that did not get reported in the newspapers. The water from the cooling system of the plant where she works got mixed in somehow with the water provided for the workers to take showers. The men and women who work with plutonium are supposed to shower so that they can be decontaminated. But that day this mixture was not detected until after they took their showers. Every one of them set off an alarm as they attempted to leave the building because the showers had made them radioactive.

Because of the introduction of firearms the radial plan is no longer essential, and fortifications which become more important in the Baroque period, are now hexagonal.

This story doesn't have an ending yet. Except an old ending we've seen and known before, and learned to accept as if the gods had made it so. There are memories that perhaps we've buried together. And, as the song goes, . . . *the faces of my friends and kin are scattered just like straw in the wind.*

EXILE

| | |

In 1827 Giovanni Battista Amici corrects the major aberrations of optical lenses. Cells become visible.

I am thinking of the wind and all it carries. A boy rides his horse through the hills, down into the valley, through thick brush. As the horse makes its way through the brush it struggles and sweats as if moving against an invisible weight. The night the boy returns he goes to bed ill. His head is aching. His skin has broken out. He is nauseous. In the morning the horse is dead. The boy learns that just on the other side of the mountain in the direction of the wind several bombs have been detonated. In a few years he too will be dead.

In 1862, a rapid-fire gun designed by Dr. Richard Gatling is tested at Indianapolis. With this gun 200 shots can be fired each minute.

It is a decade before the boy rides his horse through those hills. There is no perceptible wind in the laboratory. Men in overalls have worked for days to make large piles of graphite and uranium. They do not know the meaning of what they do. Enrico Fermi is about to create the first chain reaction. The general has asked him if there is any danger that the chain reaction will go on forever, blowing up Chicago, destroying Illinois, North America, the world. Fermi tells him the risk is negligible. He has designed certain safety measures. A mechanical apparatus will insert a rod to still the reaction after just a few moments. During those moments some of the scientists present will fear the reaction is going to be infinite. But even if the mechanical apparatus were to fail, Fermi has assigned a man to stand with an ax next to a rope which has the rods suspended from it. And if the ax should fail, two other men stand nearby with buckets of a chemical which will also stop it. The experiment is successful. At Enrico Fermi's bidding a chain reaction is started, and then it is stopped.

Every cell arises from a cell.

It is Thursday, the twelfth of July 1945. Many objects are taken out of the laboratory at Los Alamos and moved along a secret road to a site simply labeled "S." In that place, the many objects are assembled into one, and this is moved to a stretch of desert known as *Jornada del Muerto,* Tract of the Dead. There it is hung on a scaffolding high up toward the sky. On July 14 and 15, heavy thunderstorms break out over Los Alamos.

The United States Army buys 100 Gatling rapid-fire guns. Within twenty years, this weapon is to be used in the Franco-Prussian War, the Russo-Turkish War, and in Egypt, Cuba, West Africa . . .

It is 5:30 A.M., July 16, and, very silent, Enrico stands just more than five and a half miles from the scaffolding. He is holding two pieces of paper, one in each hand. There is a white light that brightens the earth. It stuns the surrounding hills and swallows the sky. Enrico Fermi lets the pieces of paper fall from each hand. A ball of fire appears and grows larger and larger. And then there is a sound so loud it seems more than sound, to be force itself. But Fermi does not hear this sound. He is watching the paper fall, looking to see how far the paper, in its trajectory toward the earth, is moved off its course by the ensuing wind. In this he hopes to guess the power of the explosion.

Like the stone in a cherry, the nucleus of the cell is in the cell's center. And inside this center are the chromosomes, the coded knowledge, genes. When the cells divide, to duplicate this knowledge, each chromosome splits in two.

There are conversations that go on wordlessly with the dead, with animals, with the very young or very old. It is years ago in Italy in the life of a boy not yet fourteen. This boy had a brother closer to him than air to skin, and this brother has just died. The two boys had spent hours alone together building electric motors, drawing designs for the engines of airplanes, the movements of their hands, their minds inseparable. The grief of the living boy is great. But now Enrico Fermi trains himself to walk past the hospital where his brother has died, without crying. To console himself he immerses his mind in the study of science.

By 1903, the year of his death, Gatling saw his weapon improve. Loose powder and percussion ignition were replaced with primed metallic cartridges, using smokeless powder. And the hand crank was replaced with an electric motor.

On this earth there have been many diasporas, many refugees, and many living, hence subtle and intricate, communities torn apart that were once whole. There is a way that we are all connected. Even through the eyes of science we can see it. One need not be a mystic to know this. Common sense gives us a daily taste of our union with all kinds of beings and phenomena which we have imagined, in other moments, to be separate from us. That gray haze which settled over the city across the bay has now been diffused and all the water and the sky are dim in color. The wind that diffuses it blows through the open doors of this room, and right now I breathe in some of that grayness.

Cells are not static. Continually they break down, rebuild the material of their own lives, always changing what they are at any given moment.

It is August 5, 1945. Carefully a pilot goes over the last details of his flight. Tomorrow he will fly over Hiroshima. He has made a decision. He gives an order to his maintenance crew. Before the night is over the name *Enola Gay* shall be painted in clear block letters on the side of his plane.

An invention made in 1986, the center fire metallic cartridge, combining propellant, primer and bullet in one case, makes possible the invention of magazine rifles, automatic pistols and machine guns.

It is years ago when the pilot was just a boy. His father wants to send him to military school. His mother, Enola Gay, known to be as gentle as his father is severe, argues for the boy to stay at home. She loses this argument. All through his childhood she will take his side. Later, she will support her son's choice to join the air force.

Cells create motion, transport other molecules, generate electricity, transmit knowledge, emit light.

On August 11, 1941, *Life* magazine publishes a photograph of Rita Hayworth. A beauty redolent with light emanates from the silvery surface of her skin. Through a gaze you feel yourself sink back with her into the deepest, most rounded region of pleasure. Over five million copies of this photograph are sent out during the Second World War. Her image travels in footlockers, in packs, in ships, airplanes, tanks to the far points of the earth. The same photograph is to be pasted on the first nuclear weapon detonated over Bikini atoll in 1946.

In 1884 a weapon invented by Hiram Maxim is advertised for sale. It will load and fire itself at the rate of over 600 rounds a minute. It is called an automatic machine gun.

There are more languages than diasporas on this earth. A vocabulary is embedded in every cell of every living being. And this is how cells are able to duplicate or how an embryo can grow from the meeting of an egg and sperm, a flower and then fruit from the seed.

I have often wondered what it would be like to be a refugee, to find oneself suddenly in a place where no one knew the same names for things. I would have to learn a new language but always there would be a longing for the old words. And perhaps at night, falling off to sleep, to comfort myself, I would whisper certain sounds: *leaf, river, doorbell, cup.*

It is an unexplained part of human nature that we delight in naming. In the eighteenth century a boy who had lived all his life in the woods emerged into civilization knowing no words. The scientist who worked with him began to teach him language. Quickly the boy learned to pronounce the word *lait,* which is French for *milk.* But he did not use this word to command the presence of the milk that was brought to him daily, as one might have guessed. Rather, he would say the word after the milk had appeared, with a kind of delight or praise, and then again, after he had consumed it, over and over, like a song.

Perhaps this is why I find myself saying over and over the name of my friend who has recently died. All those we lose, and all that we love works its way into our language. We live our lives in a fabric of shared meanings. The commonality of words gives even our most inner thoughts resonant tones. And there are other languages, words, gestures, the small rituals of daily life that connect us to others, both the living and the dead. This afternoon I drink my tea from a ceramic cup. It is useful and also beautiful.

And part of its use, part of its beauty, lies in the long history of the cup, so that as I drink I participate for a moment in other lives.

The cell is constantly exchanging matter with the world around it.

There is a matrix of meaning in the material world. Is it this matrix that culture reflects? Just as our lives are defined by the intricate connections we are born to and have made, any given particle, a neutron for instance, derives its significance from its environment, the "atom." This environment is not fixed but is instead a chemical process, a constantly changing field of matter and energy. Yet even these constant changes possess some order, some still ineffable reason. It is a reason derived from connection, and it is this reason which is destroyed by a chain reaction. Neutrons bombard atoms and these atoms release other neutrons which in turn bombard other atoms. The matrix in which the neutron lived is torn apart, and the world of connection becomes a diaspora.

The neutron does not travel very far when it is driven from the atom. The distance is not perceivable to our eyes, or even imaginable. When we try to understand the neutron we draw pictures of it which are enlarged many thousands of times. But these pictures fail us too. For the neutron exists someplace in its smallness, someplace as precise and exact as our own bedrooms, our kitchens, a place that is a world with its own laws, its own being. To the neutron the space through which it travels is vast. Like a void, a great immeasurable emptiness. Does the neutron have consciousness? Where does our own consciousness live? In the cells? In the animal alone? I can't answer this. Only, I know that the neutron does belong to a world of meaning, a meaning that is in us too, in our bodies, and in all that surrounds us. As the neutron leaves the atom, does it feel senseless and without purpose? Does it feel the anguish of separation? Does it despair?

I know such a loneliness as I imagine the neutron possesses in its journey through the void. Sometimes it feels a part of my flesh.

As a child, I saw everyone I loved leave me in one day. My parents separated; I was sent to my grandmother, and my sister to my great-aunt. My memory is of an endless chill descending, sweeping all my family away, even as if by violence, though no one had really died, and for a few months we were all still just a few miles apart. But time and distance cannot be measured except as we know them. Distance is relative to feeling.

In 1945 experiments are begun to improve the Gatling ten-barrel gun. It is fitted with an electric motor. After ten years, this weapon can fire 5,800 rounds each minute.

When my father was separated from his mother, he learned the lessons of loss and abandonment, and he passed this knowledge on to me. In a sense, when Enrico Fermi created the first chain reaction, he too taught the neutron a lesson, which it in turn passed on, unto many generations.

In spring, I decided to travel to the island where my father was born, and where he parted from my grandmother. I hoped to find some mention of her there, proof of her existence, in the town records, in old newspapers, buildings bought and sold, some sign. I wanted to know why my grandfather had left her, and even more, simply to affirm to myself she had lived. For me she had receded into a cloud of unknowing. All I had learned of her were fragments from my sister or my mother. I cannot remember my father ever speaking to me of her, except just before his death, when he showed me that photograph she had sent him in the mail. She had written to him over the years, but this was the first and only letter he answered. Still, for me she scarcely inhabited this world. She belonged instead to the world of speculation and dream.

Is it possible that for Fermi the world of matter had become unreal? He spent the greater part of his waking hours considering what we call the physical properties of things. What was it that kept the neutron bound to its inner path? What is the nature of this that we call real? In a certain sense, the answers that he provided for these questions were proved accurate. But I am arrested by the image of a man who is himself transfixed, not just for a moment, or for a few hours, but for a lifetime. He is staring at a view somewhat distant from himself. He will never journey into this territory. He will always keep his distance.

Do our thoughts belong to another realm eternally divided from matter? For many centuries it has been the opinion of science that matter is inanimate and therefore has no possibility at all of possessing that quality we call *spirit*. The soul was said to emanate from heaven and to give life to dead matter. The mixing of wine with water in the holy sacraments was meant to signify this union. But an earlier view says that wine and water are of their nature indivisible. What a strange pass we have come to now concerning this question. By the same discovery through which science has finally learned that the enspiriting force and matter are one, science has also discovered a way to separate energy from matter, rending apart thus the fabric that we now know holds existence together.

In the days before the first atomic bomb was tested at Alamogordo, Enrico Fermi was said to have taken side bets on the possibility that the whole state of New Mexico would be incinerated. Such a bet produces an obvious problem. But only for a mind that believes itself to be part of a body. Had the entire state of New Mexico been incinerated, Fermi, who was watching the test in New Mexico that day, would have perished. He would not have been able to collect his debt, or even understand that he had won. His gamble enters the region of Heisenberg's principle of uncertainty which has it that the experimenter affects the reality he observes. But in this case, it is the observed which would have affected the scientist. And in fact, as history has it, Fermi was not unaffected by what he saw that day.

In every scientific experiment there is some risk that events will not proceed as they have been predicted. Otherwise the experiment itself would have no purpose. Concerning whether or not the bomb would explode at all, Hans Bethe, the head of the theoretical division at Los Alamos, said, *Human calculation indicates that the experiment must succeed. But will nature act in conformity to our calculations?*

Until an error was discovered in their calculations, the scientists at Los Alamos feared the possibility of an infinitely expanding explosion. Repeated equations had led them to this conclusion. But finally the scientists made calculations that convinced them the explosion would be finite.

Still, the blast was far more powerful than the scientists had predicted. Nature exceeded their calculations by so far that the instruments designed to measure the explosion were destroyed by it. The scientist operating these instruments was reduced to tears. During the experiment Fermi concentrated on the pieces of paper he was using to measure the explosion. He was perhaps like another physicist there that day named Frisch who told himself he could memorize this phenomenon without being affected by emotion. Yet, though he did not hear the sound of the blast, Fermi was affected. At what moment did his feelings reach him? Was it when he lifted his eyes from the fallen paper, or was it after he explored the region of the blast?

Whenever it was, he was shaken. So much so that, though he never permitted anyone else to drive his car, now he had to be driven. He left the site of the experiment as a passenger. Months later, after the bomb had been dropped over Hiroshima, he told his wife Laura that during this journey it had seemed to him as if his car were jumping from curve to curve and skipping the straight stretches in between.

If Fermi was shocked at the disparity between how he thought he would feel and how he did feel, at least he was able to confess this shock to his wife, and thus, knowing himself in this way, regain composure, as in the telling he wedded together two parts of his being. For Fermi underwent two shocks that day. The first was on seeing the power of the blast, and the second was on meeting an undiscovered part of himself.

Perhaps such a moment is like a dream whose images wake you in the middle of the night. The dream itself has been terrifying and for a moment it is a relief to be awake, but then another terror follows upon this relief when you realize that the feelings and images in the dream were your own.

After certain nights one is glad to wake to a daylight which diminishes the gigantic proportions of dreams. This kind of night is filled with a sense of menace that we believe belongs to darkness. Yet we also entrust sexuality to the night. It is the time when lovers embrace and when even sleep leads to the realm of passion. Night is an intricate landscape where passion and joy cohabit with terror and menace. This is part of the territory of nightmare but it also belongs to waking thought and is woven by day in a more subtle fashion into myth, into story and legend.

I learned the Greek myths in school. The older I grow I read more and more into the shapes of these myths and they become radiant. In this way it is as if time takes me backward and gradually joins me in a circle with antiquity. But the figures from my childhood who glow most brightly are film stars. Childhood memory is the bedrock under all we see. There is the youth and beauty of Achilles. And then the tough and blazingly handsome face of Alan Ladd, framed by his leather jacket, as he moves gracefully into the cockpit of his airplane. Achilles wounded in his heel. Ronald Reagan, his legs severed, crying out, "Where is the rest of me?" Penelope waiting bravely, patiently weaving and unweaving her threads. Paulette Goddard forever making a home, forever saying goodbye. Helen, a thousand ships at sea because of her beauty, Rita Hayworth hotly burning herself into a region of desire.

There was much that Enrico Fermi could not tell his wife. She heard rumors. A sleepless patient at a hospital awake in the early morning hours sees a strange light. A blind girl sees a flash of brightness. A newspaper speculates that a hidden ammunition dump exploded. One day all the men at Los Alamos disappear together with no explanation. When they return they do not say where they have been. What does she think? It is wartime. There is much that is unexplained. And this creates a chasm of speechlessness between her and the man she has married.

There is a party at the Fermi home. This party is held after Fermi has created the first chain reaction. But none of those present speak of this event. And the hostess, Laura Fermi, does not know the reason for the celebration. Later, she is to write a history of these events which she saw but did not witness.

What do the guests at this party do? Because the husbands know something the wives do not, is the atmosphere strained? Or is the party like so many others, where the husbands congregate in another room and hold a separate conversation, speaking as usual about things the wives never know? Do they dance?

Later, when Fermi is alone with his wife, do they undress together, their bodies become suddenly so innocent, simple, unclothed, being naked, and undisguised as truth, do they lie down together, does he open his mouth to her, put his tongue in her mouth, her vagina, his penis in her, hearing her cries, does he also cry, even from someplace unwilled in him, his flesh, the cells washed, as if by light, or life, with pleasure, and more the pure sense of being, and at the same time, his skin like a cloud diffusing into her skin, through her flesh, the room, the bedroom curtains, the horizon? At this moment, where is his secret? Does he let it go, believe it never happened? Bury it deeper inside himself, in a wordless place, in a place described only by formula and the vocabulary of science, a vocabulary he keeps apart from all the words he uses at home: *breast, leaf, river, doorbell, cup, child, love?* Fermi. Does he ever tell his secret to himself in this plain language?

Though I never put my feelings into words, I had trouble preparing for my trip to my father's birthplace. The island of Grand Manan, like my grandmother, had never been real to me. I made a desultory attempt to find it in an atlas. Grand Manan was not in the index. Nor on the map of the region surrounding Nova Scotia. When I reached Maine, I did find it on a map, and I dialed a telephone number to hear the recorded times of ferry crossings. But still the place and even the ferry seemed half mythic for me. It was only when my daughter and I crossed over the Canadian border, and I found pictures of Grand Manan in a tourist office, that I began to believe in the existence of this island. Then a shock of energy went through me, and I was astonished. It was as if I had just awakened, or rather, as if a dream had suddenly become real.

The physicist David Bohm speaks of an illusory perception that we have of nature shaped by our fragmentary thought. Because we think in a fragmentary way, we see fragments. And this way of seeing leads us to make actual fragments of the world.

While Enrico Fermi worked with a team of physicists to design and construct the weapon which would, by means of a chain reaction, create a vast explosion, Paul Tibbets trained a crew of men to maintain and fly the necessary airplanes, navigate, operate the radar, aim and release this weapon. The atomic bomb dropped over Hiroshima was aimed with the human eye. Following the directions of Tibbets, who was his commanding officer, Thomas Ferebee, the bombardier, practiced dropping bomb casings, designed to weigh what the atomic bomb would weigh, again and again and again over the deserts of Nevada. He and the pilot made many careful observations of this procedure and numerous minute changes—adjusting the height of the seat, the placement of a headrest over the site. After this, guided by what he had learned, the bombardier practiced until his eyes and hands were educated and could achieve a certain accuracy.

WHAT YOU HEAR HERE, WHAT YOU SEE HERE, WHEN YOU LEAVE HERE, LET IT STAY HERE. These words were displayed next to the gate at Wendover, the base where Paul Tibbets assembled his battalion for their training. Just as in the desert at Los Alamos, the base at Wendover was chosen because it was isolated. The men who were trained there were not told of the existence of an atomic weapon, nor of the purpose of their mission. *Stop being curious,* the pilot told them. *Never mention this to anybody,* he said. *That means your wives, girls, sisters, family.*

Paul Tibbetts was known to be a laconic man. *Laconic.* The word has a military history. It was derived from the Greek word meaning to imitate the Spartan manner of speech, which was terse, and Sparta was a military state. This nation was frugal with more than words. All its resources, human and material, were marshaled for war.

That the pilot was keeping military secrets from his wife fit almost imperceptibly into the pattern of their married life. He was habitually silent about his thoughts, his feelings, or what he did during the day.

In this way he was not unlike my stepfather, a man who, though once present in my life, fades easily from my memory. He was always vanishing. Either he did not come home until very late, or he returned only to eat and fall asleep on the living-room couch. Seated at the table, or behind the wheel of his car, he would say very little. Sometimes he would tell me jokes. I did not dislike him. He smiled, and at times his eyes shone with a rough tenderness.

The tips of my stepfather's fingers were swollen, and this kept him from doing the fine mechanical work on cars for which he was trained. He had fixed machines in the war. But his fingers became forever swollen in the same war, from some unnamed and mysterious ailment he contracted while sleeping in wet fields. He was never in battle. He loved the time he spent in war because he loved the company of men. It was not so much that he spoke with them any more than he did with my mother or me that drew him but simply the way he was with them. When he came together with men in bars or on the occasions his friends would visit the house, I would watch him do a silent dance of comradeship, a swelling of his chest, a movement forward, a gesture with his hand to another man's shoulder, the middle of a back, an unexplained but shared laughter. It was as if they shared a secret.

The pilot could not, did not tell his wife why they were in the desert. She complained about his silence, not so much that he withheld the nature of his work, but that he withheld himself. To one man he admitted that he preferred to be among his men or in the air. He seldom spoke with his children. At Christmas he picked up presents at the last minute from the base supply depot. He gave each child a model plane. In many small ways he communicated his distance.

This man and my stepfather were alike in another way too. When he was just a boy my stepfather's father took him to pool halls. He must have been very small because to practice his first shots he had to stand on a box. But this friendship between father and son was soon interrupted by violence. Again and again for small infractions, or no reason at all, my stepfather's father beat his son. His mother could not protect him. But she gave him a special tenderness for what he suffered. And he loved her.

This must have been like the love Paul Tibbetts felt for his mother. Enola Gay had given her son a special tenderness to make up for his father's severity. On the night before he flew over Hiroshima, the pilot remembered that once his mother told him that everything he did would turn out all right, and that was why he named his plane after her.

He was worried that night. There were fears he could tell no one. The crew was trained to fly away from the bomb as fast as possible. In practice sessions they had been able to fly seven miles from the bomb before it was calculated to explode. But the scientists could not promise that at this distance the plane would be safe. While they were trained, the men who were to fly with Paul Tibbetts knew nothing of this fear, nor of the weapon they would carry. But they sensed a danger from the fact that their mission was extraordinary.

Men going into warfare are always going into danger and, knowing this, they enter a realm of recklessness, where many truths—the laws of gravity or the laws of mortality—are suspended as if by this very choice to move toward rather than away from death. There are soldiers' uniforms on which a figure of death is emblazoned with pride. There are soldiers who wear shrunken heads and ears around their necks, as if embracing death. And, at the same time, as if standing between life and death, soldiers preparing to go for battle will reach out for what they call *life* as if life were a substance that could be devoured once and for all time.

The battalion of men who readied themselves to drop the bomb over Hiroshima were known as "hell-raisers." They drank. Claude Eatherly, who flew the weather plane, was famous for his gambling. On his airplane, which he named the *Straight Flush,* he had drawn a cartoon of a Japanese man immersed in a toilet. Tom Ferebee, the bombardier, was known as a ladies' man. Near the base at Wendover, many of the men got into trouble in the town, going after other men's wives, or daughters, or prostitutes.

A man—perhaps he is a soldier, and nearly ready to go into battle—goes to see a prostitute. He goes first to a bar, or to two or three or many bars, and drinks among men. Then when he is tight enough, but still able to walk, still able to feel himself in his sex, he searches, in the last bar, or the neighborhood surrounding it. What is he looking for—a color of hair, the shape of a face, a way of moving, large breasts, or a lean body, light or dark skin—none of this matters. Some bit of her, her laugh, the way she looks, will reach him and eat into his imagination until he is drawn. Not knowing this woman, he is drawn inevitably toward that which he remembers, or that which he has always dreamed of and learned in some way to associate with the turn of a head, the purely physical inflection of a voice. He follows as a force that seems to be hers takes him closer and closer. Who is she? He learns very little. Whatever she tells him she invents. In the darkened rooms where they meet he is not able to tell that she has taken drugs, enough to take the edge away from her awareness, or more, to make her nearly insensible. He will not have to remember her name. She only pretends to learn his name. He may ask to be beaten or to beat her. He may want to caress her, to pull her to him roughly and quickly. Perhaps he asks her to put his sex in her mouth. He may want to swear at her or give her orders. As the sex comes into him a certain sharpness enters his mind, like windows, doors opening. There is a place in him, between his chest and thighs, inside and through and in his belly, his penis, his testicles, that starts to unwind as he grows larger, as if space itself became larger, even infinite, and inside him, like someone dying, images enter his mind unbidden; he is more drunken than drunk, perhaps he cries out, or shouts, he thinks of his own death, he puts his sex, large with wanting, inside her, and despite himself, his body sighs sinking into pleasure and then into more desire as he moves in her, wanting, his skin intense with feeling; he senses death, something in him almost breaking, he may shout again, and then it is warm, it breaks, it is sweet, it is gone. He rolls away from her, surviving. He has vanquished this small death. And now he hardly notices her. His mind is racing back to where he came from. Feeling cold, saying nothing of what he has seen, what he has felt, he stands and puts on his clothes. He will give her money now and quickly make his way back to the street where he can be among the other men again.

The story of atomic warfare began in silence. While scientists designed a nameless weapon, and a battalion of men trained for an unknown mission, a whole city was built in Tennessee whose purpose was hidden.

Is it possible that a mind can break from the weight of what is known and yet unknown? Those who worked in the factories at Oak Ridge were not told that they were making the fissionable material to be used in atomic weapons. Almost none of the military men assigned to this project knew its purpose. But wherever a secret is kept it will make its way, like an object lighter than water and meant to float, to the surface. A navy ensign posted to Oak Ridge suffers a mental breakdown. Is he the repository for the unspoken fears of others? He begins to rave about a terrible weapon that will soon bring about the end of the world. Because his ravings are close to the truth, the navy builds a special wing of the hospital at Oak Ridge for him, staffed with psychiatrists, physicians, orderlies and janitors, each chosen especially for this work, judged trustworthy and able to keep secrets. The ensign is given continual sedation. Whenever he begins to speak, he receives another injection. His family is told that he is on a long mission at sea.

How strange it is that some lives become emblematic of our times. What is it that makes us recognize madness in another? I imagine the speech of this man. He utters only fragments, broken phrases, that do not make sense. Perhaps he repeats the word *Terrible* over and over, punctuating his speech only occasionally with the word *weapon* or *death*. Perhaps he uses the phrase *end of the world* but surrounded in a labyrinth of personal associations, a childhood name for a brother, a fearful memory from a nightmare, a word known only to him but meant as a key to unlock his private suffering, the experience that sometime in his past broke him. Not only what he says, but also his broken mind evokes a story that is true—neutrons released from atoms fracture other atoms until the circumference does not hold and there is one vast breaking.

Oak Ridge was a closed city. Its occupants had to carry identification badges. They would enter and leave through an armed guardhouse. Regular buses would take wives into Knoxville so that they could carry back the small necessities of life; groceries, a pair of socks, electric light bulbs. Otherwise what they needed was provided for them inside the city walls—schools, churches, movies, dances. The gates stayed closed for three years after the war. When they were opened a parade was arranged down the main street. Marie ("The Body") McDonald rode in an open car through the gates. She was followed by a brass band. And speeches. At Elza Gate a circle of children cowered into the arms of their parents as they watched a magnesium flare produce a miniature mushroom cloud.

A photograph of this occasion was published in a book celebrating the twenty-fifth anniversary of Oak Ridge. I was given this book by a woman I met in Oak Ridge last winter. I met her through Lee's lover, Iris, whose mother she is. I sat in her living room with her and her daughter as she told me the story of her life. I will call her Edna.

She was born in North Carolina. Both her parents worked in the cotton mills. Her mother started when she was just nine years old. Edna's grandparents had owned a small farm. Because they had depended on the labor of slaves to work this land, after the Civil War it became useless to them. In 1900 they moved to town. Edna's grandfather started a small truck farm there, and all the children, including Edna's mother, were sent to work. Edna's mother and father met in the mill just before World War I. She was born in 1914.

Her father was a sample weaver. He wove the sample patterns drawn for him by designers. On several occasions he brought home cloth for the family. He wove the cloth for Edna's first prom dress. It was damask, she told me, with a pattern of white flowers embossed on it. Edna's father had been orphaned young. His father died when he was six, and his mother when he was twelve. After that he began to wander all over the country. Somewhere, Edna told me, someone must have started him learning. He had no formal education but he was always reading. The range of his interest was wide. Physics. The Apocrypha, or what she called the forgotten books of the Bible. Edna always wanted to know where it was that he had gone as a young man.

My father had little education, and he spoke in the grammar of workingmen, but he had the same hunger to know, a curiosity, and an openness. We would speak of many subjects together, arguing dispassionately, never with rancor. He often agreed with my perceptions, which gave me a confidence rare in a girl.

Edna took after her father, reading and thinking. Her brother

Jack was like him too. Edna's father adored this son. In 1941, against his father's wishes, Jack enlisted. Later that year, after the Japanese attack on Pearl Harbor, America entered the war. When he heard the news of this attack, Edna's father had a stroke. And that Christmas Eve he died. Edna believed her father chose to die so that he would not have to suffer the death of his own son. Jack died on D-Day in Normandy. The young man who came to tell Edna's mother of this death could say nothing. He just sat and cried, as did Edna when she told me of these two deaths. I had asked her what she thought when she learned of the atomic bomb. *I didn't think,* she said. *I was just glad the war was over.*

Edna met her husband before this war, when she was just sixteen. She was already graduated from high school and had gone to work in the hosiery mill. She made the seams of the stockings that eventually were carried by soldiers going overseas. She married at seventeen. Her husband worked in the cotton mill. Bill drank and one night he got into serious trouble. By then they had two children and one more on the way. He said he was forced to do what he did by the two men who gave him a lift. She never knew whether or not he was telling her the truth. The charge was serious because a gun was used. But he was young, so he was sent to reform school, and that was where he learned to be a machinist.

Jobs were hard to find. And then he was offered a job with very good pay. The management paid for the whole family to visit Oak Ridge. They were put up in a hotel, and a limousine came to drive them to the plant. Edna understood almost nothing of what she saw as they passed through the plant. Over the years, her husband told her little. She picked up a bit of information here and there. That uranium is a soft metal when it is machined. That the doctors found high levels of mercury in Bill's blood. He had dropped a beaker of it and had been tracking it home on the bottoms of his shoes. It was on the carpet where the children played.

He was told to keep the work he did a secret from everyone,

even his family. But, like Paul Tibbetts, he was a habitually silent man who seldom talked to his family anyway about what he did or felt. He took after his father, who was an overseer in the cotton mill, and who used to tell his mother, *Just so you don't bother me, that's all I want.*

Bill himself did not know the whole truth, and he accepted this. But his mind worked all the time, even so. He was an intelligent man. He had constructed a valve essential for the manufacture of uranium into fissionable material. He never knew what the valve was for but he pieced together an idea from incidents and rumors. A boy shut out by his father's silence learns not to ask questions but to find his answers in other ways. One day a man dropped a block of ice while he was delivering it. It fell with a loud crashing sound and the scientists he worked with panicked, running in all directions. From what he gathered to be the truth, he made his own decision. He moved his wife Edna and their children back to Carolina until the war was over. He did not tell her why.

After the war, Edna's husband returned briefly to Carolina, but he could find no work. Edna stopped working in the mills after her fourth child. The family moved back to Oak Ridge. Now, six of her ten children work there, some as scientists and engineers, tutored by their mother's love of knowledge. Edna's husband is retired now with a lung disease the plant doctors tell him came from smoking. A few years ago Edna discovered the stream in back of their house, where the children played and caught fish, was polluted with chemicals and radiation. She and her husband lead separate lives, rarely speaking, except for practical reasons.

I was born in 1943, the year Edna came to Oak Ridge. My mother and father were troubled in their marriage and I was conceived to hold them together. In marrying my mother, my father drew into his life all the hidden sorrows of his childhood and made for me the same circumstances he had suffered. Long before

I was born my mother began to have a problem with drinking. This problem grew worse. We shared a house with my mother's parents. Just as my great-grandmother had dominated her family, so my mother's mother ruled our household, according to strict ideas of propriety. In an attempt to be free, my parents moved away, but once in their freedom, my mother fell in love with another man. This was scarcely mentioned except in whispers. But it was part of the cause and reason for my sister and me to be separated, as was my father, from our mother. I was six.

For years I lived with my grandmother. My father would come to visit me on weekends. He was often late. And I was often waiting for him. Since his death I have had many dreams in which he returns to me. He comes with many faces, but he is always dead. When he died I had the feeling that he had never really lived, and left the earth, unfinished. We spent many hours together and had many conversations but never once did he speak to me of the pain that I could see at times in his eyes. Repeatedly I asked him to tell me about his childhood. He told me about pranks he pulled, or the day he stole a melon from a neighbor's garden and was caught, but never once did he say the name of the island where he was born, or speak of his mother. He had a loneliness as of a man who seems in solitary confinement even when among others. Was he a vague presence even to himself, a fragment leaving only traces on the face of this earth, trailing unclaimed ghosts?

One of his ghosts inhabits me. In our hours together I breathed in the irresolution of his unspoken feelings. Like my father, I have committed small suicides daily. Not going to the heart of all I feel, I have erased my real presence, sexuality, intelligence from language and expression.

Perhaps it was because there was so much unspoken between my father and me that we loved to go to the movies. We would go to Grauman's Chinese, the famous theater where the stars had molded their hands into unsettled concrete. I would fit my smaller hand into these depressions. And then go with my father into the dark theater, where we waited to see the screen light up with color, motion and momentous feeling.

To say one of their names was to evoke a world of feeling. Alan Ladd. We watched them all. Katharine Hepburn. Cary Grant. Brilliant and luminous. They were our icons. Rita Hayworth.

Tilted back away from the camera, so that you can see the line of where her breasts meet, caressed and framed by lace, one shoulder, one thin eyebrow raised, smile of knowing on her face, reddened lips, she rests on the unmade sheets of a bed. The love goddess. Posed for this photograph on a prop bed, wearing a negligee from the wardrobe department, from birth she was groomed to be a film star.

We can all trace the shapes of our lives back to our families. She was as much shaped by her father as I was by mine. Eduardo Cansino was a professional dancer. He taught his daughter Margarita all that he knew. Then, at the age of thirteen, she began to dance as his partner. No one in the audience knew she was a child. She was dressed seductively. Onstage they performed a romantic duet, dancing in lockstep, ending faces in profile, kissing. Offstage Eduardo locked her in her dressing room, while he would go to drink and gamble. For years he managed her career, introducing her to men who made films. When she was first married, it was to a man her father's age, who controlled her in the way her father had done before.

But there was more, another more violent aspect of her education. The duet pictured on the stage had a grim reality, a secret both dancers kept. Throughout those years of her childhood, Rita Hayworth's father had been raping her.

What is it like for a girl to be forced to keep such a secret? The shame of it invades her. She feels she is the cause of her own suffering, a suffering for which she must make amends in the world, complying ever after with whatever the world asks of her. And she is caught by this shame in a terrible paradox. At the heart of what makes her wrong is her sexuality, but it is this the world demands of her.

I remember the night my father discovered I had made love with a boy. I never saw him so angry with me. He shouted at me. Slapped me. Then, when he tucked me into bed, he put his lips over my ear and blew softly. Who was I to him at this moment? This was the only sexual gesture he ever made toward me. But still, we did our own lockstep. I felt guilty toward him, at his death, as if somehow I had caused it, even, somewhere in an unstated region of my mind, believing that the intensity of my youthful passion, which I could not separate from the intensity of my being, had mortally endangered him.

I am thinking now of Emilio Segre, and a remark I heard him make as he described the way he and Enrico Fermi discovered how to create the first chain reaction. He was speaking to a small seminar on nuclear technology I regularly attended at the university in the city where I live. He told us that the real secret to penetrating the seemingly impenetrable nucleus of the atom had been to slow down the neutrons aimed at it. *But why slowness?* one of us asked. *If you have a lion passing with the velocity of light through this room,* he said, *it will not eat us, it does not have the time, but if it starts walking around leisurely, well* . . . Even then I was struck by this portrait of the inner nature of matter as a ferocious beast.

Just as atomic structure has been altered in our century to mirror our civilization's idea of the true nature of matter, the movie studios reshaped Rita Cansino to fit an ideal. Given a new anglicized name, Rita Hayworth, she was remade to look at one and the same time more sultry and less Hispanic, her browline moved back, hair dyed, eyebrows removed. Did she know that these changes echoed an older chapter in her family history? Eduardo Cansino had descended from Muranos, those Spanish Jews forced to convert to Catholicism during the Inquisition. Though they continued to practice Judaism in secret, for most the knowledge of who they once were was eventually lost.

A few years after the end of the war, when I was five years old, Rita Hayworth made a famous film called *The Lady from Shanghai*. It was directed by Orson Welles, who was then her husband. He played the hero and she the heroine, a lady named after *the most wicked city in the world*. The hero, a detective, is drawn by the heroine's beauty into danger. Slowly she entraps him. They enter a house of mirrors. She points her gun outward at him and at us who watch as the story concludes. A gun explodes and the mirror is shattered. But the hero lives. It is the evil lady who dies, and of course we too, who are the witnesses, survive.

Three years earlier, in August 1945, two atomic bombs had been dropped over Japan, in Hiroshima and then Nagasaki. I remember a faded bookmark from this time. I found it in my grandmother's books. A caricature of a Japanese man, painted yellow, glowers over a lighted match. Behind him a small green forest bursts into flame.

At least once that I know of, Rita Hayworth complained about the image Hollywood produced of her. What troubled her enough to speak out was the decision the studio made to put her image on a nuclear weapon. Her brothers had been in the Second World War and come back different, scarred. This had made her against all war, she said, and she wept when the bomb bearing her image was detonated.

Is it possible that Helen of Troy was only a caricature of a woman? In one version of that story it is said that she was never really in Troy at all, and that what the Greek armies saw was only a phantom. The blast at Hiroshima left phantoms of a kind, shadows instantly impressed by objects, parts of buildings, fleeing people, who existed in one moment and then in the fraction of a second vanished into vapor.

In the fall, when I traveled to Hiroshima, I asked to meet a woman my age, who, like me, would have been two years old when the bomb exploded. Yōko was thrown through the air and out a window on August 6, 1945. She still has two small scars on her face, where the glass was embedded. But she does not remember the blast.

Her first memories are of grade school. She was living with her older sister, a brother and a cousin. Her father had disappeared in the explosion. They searched for his bones or his ashes but no sign of him could be found. His passage from life could not be consecrated. Her mother, very badly burned, lived until August 23, when she died of radiation sickness.

Yōko's sister worked to support them all. But she was also sick of radiation exposure, the work was hard, the wages small. They lived frugally with no electric lights, no heat, the barest minimum of food and clothing. Then Yōko's sister became very ill. She was taken to the hospital. Yōko's brother, who was older, abandoned the two younger children. As a boy, he had been raised to be taken care of, and he could not face the responsibility. The two small children were left alone. Yōko's cousin would go to help in the grocery for some food. And then, for long periods, she would not return. Yōko remembers one New Year's Eve. Her cousin was gone. It was cold. She went outside to make a fire, and when she looked at the night sky, she told me, she felt very alone.

After this, the two children were taken in by relatives, the cousin to one home and Yōko to another. But her loneliness did not end. She moved in rotation among five different houses. An extra child was a burden. She carried her belongings in a scarf and opened them in a corner of a room. She had no room or bed of her own. Many times she sat and listened as her relatives argued over who should take her next. She saw how the natural children of each family were treated differently. If she had a quarrel with one of them, she would be told, *Our parents are raising you*. In one family she had to work until late at night or, on special days, until midnight. When she began to menstruate she had no one to approach with her questions.

Somewhere inside herself, she felt she had no reason to exist. She was like a neutron, lost from its path of meaning, without a matrix, with no world of relation. She went to her middle school by a train that passed over a bridge. And while the train made its way over this bridge, she would think of taking her own life.

I nodded as she told me this story. Between us a kind of knowledge passed, half spoken, half unspoken. From our meeting we both understood that what we felt had come from circumstances outside our control. Such a childhood settles into flesh and bone. It can be seen. It is not invisible but present in the line of shoulders, the measure of breath, a hand moving to lips, words spoken or unspoken, so that even a story not told is told over and over again in mimed gestures of shyness and fear and conscribes a place in the body which holds this old suffering almost with tenderness. Yōko has not spoken of her childhood to her husband or to her children.

How much do we know or not know in those we love? Love is, in some way, a kind of seeing through which many intricate facts are embraced. What is hidden, kept secret, cannot be loved. It exists in a place of exile, outside the realm of response.

In a famous short story written about the bombing of Hiroshima, a man who is poisoned with radiation returns home to his village. He tells his family and friends what he has seen. No one believes him until news reports arrive. Then they listen to his story with shock and grief. But after a time they no longer want to hear his story. He is condemned to repeat what he has witnessed over and over to those who do not listen.

Some argued that, because of the high intelligence of the people of Kyoto, this city would be the best target for the first atomic bomb. These citizens, it was said, would best be able to appreciate the significance of the new weapon. But Kyoto was not chosen. Secretary of War Henry L. Stimson felt the city too beautiful to be destroyed. Kyoto has for many centuries been the home for an ancient and gracious culture. Its streets are resplendent with temples, gardens; it is a center for the manufacture of silk and the practice of the tea ceremony.

Beauty lies at the heart of the tea ceremony. Each object used must be beautiful. Special cups are made for this ceremony. Even to look on these cups is to be brought into a wider, calmer realm of the self. The tea master Okakura Kakuzo has said that beauty evokes harmony and the mystery of mutual charity. What became at one point in history an art reserved for the samurai warrior is really the distillation of all the ways that women had of shaping life. Ways of setting a table, design in fabric, old recipes, songs, ways of bowing, of serving, of sitting. All that we call beautiful— the shape of a balcony, a certain landscape, a phrase, an alphabet, the curve of an airplane wing, a mathematical formula—is a kind of vessel, like love, that holds what we know.

There is a museum for children in Oak Ridge, Tennessee. One room of this museum holds objects left behind from Wheat, the farming community that once stood on the site of Oak Ridge —scythes, plows, butter churns, wooden chairs, hand-carved toys and musical instruments—and they are beautiful. When I was there I saw two temporary exhibits. A room was filled with pottery made throughout the Southern states and it had a haunted quality. I had just returned from Japan and could not help noticing how many of these objects resembled Japanese ceramics. In a long corridor, photographs were displayed from Oak Ridge during the war. *April 14, 1944, a church service held in the central cafeteria. December 13, a Sergeant back from the war in Germany urges a crowd of assembled workers to get the job done.*

The weapon the young navy ensign had raved about was taken on a long voyage over several oceans. Bit by bit essential pieces were assembled from many places. A heavy crane from England. Fissionable matter from Oak Ridge. A crate, fifteen feet long, carrying the inner cannon of the bomb, a leaded cylinder two feet high, a foot and a half wide, holding a uranium projectile, all journeying toward the island of Tinian, near Japan.

Hiroshima is on an inland sea. And there are several islands in its harbor. One of these is a famous shrine, some say to an ancient female deity. Another, Ninoshima, was the site of a quarantine station for homecoming soldiers during the Russo-Japanese War. After the atomic bomb was dropped over Hiroshima, many of the most severely wounded were taken to this island to die. Few buildings in the city itself were left standing. On the island, the old hospital was still intact, though its corridors and rooms were almost empty. There were few doctors, or medical supplies. Those who were very badly burned were taken there by rowboat. The trip took two hours. Often the dying crawled into the woods or back into caves and tunnels. Even today bodies are still discovered there.

I went by ferry to Ninoshima. The trip across the water was brief. It was November and just beginning to turn cold. The sky was gray and white. The water, waved, shimmering with a silver reflection of muted light, a green darkness beneath. I stood on the deck watching as we made our progress toward the island, remembering suddenly my ferry trip to another island earlier that year, the island of my father's birth.

That day, though it was midsummer, the sky was gray and white and there was light on the water. And it was there on that water, in the midst of the reverie of travel, that I found in myself a feeling of urgency, under the calm surface, and beneath that an indefinable pain, sharp as a bud. This island of my imaginings was real. And so then were the stories I had heard. The water we navigated became then like the water of legend, between one kind of knowledge and another.

Even the trees, green and orange, growing over the hills of Ninoshima, reminded me of Grand Manan. And here too legend sprang to life as if time had stopped and the dying who had for two hours of agony looked to this island for hope and refuge, who lay near the water or crawled into caves or forests, were still there, in suspension for a moment from physical pain, without weeping or admonitions to heaven, the air itself pregnant with the breath of words impossible to speak or hear or, even, to forget.

Perhaps every moment of time lived in human consciousness remains in the air around us. Mitsukuni Akiyami, who was a schoolboy at the time of the blast, has written of the moment that the bomb exploded. He felt an eerie silence. Sound and color stopped. Then it was as if an instant of time had frozen and within that instant—*a fraction of a thousandth of a second,* he called it—he said that an *unimaginable number of incidents took place.* He looked toward the city. In this instant it had disappeared. And before the instant had passed the boy had already prayed, *Please let this all be a bad dream.*

There is a territory of the mind, vacant and endless as the miles and miles of rubble the city of Hiroshima had become. One enters this territory as one speculates for instance over a disaster. If I had traveled a different road would there have been no accident? A life can be gone in an instant. To grasp the meaning of the explosion of one atomic weapon at Hiroshima would take more than one lifetime. One would have to hear every story, and take in the memories too, how the vanished repeat themselves in the minds of the living. The telephone ringing in the early morning. The sound of feet on a certain staircase. Echoes resounding for years in the experience of each woman, each man, each child who survived.

I went to the island of Ninoshima to hear a man tell his story. He was a boy of twelve when the bomb exploded. His father had died of illness earlier in the war. With his younger brother and sister he tried to get back to their house. His mother must have died instantly there. They lived close to the center of the explosion. The great mass of those fleeing, injured severely, skin hanging from arms, legs, faces, stunned, silent, moved out of the city and toward the hills. They found themselves in a crowd walking toward Yaga, three kilometers away. Soon Ota had to be carried. He was burned over half of his body, his back, legs, arms.

When there is death, even one death, time seems to stop, as if perhaps, in stopping, the dead could be called back into life, or events could be erased before sinking irrevocably into knowledge. He did not know at what hour they finally arrived. People hovering between life and death were spread out everywhere, lying on the grass where he, too, would rest.

Between each cell, and neighbor cell, there is an elaborate network of membranes, closed, resembling pockets. These structures can make fleeting connections with each other, or with the plasma membrane surrounding them.

We sat together almost forty years later, circling a low table, Ota, Mr. Masako, a reporter who, like me, wanted to make a record of this story, Becky, who interpreted for me, and Mr. Kikawa, director of this school, once an orphanage for children cast into a state of abandonment by the explosion of the atomic bomb over Hiroshima. The island of Ninoshima had to be cleared of corpses to make way for the children, several weeks after the bombing. Years later, mass burial sites were still being discovered. *Now to speak of it,* he told us, *is almost unbelievable.*

They lay there, Ota and the others who were wounded and dying, endlessly, day after day. A list of names was posted. Each time someone died, another name was struck from the list. Many vomited blood or lost hair. Bodies were swollen. These are symptoms of radiation poisoning. Burns became infected and filled with pus. Maggots grew in the open, unhealing wounds. Ota told me he believes he survived only because his younger brother picked the maggots from his body every day. Those with no one to do this died. Because of his burns, he lay on his left side. In this way, as it healed, his ear was fixed to the back of his head, as it still is today. His mouth was filled with dust unsettled by the blast. But he had been told not to drink the water.

All over Hiroshima people were warned about the water. Those too badly injured to move would cry out again and again for water that never came. And in moments of extreme pain people of all ages would cry for their mothers.

How did he bear the pain? Everyone was in the same pain, he said. At times they would cry out together. The most severely injured could not cry. Over time, it was better for all of them to lie there quietly. Then, the pain was felt, not as if in one body alone, but in all bodies at once. Together they floated in a timeless element, suffused with agony, ringed with death, held in one another's presence.

After an immeasurable period of time he was taken away into the home of strangers in the country. Here he would be cared for, for a few weeks. From that time, until the spring of the next year, when he could once more walk, he was moved from one house to another so that the burden of his care could be shared.

The day that he gained sanctuary in the countryside, he lost his brother and sister. A few years later he was able to find his brother again. He believed his sister had died. He did not ask about her. There were so many dead, and for each the same question was held mute within, *Where?* Even if you have witnessed a death, this is not a question that can be answered.

Thirty-two years later, when he was a grown man and teaching children in the same school he had attended as a child, he saw a woman's face on television. She had appeared to ask if anyone remembered her, if anyone could claim her as part of a family. She had been so young when she was separated from her two brothers that she did not know her family name. Something about her face seemed familiar to Ota. Her personal name sounded the same, but she was spelling it with different characters. She did not immediately recognize him when he called. In her infancy he was older and gone at school much of the time. She had played with her younger brother. But she remembered that she had two brothers. Slowly the pieces fell together and they were re-united.

His feeling is not easy to describe. Had only ten years passed their meeting would have been different. He felt sorrow, happiness and confusion at once. He said his heart was filled, that he cried, and he touched his throat and said he was not able to speak.

Knowing how many years had gone, knowing both parents had died, they embraced in silence. A place of quiet had been broken into, in this reunion, as if the sharp edge of separation had only now penetrated what they had taken to be ordinary.

The dimensions of Ota's suffering, great with the magnitude of that terrible explosion, were beyond my comprehension, except as we who sat in his presence that day were infused with this story which found a stillness in all of us who listened. Yet still there was something in his story familiar to me. A few months earlier I too had found one of my family, someone who belonged to me, but whom I had never met. As that ferry made its way to Grand Manan, I questioned the woman sitting next to me. Did she live there? Had she heard of anyone bearing my family name? She pointed to a man on the other side of the cabin who sat talking with his wife. Full of apprehension, I approached him and told him who I was. *My father,* he told me, *would be able to answer your questions, and he lives just one thousand yards from where the boat docks.*

A more recent development, the Vulcan gun fires ammunition that is incendiary and pierces armour at the rate of 7,200 shots each minute.

My daughter beside me in our rented car, I followed him on this short drive. Time was not passing. It had become a more flexible element. I entered the door. At the end of the narrow kitchen, sitting at a small table, I saw an elderly man who looked just as my father would have looked today, had he lived. This man looked at me with a face of shock, before he assembled himself into cordiality. Later, near tears, he said to me that it had seemed to him that his mother walked into the room when I entered.

My daughter and I sat in the living room. It reminded me of my great-aunt's house. We were surrounded by our family, who asked and answered questions. Arnold remembered my great-aunt Alta playing the organ. His son told me where my great-uncle Wesley was buried, and promised to take me there. My sister still had a seascape he had painted on the island. My father's brother Roland, they told me, had stayed on the island for a while longer than my father, with another family, until someone was sent to fetch him. He was remembered better than my father. And my grandmother? Her name before she was married to my grandfather, I told them, was Ina Tatum.

Ina Tatum. Arnold's wife repeated her name, and thought, then, looking at Arnold and nodding, she said to me, *Oh, that would be Ina Benson.* She had remarried. And she was here. On the island. In a rest home. Just up the hill.

Whatever had held me in disbelief for years in this instant vanished. The air in that house, in the graveyard, in the rooms my daughter and I took by the sea, seemed sharp to breathe. As if by a magnifying glass my life was brought into focus. Yet with this new vision, I felt strangely out of balance.

It was dark now. Waiting for the morning hours when the old-age home where my grandmother was would be open for visitors again, my daughter and I ate our dinner with another cousin. Robbie, Arnold's second son, was compiling a history of our family. Each of us had different pieces of the puzzle. Searching through his genealogical charts, I found my father's name penciled in on the back of a page belonging to my grandmother. The writing was not in her hand but in Robbie's. Thus she had disowned my father. Only one child was listed for her in her own hand, a daughter, born after my grandfather left the island.

Robbie and I guessed at the reasons for the rupture in my grandparents' marriage, and why my grandmother's children were taken from her. Was there a secret affair? A child conceived outside the bonds of marriage? For years everyone on the island has speculated. And no one knows.

That night I lay awake, shaken by how intensely now I wished to see my grandmother. I wept with a strange grief whose source eluded me and which, like Ota's grief, was mixed with joy, an elation which seemed to move beyond what I had thought to be myself. And inside a child began to weep with bitterness that she had been disowned, not written on the page, in any hand.

The pockets between cells take in substance from outside the cells which will become part of the cells.

In the spring after the year the bomb exploded, when Ota was able to walk, he was released into the world alone. For months he wandered Japan. After the war, travel by train was free for children. The trains were warm. The seats were clean. Food could sometimes be had from the plates of other travelers. Ota would board a train with others who were orphaned by the war, and they would stay there as long as they could, before being discovered, or until the end of the line. He went in every direction, east Tokyo and beyond, to the far end of Northern Honshu, Aomori, and south even to the island of Kyushu. He would read a comic book, talk with his friends, look for food, sleep and wake to find himself some place unknown. Often he was without any sense of direction.

In the Second World War many machine guns could be fired from airplanes, or from the ground toward the sky, as well as over land.

How is it that we know where we are? Antoine de Saint-Exupéry writes that in the early days of flying the ships were open and in bad weather a pilot would simply thrust his head out around the windshield to take his bearing. Then the wind would whistle in his ears, and this whistling would remain there for a long time.

———

Certain voices, certain names remain in the ears long after those whom they recall have died. But my grandmother did not remember my father's name. I sat on the bed and spoke quietly to her. She was cordial to me and, after a while, asked if I worked there. Then I told her who I was.

Her mind had become ancient, part like a child, part wise, and emptied, in a certain way, of her own past. She accepted me as her granddaughter, though she could not trace the lineage. When my daughter walked into the room she looked up to her face with eyes of joy. What she did not know, she knew in another way. The undercurrent of this knowledge held us through this day, as if an old power had risen up finally to claim us.

And what the cells relinquish flows into these pockets to be taken to other places in the body.

We had come to visit her just before lunch. The nurse came to help her into the dining room. She was ninety-six years old and just learning to use a walker. My daughter and I promised to return in the afternoon. I drove about the island. I was looking for paintings by my uncle Wesley. They were supposed to be in the school library. After a time I found them. But my search was frantic, as if I could not yet understand that I had found what I had come for, and frantic searching had become a habit.

When we returned to the rest home we entered a strange circle of quiet that seemed to exist outside time. My grandmother searched my face, her own face filled with longing and confusion. We sat with her friend, who made us laugh about forgetfulness and old age. The sea and much of the island lay in a thick fog, and together we sat, four women, arranged in front of a picture window, staring into the soft, white mist.

Machine guns used against airplanes were often mounted in groups. With hydraulic power they could be set to fire with the guidance of one sight.

I asked her what she remembered. She remembered her mother and father. And Walden, *my* father? I drew her a chart tracing her marriage to my grandfather, the birth of her two sons, and my birth. I wrote my father's name in large block letters for her.

I placed the drawing in her hand. She took it gently, stared at it for a while in silence, and then began to praise me for the fine job I had done. I traced the lines I had made with my finger for her, stopping to say each name. Then her eyes rested deeply on the page. For the next few moments she was silent again, and while her friend continued speaking with wry humor, my grand-mother looked from me to the page and back, and finally, with tears beginning to show in her eyes, she started speaking, almost singing, again, and then again and again, my father's name. *Walden, Walden, Walden,* she said.

As exchanges occur between the cells and the pockets between the cells, there is no tear nor gap in the membrane.

The ferry was soon to leave. I crossed the room. I leaned toward her and then hesitated, but she pulled my face to hers, and when I kissed her, she kissed me back with a passion passed through many years, that now belonged to us both. Then she gestured to my daughter and they kissed goodbye. As the ferry pulled into the bay, I walked over its deck back toward the land, and called out over widening water, silently.

The mechanisms used in machine guns could also be used to create faster firing pistols.

Saint-Exupéry writes of the several generations of craftsmen who have experimented with the curve of the fuselage of an airplane until it has been made to resemble the elementary purity of the curve of a human breast or shoulder.

All cells are immersed in liquid, either blood, or a fluid originating from blood.

What was told to me in Hiroshima, I heard in a language I do not speak. Because I could not decipher sounds, I looked at gestures and expressions. A face held down, hands held up as if to ward off force. These were the truths that were mimed before my eyes. Now, looking out toward the bay I live above, I accept this silence. Argument and explanation have faded into stillness too. I see a man letting pieces of paper fall to the ground, a flash of light, a boy, blackened and numb, carried up a long hill, a pilot climbing into his airplane, a girl and her father dancing, a flat and ashen landscape stretching for miles in every direction.

From 1898 to 1942 a pistol developed by Georg Lugar is manufactured. A box magazine, loaded before use, fits into the grip of this weapon.

What are the words, the sounds we might whisper to ourselves in this new territory, *leaf, river,* this place of whistling wind, *doorbell, cup,* this place of ever widening concentric circles drawn in the air above us, this strange place we have come to, and witness?

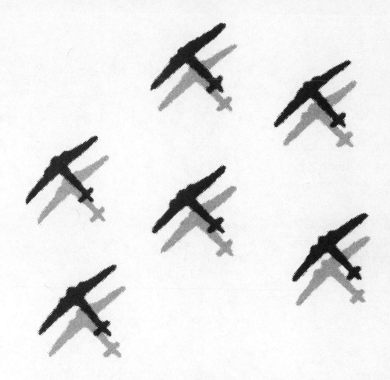

OUR SECRET

IV

The nucleus of the cell derives its name from the Latin nux, *meaning nut. Like the stone in a cherry, it is found in the center of the cell, and like this stone, keeps its precious kernel in a shell.*

She is across the room from me. I am in a chair facing her. We sit together in the late darkness of a summer night. As she speaks the space between us grows larger. She has entered her past. She is speaking of her childhood. Her father. The war. Did I know her father fought in the Battle of the Bulge? What was it for him, this great and terrible battle? She cannot say. He never spoke of it at home. They knew so little, her mother, her brothers, herself. Outside, the sea has disappeared. One finds the water now only by the city lights that cease to shine at its edges. California. She moved here with her family when her father became the commander of a military base. There were nuclear missiles standing just blocks from where she lived. But her father never spoke about them. Only after many years away from home did she learn what these weapons were.

The first guided missile is developed in Germany, during World War II. It is known as the Vergeltungswaffe, *or the Vengeance weapon. Later, it will be called the V-1 rocket.*

She is speaking of another life, another way of living. I give her the name Laura here. She speaks of the time after the war, when the cold war was just beginning. The way we are talking now, Laura tells me, was not possible in her family. I nod in recognition. Certain questions were never answered. She learned what not to ask. She begins to tell me a story. Once when she was six years old she went out with her father on a long trip. It was not even a year since the war ended. They were living in Germany.

They drove for miles and miles. Finally they turned into a small road at the edge of a village and drove through a wide gate in a high wall. The survivors were all gone. But there were other signs of this event beyond and yet still within her comprehension. Shoes in great piles. Bones. Women's hair, clothes, stains, a terrible odor. She began to cry a child's frightened tears and then to scream. She had no words for what she saw. Her father admonished her to be still. Only years later, and in a classroom, did she find out the name of this place and what had happened here.

The shell surrounding the nucleus is not hard and rigid; it is a porous membrane. These pores allow only some substances to pass through them, mediating the movement of materials in and out of the nucleus.

Often I have looked back into my past with a new insight only to find that some old, hardly recollected feeling fits into a larger pattern of meaning. Time can be measured in many ways. We see time as moving forward and hope that by our efforts this motion is toward improvement. When the atomic bomb exploded, many who survived the blast say time stopped with the flash of light and was held suspended until the ash began to descend. Now, in my mind, I can feel myself moving backward in time. I am as if on a train. And the train pushes into history. This history seems to exist somewhere, waiting, a foreign country behind a border and, perhaps, also inside me. From the windows of my train, I can see what those outside do not see. They do not see each other, or the whole landscape through which the track is laid. This is a straight track, but still there are bends to fit the shape of the earth. There are even circles. And returns.

The missile is guided by a programmed mechanism. There is no electronic device that can be jammed. Once it is fired it cannot stop.

It is 1945 and a film is released in Germany. This film has been made for other nations to see. On the screen a train pulls into a station. The train is full of children. A man in a uniform greets the children warmly as they step off the train. Then the camera cuts to boys and girls who are swimming. The boys and girls race to see who can reach the other side of the pool first. Then a woman goes to a post office. A man goes to a bank. Men and women sit drinking coffee at a café. The film is called *The Führer Presents the Jews with a City*. It has been made at Terezin concentration camp.

Through the pores of the nuclear membrane a steady stream of ribonucleic acid, RNA, the basic material from which the cell is made, flows out.

It is wartime and a woman is writing a letter. *Everyone is on the brink of starvation,* she says. In the right-hand corner of the page she has written *Nordhausen, Germany 1944.* She is writing to Hans. *Do you remember,* she asks, the day this war was declared? The beauty of the place. The beauty of the sea. *And I bathed in it that day, for the last time.*

In the same year, someone else is also writing a letter. In the right-hand corner he has put his name followed by a title. *Heinrich Himmler. Reichsführer, SS. Make no mention of the special treatment of the Jews,* he says, use only the words Transportation of the Jews Toward the Russian East.

A few months later this man will deliver a speech to a secret meeting of leaders in the district of Posen. *Now you know all about it, and you will keep quiet,* he will tell them. Now we share a secret and *we should take our secret to our graves.*

The missile flies from three to four thousand feet above the earth and this makes it difficult to attack from the ground.

The woman who writes of starvation is a painter in her seventy-seventh year. She has lost one grandchild to this war. And a son to the war before. Both boys were named Peter. Among the drawings she makes which have already become famous: a terrified mother grasps a child, *Death Seizes Children;* an old man curls over the bent body of an old woman, *Parents;* a thin face emerges white from charcoal, *Beggars.*

A small but critical part of the RNA flowing out of the pores holds most of the knowledge issued by the nucleus. These threads of RNA act as messengers.

Encountering such images, one is grateful to be spared. But is one ever really free of the fate of others? I was born in 1943, in the midst of this war. And I sense now that my life is still bound up with the lives of those who lived and died in this time. Even with Heinrich Himmler. All the details of his existence, his birth, childhood, adult years, death, still resonate here on earth.

The V-1 rocket is a winged plane powered by a duct motor with a pulsating flow of fuel.

It is April 1943. Heinrich Himmler, Reichsführer SS, has gained control of the production of rockets for the Third Reich. The SS Totenkampf stand guard with machine guns trained at the entrance to a long tunnel, two miles deep, fourteen yards wide and ten yards high, sequestered in the Harz Mountains near Nordhausen. Once an old mining shaft, this tunnel serves now as a secret factory for the manufacture of V-1 and V-2 missiles. The guards aim their machine guns at the factory workers who are inmates of concentration camp Dora.

Most of the RNA flowing out of the cell is destined for the construction of a substance needed to compensate for the continual wearing away of the cell.

It is 1925. Heinrich Himmler, who is now twenty-five years old, has been hired as a secretary by the chief of the Nazi Party in Landshut. He sits behind a small desk in a room overcrowded with party records, correspondence and newspaper files. On the wall facing him he can see a portrait of Adolf Hitler. He hopes one day to meet the Führer. In anticipation of that day, while he believes no one watches, he practices speaking to this portrait.

It is 1922. Heinrich visits friends who have a three-year-old child. Before going to bed this child is allowed to run about naked. And this disturbs Heinrich. He writes in his diary, *One should teach a child a sense of shame.*

It is the summer of 1910. Heinrich begins his first diary. He is ten years old. He has just completed elementary school. His father tells him his childhood is over now. In the fall he will enter Wilhelms Gymnasium. There the grades he earns will determine his prospects for the future. From now on he must learn to take himself seriously.

Eight out of ten of the guided missiles will land within eight miles of their targets.

His father Gebhard is a schoolmaster. He knows the requirements. He provides the boy with pen and ink. Gebhard was once a tutor for Prince Heinrich of Wittelsbach. He has named his son Heinrich after this prince. He is grateful that the prince consented to be Heinrich's godparent. Heinrich is to write in his diary every day. Gebhard writes the first entry in his son's diary, to show the boy how it is to be done.

July 13 Departed at 11:50 and arrive safely on the bus in L. We have a very pretty house. In the afternoon we drink coffee at the coffee house.

I open the cover of the journal I began to keep just as I started my work on this book. I want to see what is on the first page. *It is here I begin a new life,* I wrote. Suffering many losses at once, I was alone and lonely. Yet suddenly I felt a new responsibility for myself. *The very act of keeping a journal,* I sensed, would help me into this life that would now be my own.

Inside the nucleus is the nucleolus where the synthesis of RNA takes place. Each nucleolus is filled with a small jungle of fern-like structures all of whose fronds and stalks move and rotate in perfect synchrony.

It is 1910. The twenty-second of July. Gebhard adds the words *first swim* to his son's brief entry, *thirteenth wedding anniversary of my dear parents.* 1911. Over several entries Heinrich lists each of thirty-seven times he takes a swim, in chronological order. *11:37 A.M. Departed for Lindau.* He does not write of his feelings. *August 8, Walk in the park.* Or dreams. *August 10, Bad weather.*

In the last few years I have been searching, though for what precisely I cannot say. Something still hidden which lies in the direction of Heinrich Himmler's life. I have been to Berlin and Munich on this search, and I have walked over the gravel at Dachau. Now as I sit here I read once again the fragments from Heinrich's boyhood diary that exist in English. I have begun to think of these words as ciphers. Repeat them to myself, hoping to find a door into the mind of this man, even as his character first forms so that I might learn how it is he becomes himself.

    The task is not easy. The earliest entries in this diary betray so little. Like the words of a schoolboy commanded to write what the teacher requires of him, they are wooden and stiff. The stamp of his father's character is so heavy on this language that I catch not even a breath of a self here. It is easy to see how this would be true. One simply has to imagine Gebhard standing behind Heinrich and tapping his foot.

His father must have loomed large to him. Did Gebhard lay his hand on Heinrich's shoulder? The weight of that hand would not be comforting. It would be a warning. A reminder. Heinrich must straighten up now and be still. Yet perhaps he turns his head. Maybe there is a sound outside. A bird. Or his brother Gebhard's voice. But from the dark form behind him he hears a name pronounced. This is his name, *Heinrich*. The sound rolls sharply off his father's tongue. He turns his head back. He does not know what to write. He wants to turn to this form and beseech him, but this man who is his father is more silent than stone. And now when Heinrich can feel impatience all around him, he wants to ask, *What should I write?* The edge of his father's voice has gotten sharper. *Why can't you remember?* Just write what happened yesterday. And make sure you get the date right. *Don't you remember?* We took a walk in the park together and we ran into the duchess. Be certain you spell her name correctly. And look here, you must get the title right. That is extremely important. Cross it out. Do it again. *The title*.

The boy is relieved. His mind has not been working. His thoughts were like paralyzed limbs, immobile. Now he is in motion again. He writes the sentences as they are dictated to him. *The park*. He crosses out the name. He writes it again. Spelling it right. *The duchess*. And his father makes one more correction. The boy has not put down the correct time for their walk in the park.

And who is the man standing behind? In a photograph I have before me of the aging Professor and Frau Himmler, as they pose before a wall carefully composed with paintings and family portraits, Frau Himmler adorned with a demure lace collar, both she and the professor smiling kindly from behind steel-rimmed glasses, the professor somewhat rounded with age, in a dark three-piece suit and polka-dot tie, looks so ordinary.

*The missile carries a warhead weighing 1,870 pounds. It has three differ-
ent fuses to insure detonation.*

Ordinary. What an astonishing array of images hide behind this
word. The ordinary is of course never ordinary. I think of it now
as a kind of mask, not an animated mask that expresses the essence
of an inner truth, but a mask that falls like dead weight over the
human face, making flesh a stationary object. One has difficulty
penetrating the heavy mask that Gebhard and his family wore,
difficulty piercing through to the creatures behind.

It must not have been an easy task to create this mask. One
detects the dimensions of the struggle in the advice of German
child-rearing experts from this and the last century. *Crush the will,*
they write. *Establish dominance. Permit no disobedience. Suppress everything in the child.*

I have seen illustrations from the books of one of these experts, perhaps the most famous of these pedagogues, Dr. Daniel
Gottlieb Moritz Schreber. At first glance these pictures recall images of torture. But they are instead pictures of children whose
posture or behavior is being corrected. A brace up the spine, a belt
tied to a waist and the hair at the back of the neck so the child will
be discouraged from slumping, a metal plate at the edge of a desk
keeping the child from curling over her work, a child tied to a bed
to prevent poor sleeping posture or masturbation. And there are
other methods recommended in the text. An enema to be given
before bedtime. The child immersed in ice-cold water up to the
hips, before sleep.

The nightmare images of the German child-rearing practices
that one discovers in this book call to mind the catastrophic events
of recent German history. I first encountered this pedagogy in the
writing of Alice Miller. At one time a psychoanalyst, she was
haunted by the question, *What could make a person conceive the plan
of gassing millions of human beings to death?* In her work, she traces
the origins of this violence to childhood.

Of course there cannot be one answer to such a monumental riddle, nor does any event in history have a single cause. Rather a field exists, like a field of gravity that is created by the movements of many bodies. Each life is influenced and it in turn becomes an influence. Whatever is a cause is also an effect. Childhood experience is just one element in the determining field.

As a man who made history, Heinrich Himmler shaped many childhoods, including, in the most subtle of ways, my own. And an earlier history, a history of governments, of wars, of social customs, an idea of gender, the history of a religion leading to the idea of original sin, shaped Heinrich Himmler's childhood as certainly as any philosophy of child raising. One can take for instance any formative condition of his private life, the fact that he was a frail child, for example, favored by his mother, who could not meet masculine standards, and show that this circumstance derived its real meaning from a larger social system that gave inordinate significance to masculinity.

Yet to enter history through childhood experience shifts one's perspective not away from history but instead to an earlier time just before history has finally shaped us. Is there a child who existed before the conventional history that we tell of ourselves, one who, though invisible to us, still shapes events, even through this absence? How does our sense of history change when we consider childhood, and perhaps more important, why is it that until now we have chosen to ignore this point of origination, the birthplace and womb of ourselves, in our consideration of public events?

In the silence that reverberates around this question, an image is born in my mind. I can see a child's body, small, curled into itself, knees bent toward the chest, head bending softly into pillows and blankets, in a posture thought unhealthy by Dr. Schreber, hand raised to the face, delicate mouth making a circle around the thumb. There is comfort as well as sadness in this image. It is a kind of a self-portrait, drawn both from memory and from a feeling that is still inside me. As I dwell for a moment with this image I can imagine Heinrich in this posture, silent, curled, fetal, giving comfort to himself.

But now, alongside this earlier image, another is born. It is as if these two images were twins, always traveling in the world of thought together. One does not come to mind without the other. In this second portrait, which is also made of feeling and memory, a child's hands are tied into mittens. And by a string extending from one of the mittens, her hand is tied to the bars of her crib. She is not supposed to be putting her finger in her mouth. And she is crying out in rage while she yanks her hand violently, trying to free herself of her bonds.

To most of existence there is an inner and an outer world. Skin, bark, surface of the ocean open to reveal other realities. What is inside shapes and sustains what appears. So it is too with human consciousness. And yet the mind rarely has a simple connection to the inner life. At a certain age we begin to define ourselves, to choose an image of who we are. I am this and not that, we say, attempting thus to erase whatever is within us that does not fit our idea of who we should be. In time we forget our earliest selves and replace that memory with the image we have constructed at the bidding of others.

One can see this process occur in the language of Heinrich's diaries. If in the earliest entries, except for the wooden style of a boy who obeys authority, Heinrich's character is hardly apparent, over time this stilted style becomes his own. As one reads on, one no longer thinks of a boy who is forced to the task, but of a prudish and rigid young man.

In Heinrich's boyhood diaries no one has been able to find any record of rage or of events that inspire such rage. Yet one cannot assume from this evidence that such did not exist. His father would have permitted neither anger nor even the memory of it to enter these pages. That there must be no visible trace of resentment toward the parent was the pedagogy of the age. Dr.

Schreber believed that children should learn to be grateful. The pain and humiliation children endure are meant to benefit them. The parent is only trying to save the child's soul.

Now, for different reasons, I too find myself on the track of a child's soul. The dimensions of Heinrich Himmler's life have put me on this track. I am trying to grasp the inner state of his being. For a time the soul ceased to exist in the modern mind. One thought of a human being as a kind of machine, or as a cog in the greater mechanism of society, operating within another machine, the earth, which itself operates within the greater mechanical design of the universe.

When I was in Berlin, I spoke to a rabbi who had, it seemed to me, lost his faith. When I asked him if he still believed in God, he simply shook his head and widened his eyes as if to say, *How is this possible?* He had been telling me about his congregation: older people, many of Polish origin, survivors of the holocaust who were not able to leave Germany after the war because they were too ill to travel. He was poised in this painful place by choice. He had come to lead this congregation only temporarily but, once feeling the condition of his people, decided to stay. Still, despite his answer, and as much as the holocaust made a terrible argument for the death of the spirit, talking in that small study with this man, I could feel from him the light of something surviving.

The religious tradition that shaped Heinrich's childhood argues that the soul is not part of flesh but is instead a prisoner of the body. But suppose the soul is meant to live in and through the body and to know itself in the heart of earthly existence?

Then the soul is an integral part of the child's whole being, and its growth is thus part of the child's growth. It is, for example, like a seed planted underground in the soil, naturally moving toward the light. And it comes into its fullest manifestation thus only when seen, especially when self meeting self returns a gaze.

What then occurs if the soul in its small beginnings is forced to take on a secret life? A boy learns, for instance, to hide his thoughts from his father simply by failing to record them in his journals. He harbors his secrets in fear and guilt, confessing them to no one until in time the voice of his father chastising him becomes his own. A small war is waged in his mind. Daily implosions take place under his skin, by which in increments something in him seems to disappear. Gradually his father's voice subsumes the vitality of all his desires and even his rage, so that now what he wants most passionately is his own obedience, and his rage is aimed at his own failures. As over time his secrets fade from memory, he ceases to tell them, even to himself, so that finally a day arrives when he believes the image he has made of himself in his diaries is true.

The child, Dr. Schreber advised, *should be permeated by the impossibility of locking something in his heart.* The doctor who gave this advice had a son who was hospitalized for disabling schizophrenia. Another of his children committed suicide. But this was not taken as a warning against his approach. His methods of educating children were so much a part of the canon of everyday life in Germany that they were introduced into the state school system.

That this philosophy was taught in school gives me an interior view of the catastrophe to follow. It adds a certain dimension to my image of these events to know that a nation of citizens learned that no part of themselves could be safe from the scrutiny of authority, nothing locked in the heart, and at the same time to discover that the head of the secret police of this nation was the son of a schoolmaster. It was this man, after all, Heinrich Himmler, Reichsführer SS, who was later to say, speaking of the mass arrests of Jews, *Protective custody is an act of care.*

The polite manner of young Heinrich's diaries reminds me of life in my grandmother's home. Not the grandmother I lost and later found, but the one who, for many years, raised me. She was my mother's mother. The family would assemble in the living room together, sitting with a certain reserve, afraid to soil the surfaces. What was it that by accident might have been made visible?

All our family photographs were posed. We stood together in groups of three or four and squinted into the sun. My grandmother directed us to smile. I have carried one of these photographs with me for years without acknowledging to myself that in it my mother has the look she always had when she drank too much. In another photograph, taken near the time of my parents' divorce, I can see that my father is almost crying, though I could not see this earlier. I must have felt obliged to see only what my grandmother wanted us to see. Tranquil, domestic scenes.

In the matrix of the mitochondria all the processes of transformation join together in a central vortex.

We were not comfortable with ourselves as a family. There was a great shared suffering and yet we never wept together, except for my mother, who would alternately weep and then rage when she was drunk. Together, under my grandmother's tutelage, we kept up appearances. Her effort was ceaseless.

When at the age of six I went to live with her, my grandmother worked to reshape me. I learned what she thought was correct grammar. The manners she had studied in books of etiquette were passed on to me, not by casual example but through anxious memorization and drill. Napkin to be lifted by the corner and swept onto the lap. Hand to be clasped firmly but not too firmly.

We were not to the manner born. On one side my great-grandfather was a farmer, and on the other a butcher newly emigrated from Ireland, who still spoke with a brogue. Both great-grandfathers drank too much, the one in public houses, the other more quietly at home. The great-grandfather who farmed was my grandmother's father. He was not wealthy but he aspired to gentility. My grandmother inherited both his aspiration and his failure.

We considered ourselves finer than the neighbors to our left with their chaotic household. But when certain visitors came, we were as if driven by an inward, secret panic that who we really were might be discovered. Inadvertently, by some careless gesture, we might reveal to these visitors who were our betters that we did not belong with them, that we were not real. Though of course we never spoke of this, to anyone, not even ourselves.

Gebhard Himmler's family was newly risen from poverty. Just as in my family, the Himmlers' gentility was a thinly laid surface, maintained no doubt only with great effort. Gebhard's father had come from a family of peasants and small artisans. Such a living etched from the soil, and by one's hands, is tenuous and hard. As is frequently the case with young men born to poverty, Johann became a soldier. And, like many young soldiers, he got himself into trouble more than once for brawling and general mischief. On one occasion he was reproved for what was called *immoral behavior with a low woman*. But nothing of this history survived in his son's version of him. By the time Gebhard was born, Johann was fifty-six years old and had reformed his ways. Having joined the royal police force of Bavaria, over the years he rose to the rank of sergeant. He was a respectable man, with a respectable position.

Perhaps Gebhard never learned of his father's less than respectable past. He was only three years old when Johann died. If he had the slightest notion, he did not breathe a word to his own children. Johann became the icon of the Himmler family, the heroic soldier who single-handedly brought his family from the obscurity of poverty into the warm light of the favored. Yet obscure histories have a way of casting a shadow over the present. Those who are born to propriety have a sense of entitlement, and this affords them some ease as they execute the correct mannerisms of their class. More recent members of the elect are less certain of themselves; around the edges of newly minted refinement one discerns a certain fearfulness, expressed perhaps as uncertainty, or as its opposite, rigidity.

One can sense that rigidity in Gebhard's face as a younger man. In a photograph of the Himmler family, Gebhard, who towers in the background, seems severe. He has the face of one who looks for mistakes. He is vigilant. Heinrich's mother looks very small next to him, almost as if she is cowering. She has that look I have seen many times on my father's face, which one can only describe as ameliorating. Heinrich is very small. He stands closest to the camera, shimmering in a white dress. His face is pretty, even delicate.

I am looking now at the etching called *Poverty,* made in 1897. Near the center, calling my attention, a woman holds her head in her hands. She stares through her hands into the face of a sleeping infant. Though the infant and the sheet and pillow around are filled with light, one recognizes that the child is dying. In a darker corner, two worried figures huddle, a father and another child. Room, mother, father, child exist in lines, a multitude of lines, and each line is filled with a rare intelligence.

Just as the physicist's scrutiny changes the object of perception, so does art transmute experience. One cannot look upon what Käthe Kollwitz has drawn without feeling. The lines around the child are bleak with unreason. Never have I seen so clearly that what we call poverty is simply a raw exposure to the terror and fragility of life. But there is more in this image. There is meaning in the frame. One can feel the artist's eyes. Her gaze is in one place soft, in another intense. Like the light around the infant, her attention interrupts the shadow that falls across the room.

The artist's choice of subject and the way she saw it were both radical departures, not only from certain acceptable assumptions in the world of art, but also from established social ideas because the poor were thought of as less than human. The death of a child to a poor parent was supposed to be a less painful event. In her depiction, the artist told a different story.

Heinrich is entering a new school now, and so his father makes a list of all his future classmates. Beside the name of each child he writes the child's father's name, what this father does for a living, and his social position. Heinrich must be careful, Gebhard tells him, to choose whom he befriends. In his diaries the boy seldom mentions his friends by name. Instead he writes that he played, for instance, with the landlord's child.

There is so much for Heinrich to learn. Gebhard must teach him the right way to bow. The proper forms of greeting. The history of his family; the history of his nation. Its heroes. His grandfather's illustrious military past. There is an order in the world and Heinrich has a place in this order which he must be trained to fill. His life is strictly scheduled. At this hour a walk in the woods so that he can appreciate nature. After that a game of chess to develop his mind. And after that piano, so that he will be cultured.

If a part of himself has vanished, that part of the self that feels and wants, and from which hence a coherent life might be shaped, Heinrich is not at sea yet. He has no time to drift or feel lost. Each moment has been spoken for, every move prescribed. He has only to carry out his father's plans for him.

But everything in his life is not as it should be. He is not popular among his classmates. Should it surprise us to learn that he has a penchant for listening to the secrets of his companions, and that afterward he repeats these secrets to his father, the schoolmaster? There is perhaps a secret he would like to learn and one he would like to tell, but this has long since been forgotten. Whatever he learns now he must tell his father. He must not keep anything from him. He must keep his father's good will at all costs. For, without his father, he does not exist.

And there is another reason Heinrich is not accepted by his classmates. He is frail. As an infant, stricken by influenza, he came close to perishing and his body still retains the mark of that illness. He is not strong. He is not good at the games the other boys play. At school he tries over and over to raise himself on the crossbars, unsuccessfully. He covets the popularity of his stronger, more masculine brother, Gebhard. But he cannot keep up with his brother. One day, when they go out for a simple bicycle ride together, Heinrich falls into the mud and returns with his clothes torn.

It is 1914. A war begins. There are parades. Young men marching in uniform. Tearful ceremonies at the railway station. Songs. Decorations. Heinrich is enthusiastic. The war has given him a sense of purpose in life. Like other boys, he plays at soldiering. He follows the war closely, writing in his diary of the progress of armies, *This time with 40 Army Corps and Russia and France against Germany*. The entries he makes do not seem so listless now; they have a new vigor. As the war continues, a new ambition gradually takes the shape of determination. Is this the way he will finally prove himself? Heinrich wants to be a soldier. And above all he wants a uniform.

It is 1915. In her journal Käthe Kollwitz records a disturbing sight. The night before at the opera she found herself sitting next to a young soldier. He was blinded. He sat *without stirring, his hands on his knees, his head erect*. She could not stop looking at him, and the memory of him, she writes now, *cuts her to the quick*.

It is 1916. As Heinrich comes of age he implores his father to help him find a regiment. He has many heated opinions about the war. But his thoughts are like the thoughts and feelings of many adolescents; what he expresses has no steady line of reason. His opinions are filled with contradictions, and he lacks that awareness of self which can turn ambivalence into an inner dialogue. Yet, beneath this amorphous bravado, there is a pattern. As if he were trying on different attitudes, Heinrich swings from harshness to compassion. In one place he writes, *The Russian prisoners multiply like vermin*. (Should I write here that this is a word he will one day use for Jews?) But later he is sympathetic to the same prisoners because they are so far away from home. Writing once of *the silly old women and petty bourgeois . . . who so dislike war,* in another entry, he remembers the young men he has seen depart on trains and he asks, *How many are alive today?*

Is the direction of any life inevitable? Or are there crossroads, points at which the direction might be changed? I am looking again at the Himmler family. Heinrich's infant face resembles the face of his mother. His face is soft. And his mother? In the photograph she is a fading presence. She occupied the same position as did most women in German families, secondary and obedient to the undisputed power of her husband. She has a slight smile which for some reason reminds me of the smile of a child I saw in a photograph from an album made by the SS. This child's image was captured as she stood on the platform at Auschwitz. In the photograph she emanates a certain frailty. Her smile is a very feminine smile. Asking, or perhaps pleading, *Don't hurt me.*

Is it possible that Heinrich, looking into that child's face, might have seen himself there? What is it in a life that makes one able to see oneself in others? Such affinities do not stop with obvious resemblance. There is a sense in which we all enter the lives of others.

It is 1917, and a boy who will be named Heinz is born to Catholic parents living in Vienna. Heinz's father bears a certain resemblance to Heinrich's father. He is a civil servant and, also like Gebhard, he is pedantic and correct in all he does. Heinrich will never meet this boy. And yet their paths will cross.

Early in the same year as Heinz's birth, Heinrich's father has finally succeeded in getting him into a regiment. As the war continues for one more year, Heinrich comes close to achieving his dream. He will be a soldier. He is sent to officer's training. Yet he is not entirely happy. *The food is bad,* he writes to his mother, *and there is not enough of it. It is cold. There are bedbugs. The room is barren.* Can she send him food? A blanket? Why doesn't she write him more often? Has she forgotten him? They are calling up troops. Suppose he should be called to the front and die?

But something turns in him. Does he sit on the edge of a neat, narrow military bunk bed as he writes in his diary that he does not want to be like a boy who whines to his mother? Now, he writes a different letter: *I am once more a soldier body and soul.* He loves his uniform; the oath he has learned to write; the first inspection he passes. He signs his letters now, *Miles Heinrich*. Soldier Heinrich.

I am looking at another photograph. It is of two boys. They are both in military uniform. Gebhard, Heinrich's older brother, is thicker and taller. Next to him Heinrich is still diminutive. But his face has become harder, and his smile, though faint like his mother's smile, has gained a new quality, harsh and stiff like the little collar he wears.

Most men can remember a time in their lives when they were not so different from girls, and they also remember when that time ended. In ancient Greece a young boy lived with his mother, practicing a feminine life in her household, until the day he was taken from her into the camp of men. From this day forward the life that had been soft and graceful became rigorous and hard, as the older boy was prepared for the life of a soldier.

My grandfather on my mother's side was a contemporary of Heinrich Himmler. He was the youngest boy in the family and an especially pretty child. Like Heinrich and all small boys in this period, he was dressed in a lace gown. His hair was long and curled about his face. Like Heinrich, he was his mother's favorite. She wanted to keep him in his finery. He was so beautiful in it, and he was her last child. My great-grandmother Sarah had a dreamy, artistic nature, and in his early years my grandfather took after her. But all of this made him seem girlish. And his father and older brothers teased him mercilessly. Life improved for him only when he graduated to long pants. With them he lost his dreamy nature too.

The soul is often imagined to be feminine. All those qualities thought of as soulful, a dreaminess or artistic sensibility, are supposed to come more naturally to women. Ephemeral, half seen, half present, nearly ghostly, with only the vaguest relation to the practical world of physical law, the soul appears to us as lost. The hero, with his more masculine virtues, must go in search of her. But there is another, older story of the soul. In this story she is firmly planted on the earth. She is incarnate and visible everywhere. Neither is she faint of heart, nor fading in her resolve. It is she, in fact, who goes bravely in search of desire.

1918. Suddenly the war is over. Germany has lost. Heinrich has failed to win his commission. He has not fought in a single battle. Prince Heinrich, his namesake, has died. The prince will be decorated for heroism, after his death. Heinrich returns home, not an officer or even a soldier any longer. He returns to school, completing his studies at the gymnasium and then the university. But he is adrift. Purposeless. And like the world he belongs to, dissatisfied. Neither man nor boy, he does not know what he wants.

Until now he could rely on a strict regimen provided by his father. Nothing was left uncertain or undefined for long in his father's house. The thoroughness of Gebhard's hold over his family comes alive for me through this procedure: every package, letter or money order to pass through the door was by Gebhard's command to be duly recorded. And I begin to grasp a sense of Gebhard's priorities when I read that Heinrich, on one of his leaves home during the war, assisted his mother in this task. The shadow of his father's habits will stretch out over history. They will fall over an office in Berlin through which the SS, and the entire network of concentration camps, are administered. Every single piece of paper issued with regard to this office will pass over Heinrich's desk, and to each page he will add his own initials.

Schedules for trains. Orders for building supplies. Adjustments in salaries. No detail will escape his surmise or fail to be recorded.

But at this moment in his life Heinrich is facing a void. I remember a similar void, when a long and intimate relationship ended. What I felt then was fear. And at times panic. In a journal I kept after this separation, I wrote, *Direct knowledge of the illusory nature of panic. The feeling that I had let everything go out of control.* I could turn in only one direction: inward. Each day I abated my fears for a time by observing myself. But what exists in that direction for Heinrich? He has not been allowed to inhabit that terrain. His inner life has been sealed off both from his father and himself.

I am not certain what I am working for, he writes, and then, not able to let this uncertainty remain, he adds, *I work because it is my duty.* He spends long hours in his room, seldom leaving the house at all. He is at sea. Still somewhat the adolescent, unformed, not knowing what face he should put on when going out into the world, in his journal he confesses that he still lacks that *naturally superior kind of manner that he would dearly like to possess.*

Is it any wonder then that he is so eager to rejoin the army? The army gave purpose and order to his life. He wants his uniform again. In his uniform he knows who he is. But his frailty haunts him. Over and over he shows up at recruiting stations throughout Bavaria only to be turned away each time, with the single word, *Untauglich.* Unfit. At night the echo of this word keeps him awake.

When he tries to recover his pride, he suffers another failure of a similar kind. A student of agriculture at the university, now he dreams of becoming a farmer. He believes he can take strength and vitality from the soil. After all his own applications are rejected, his father finds him a position in the countryside. He rides toward his new life on his motorcycle and is pelted by torrents of rain. Though he is cold and hungry, he is also exuberant. He has defeated his own weakness. But after only a few weeks his body fails him again. He returns home ill with typhus and must face the void once more.

What Germany needs now is a man of iron. How easy it is to hear the irony of these words Heinrich records in his journal. But at this moment in history, he is hearing another kind of echo. There are so many others who agree with him. The treaty of Versailles is taken as a humiliation. An unforgivable weakness, it is argued, has been allowed to invade the nation.

1920. 1922. 1923. Heinrich is twenty, twenty-two, twenty-three. He is growing up with the century. And he starts to adopt certain opinions popular at this time. As I imagine myself in his frame of mind, facing a void, cast into unknown waters, these opinions appear like rescue ships on the horizon, a promise of *terra firma,* the known.

It is for instance fashionable to argue that the emergence of female equality has drained the nation of its strength. At social gatherings Heinrich likes to discuss the differences between men and women. That twilight area between the certainties of gender, homosexuality, horrifies him. A man should be a man and a woman a woman. Sexually explicit illustrations in a book by Oscar Wilde horrify him. Uncomfortable with the opposite sex, so much so that one of his female friends believes he hates women, he has strong feelings about how men and women ought to relate. *A real man,* he sets down in his diary, *should love a woman as a child who must be admonished perhaps even punished, when she is foolish, though she must also be protected and looked after because she is so weak.*

As I try to enter Heinrich's experience, the feeling I sense behind these words is of immense comfort. I know who I am. My role in life, what I am to feel, what I am to be, has been made clear. I am a man. I am the strong protector. And what's more, I am needed. There is one who is weak. One who is weaker than I am. And I am the one who must protect her.

And yet behind the apparent calm of my present mood, there is an uneasiness. Who is this one that I protect? Does she tell me the truth about herself? I am beginning to suspect that she hides herself from me. There is something secretive in her nature. She is an unknown, even dangerous, territory.

The year is 1924. And Heinrich is still fascinated with secrets. He discovers that his brother's fiancée has committed one or maybe even two indiscretions. At his urging, Gebhard breaks off the engagement. But Heinrich is still not satisfied. He writes a friend who lives near his brother's former fiancée, *Do you know of any other shameful stories?* After this, he hires a private detective to look into her past.

Is it any coincidence that in the same year he writes in his diary that he has met a *great man, genuine and pure?* This man, he notes, may be the new leader Germany is seeking. He finds he shares a certain drift of thought with this man. He is discovering who he is now, partly by affinity and partly by negation. In his picture of himself, a profile begins to emerge cast in light and shadow. He knows now who he is and who he is not. He is not Jewish.

And increasingly he becomes obsessed with who he is not. In this pursuit, his curiosity is fed by best-selling books, posters, films, journals; he is part of a larger social movement, and this no doubt gives him comfort, and one cannot, in studying the landscape of his mind as set against the landscape of the social body, discover where he ends and the milieu of this time begins. He is perhaps like a particle in a wave, a wave which has only the most elusive relationship with the physical world, existing as an after-image in the mind.

I can imagine him sitting at a small desk in his bedroom, still in his father's home. Is it the same desk where he was required to record some desultory sentences in his diary every day? He is bent over a book. It is evening. The light is on, shining on the pages of the book. Which book among the books he has listed in his journal does he read now? Is it *Das Liebnest* (*The Lovenest*), telling the story of a liaison between a Jewish man and a gentile woman?

Rasse? Explaining the concept of racial superiority? Or is it *Judas Schuldsbach* (*The Book of Jewish Guilt*). Or *Die Sünde wider das Blut* (*The Sin Against the Blood*).

One can follow somewhat his train of thought here and there where he makes comments on what he reads in his journal. When he reads *Tscheka,* for instance, a history of the secret police in Russia, he says he is disappointed. *Everyone knows,* he writes, that the Jews control the secret police in Russia. But nowhere in the pages of this book does he find a mention of this "fact."

His mind has begun to take a definite shape, even a predictable pattern. Everywhere he casts his eyes he will discover a certain word. Wherever his thoughts wander he brings them back to this word. *Jew. Jude. Jew.* With this word he is on firm ground again. In the sound of the word, a box is closed, a box with all the necessary documents, with all the papers in order.

My grandfather was an anti-Semite. He had a long list of enemies that he liked to recite. Blacks were among them. And Catholics. And the English. He was Protestant and Irish. Because of his drinking he retired early (though we never discussed the cause). In my childhood I often found him sitting alone in the living room that was darkened by closed venetian blinds which kept all our colors from fading. Lonely myself, I would try to speak with him. His repertoire was small. When I was younger he would tell me stories of his childhood, and I loved those stories. He talked about the dog named Blackie that was his then. A ceramic statue of a small black dog resembling him stood near the fireplace. He loved this dog in a way that was almost painful to hear. But he could never enter that intricate world of expressed emotion in which the shadings of one's life as it is felt and experienced become articulated. This way of speaking was left to the women of our family. As I grew older and he could no longer tell me the story of his dog, he would talk to me about politics. It was then that, with a passion he revealed nowhere else, he would recite to me his long list filled with everyone he hated.

I did not like to listen to my grandfather speak this way. His face would get red, and his voice took on a grating tone that seemed to abrade not only the ears but some other slower, calmer velocity within the body of the room. His eyes, no longer looking at me, blazed with a kind of blindness. There was no reaching him at these moments. He was beyond any kind of touch or remembering. Even so, reciting the long list of those he hated, he came temporarily alive. Then, once out of this frame of mind, he lapsed into a kind of fog which we called, in the family, his retirement.

There was another part of my grandfather's mind that also disturbed me. But this passion was veiled. I stood at the borders of it occasionally catching glimpses. He had a stack of magazines by the chair he always occupied. They were devoted to the subject of crime, and the crimes were always grisly, involving photographs of women or girls uncovered in ditches, hacked to pieces or otherwise mutilated. I was never supposed to look in these magazines, but I did. What I saw there could not be reconciled with the other experience I had of my grandfather, fond of me, gentle, almost anachronistically protective.

Heinrich Himmler was also fascinated with crime. Along with books about Jews, he read avidly on the subjects of police work, espionage, torture. Despite his high ideals regarding chastity, he was drawn to torrid, even pornographic fiction, including *Ein Sadist im Priesterrock* (*A Sadist in Priestly Attire*) which he read quickly, noting in his journal that it was a book *about the corruption of women and girls . . . in Paris.*

Entering the odd and often inconsistent maze of his opinions, I feel a certain queasiness. I cannot find a balance point. I search in vain for some center, that place which is in us all, and is perhaps even beyond nationality, or even gender, the felt core of existence, which seems to be at the same time the most real. In Heinrich's morass of thought there are no connecting threads, no integrated whole. I find only the opinions themselves, standing in an odd relation to gravity, as if hastily formed, a rickety, perilous structure.

I am looking at a photograph. It was taken in 1925. Or perhaps 1926. A group of men pose before a doorway in Landshut. Over this doorway is a wreathed swastika. Nearly all the men are in uniform. Some wear shiny black boots. Heinrich is among them. He is the slightest, very thin. Heinrich Himmler. He is near the front. At the far left there is the blurred figure of a man who has been caught in motion as he rushes to join the other men. Of course I know his feeling. The desire to partake, and even to be part of memory.

Photographs are strange creations. They are depictions of a moment that is always passing; after the shutter closes, the subject moves out of the frame and begins to change outwardly or inwardly. One ages. One shifts to a different state of consciousness. Subtle changes can take place in an instant, perhaps one does not even feel them—but they are perceptible to the camera.

The idea we have of reality as a fixed quantity is an illusion. Everything moves. And the process of knowing oneself is in constant motion too, because the self is always changing. Nowhere is this so evident as in the process of art which takes one at once into the self and into *terra incognita,* the land of the unknown. *I am groping in the dark,* the artist Käthe Kollwitz writes in her journal. Here, I imagine she is not so much uttering a cry of despair as making a simple statement. A sense of emptiness always precedes creation.

Now, as I imagine Himmler, dressed in his neat uniform, seated behind his desk at party headquarters, I can feel the void he feared begin to recede. In every way his life has taken on definition. He has a purpose and a schedule. Even the place left by the cessation of his father's lessons has now been filled. He is surrounded by men whose ideas he begins to adopt. From Alfred Rosenberg he learns about the history of Aryan blood, a line Rosenberg traces back to thousands of years before Christ. From

Walther Darré he learns that the countryside is a source of Nordic strength. (And that Jews gravitate toward cities.)

Yet I do not find the calmness of a man who has found himself in the descriptions I have encountered of Heinrich Himmler. Rather, he is filled with an anxious ambivalence. If there was once someone in him who felt strongly one way or the other, this one has long ago vanished. In a room filled with other leaders, he seems to fade into the woodwork, his manner obsequious, his effect inconsequential. He cannot make a decision alone. He is known to seek the advice of other men for even the smallest decisions. In the years to come it will be whispered that he is being led by his own assistant, Reinhard Heydrich. He has made only one decision on his own with a consistent resolve. Following Hitler with unwavering loyalty, he is known as *der treuer Heinrich,* true Heinrich. He describes himself as an instrument of the Führer's will.

But still he has something of his own. Something hidden. And this will make him powerful. He is a gatherer of secrets. As he supervises the sale of advertising space for the Nazi newspaper, *Der Völkischer Beobachter,* he instructs the members of his staff to gather information, not only on the party enemies, the socialists and the communists, but on Nazi Party members themselves. In his small office he sits surrounded by voluminous files that are filled with secrets. From this he will build his secret police. By 1925, with an order from Adolf Hitler, the Schutzstaffel, or SS, has become an official institution.

His life is moving now. Yet in this motion one has the feeling not of a flow, as in the flow of water in a cell, nor as the flow of rivers toward an ocean, but of an engine, a locomotive moving at high speed, or even a missile, traveling above the ground. History has an uncanny way of creating its own metaphors. In 1930, months after Himmler is elected to the Reichstag, Wernher von Braun begins his experiments with liquid fuel missiles that will one day soon lead to the development of the V-2 rocket.

————

The successful journey of a missile depends upon the study of ballistics. Gravitational fields vary at different heights. The relationship of a projectile to the earth's surface will determine its trajectory. The missile may give the illusion of liberation from the earth, or even abandon. Young men dreaming of space often invest the missile with these qualities. Yet, paradoxically, one is more free of the consideration of gravity while traveling the surface of the earth on foot. There is no necessity for mathematical calculation for each step, nor does one need to apply Newton's laws to take a walk. But the missile has in a sense been forced away from its own presence; the wisdom that is part of its own weight has been transgressed. It finds itself thus careening in a space devoid of memory, always on the verge of falling, but not falling and hence like one who is constantly afraid of illusion, gripped by an anxiety that cannot be resolved even by a fate that threatens catastrophe.

The catastrophes which came to pass after Heinrich Himmler's astonishing ascent to power did not occur in his own life, but came to rest in the lives of others, distant from him, and out of the context of his daily world. It is 1931. Heinz, the boy born in Vienna to Catholic parents, has just turned sixteen, and he is beginning to learn something about himself. All around him his school friends are falling in love with girls. But when he searches inside himself, he finds no such feelings. He is pulled in a different direction. He finds that he is still drawn to another boy. He does not yet know, or even guess, that these feelings will one day place him in the territory of a target.

It is 1933. Heinrich Himmler, Reichsführer SS, has become President of the Bavarian police. In this capacity he begins a campaign against *subversive elements*. Opposition journalists, Jewish business owners, Social Democrats, Communists—names culled from a list compiled on index cards by Himmler's deputy, Reinhard

Heydrich—are rounded up and arrested. When the prisons become too crowded, Himmler builds temporary camps. Then, on March 22, the Reichsfürhrer opens the first official and permanent concentration camp at Dachau.

It is 1934. Himmler's power and prestige in the Reich are growing. Yet someone stands in his way. Within the hierarchy of the state police forces, Ernst Röhm, Commandant of the SA, stands over him. But Himmler has made an alliance with Hermann Göring, who as President Minister of Prussia controls the Prussian police, known as the Gestapo. Through a telephone-tapping technique Göring has uncovered evidence of a seditious plot planned by Röhm against the Führer, and he brings this evidence to Himmler. The Führer, having his own reasons to proceed against Röhm, a notorious homosexual and a socialist, empowers the SS and the Gestapo to form an execution committee. This committee will assassinate Röhm, along with the other leaders of the SA. And in the same year, Göring transfers control of the Gestapo to the SS.

But something else less easy to conquer stands in the way of his dreams for himself. It is his own body. I can see him now as he struggles. He is on a playing field in Berlin. And he has broken out in a sweat. He has been trying once again to earn the Reich's sports badge, an honor whose requirements he himself established but cannot seem to fulfill. For three years he has exercised and practiced. On one day he will lift the required weights or run the required laps, but at every trial he fails to throw the discus far enough. His attempt is always a few centimeters short.

And once he is Reichsführer, he will set certain other standards for superiority that, no matter how heroic his efforts, he will never be able to meet. A sign of the *Übermensch,* he says, is blondness, but he himself is dark. He says he is careful to weed out any applicant for the SS who shows traces of a mongolian ancestry, but he himself has the narrow eyes he takes as a sign of such a descent. *I have refused to accept any man whose size was below six feet because I know only men of a certain size have the necessary quality of blood,* he declares, standing just five foot seven behind the podium.

It is the same year, and Heinz, who is certain now that he is a homosexual, has decided to end the silence which he feels to be a burden to him. From the earliest years of his childhood he has trusted his mother with all of his secrets. Now he will tell her another secret, the secret of whom he loves. *My dear child,* she tells him, *it is your life and you must live it.*

It is 1936. Though he does not know it, Himmler is moving into the sphere of Heinz's life now. He has organized a special section of the Gestapo to deal with homosexuality and abortion. On October 11, he declares in a public speech, *Germany's forebears knew what to do with homosexuals. They drowned them in bogs.* This was not punishment, he argues, but *the extermination of unnatural existence.*

As I read these words from Himmler's speech, they call to mind an image from a more recent past, an event I nearly witnessed. On my return from Berlin and after my search for my grandmother, I spent a few days in Maine, close to the city of Bangor. This is a quiet town, not much used to violence. But just days before I arrived a young man had been murdered there. He was a homosexual. He wore an earring in one ear. While he walked home one evening with another man, three boys stopped him on the street. They threw him to the ground and began to kick him. He had trouble catching his breath. He was asthmatic. They picked him up and carried him to a railing of a nearby bridge. He told them he could not swim. Yet still, they threw him over the railing of the bridge into the stream, and he drowned. I saw a picture of him printed in the newspaper. That kind of beauty only very graceful children possess shined through his adult features. It was said that he had come to New England to live with his lover. But the love had failed, and before he died he was piecing his life back together.

When Himmler heard that one of his heroes, Frederick the Great, was a homosexual, he refused to believe his ears. I remember the year when my sister announced to my family that she was a lesbian. I can still recall the chill of fear that went up my spine at the sound of the word "queer." We came of age in the fifties; this was a decade of conformity, awash with mood both public and private, bearing on the life of the body and the body politic. Day after day my grandfather would sit in front of the television set watching as Joseph McCarthy interrogated witnesses about their loyalty to the flag. At the same time, a strict definition of what a woman or a man is had returned to capture the shared imagination. In school I was taught sewing and cooking, and I learned to carry my books in front of my chest to strengthen the muscles which held up my breasts.

I was not happy to hear that my sister was a homosexual. Moved from one member of my family to another, I did not feel secure in the love of others. As the child of divorce I was already different. *Where are your mother and father? Why don't you live with them?* I dreaded these questions. Now my sister, whom I adored and in many ways had patterned myself after, had become an outcast, moved even further out of the circle than I.

It is March 1938. Germany has invaded Austria. Himmler has put on a field-gray uniform for the occasion. Two hand grenades dangle from his Sam Browne belt. Accompanied by a special command unit of twenty-eight men armed with tommy guns and light machine guns, he proceeds to Vienna. Here he will set up Gestapo headquarters in the Hotel Metropole before he returns to Berlin.

It is a Friday, in March of 1939. Heinz, who is twenty-two years old now, and a university student, has received a summons. He is to appear for questioning at the Hotel Metropole. Telling his mother it can't be anything serious, he leaves. He enters a room and stands before a desk. The man behind the desk does not raise his head to nod. He continues to write. When he puts his pen down and looks up at the young man, he tells him, *You are a queer, homosexual, admit it.* Heinz tries to deny this. But the man behind the desk pulls out a photograph. He sees two faces here he knows. His own face and the face of his lover. He begins to weep.

I have come to believe that every life bears in some way on every other. The motion of cause and effect is like the motion of a wave in water, continuous, within and not without the matrix of being, so that all consequences, whether we know them or not, are intimately embedded in our experience. But the missile, as it hurls toward its target, has lost its context. It has been driven farther than the eye can see. How can one speak of direction any longer? Nothing in the space the missile passes through can seem familiar. In the process of flight, alienated by terror, this motion has become estranged from life, has fallen out of the natural rhythm of events.

I am imagining Himmler as he sits behind his desk in January of 1940. The procedures of introduction into the concentration camps have all been outlined or authorized by Himmler himself. He supervises every detail of these operations. Following his father's penchant for order, he makes many very explicit rules, and requires that reports be filed continually. Train schedules, orders for food supplies, descriptions of punishments all pass over his desk. He sits behind a massive door of carved wood, in his office, paneled in light, unvarnished oak, behind a desk that is normally empty, and clean, except for the bust of Hitler he displays at one end, and a little drummer boy at the other, between which he reads, considers and initials countless pieces of paper.

One should teach a child a sense of shame. These words of Himmler's journals come back to me as I imagine Heinz now standing naked in the snow. The weather is below zero. After a while he is taken to a cold shower, and then issued an ill-fitting uniform. Now he is ordered to stand with the other prisoners once more out in the cold while the commandant reads the rules. All the prisoners in these barracks are homosexuals. There are pink triangles sewn to their uniforms. They must sleep with the light on, they are told, and with their hands outside their blankets. This is a rule made especially for homosexual men. Any man caught with his hands under his blankets will be taken outside into the icy night where several bowls of water will be poured over him, and where he will be made to stand for an hour.

Except for the fact that this punishment usually led to death from cold and exposure, this practice reminds me of Dr. Schreber's procedure for curing children of masturbation. Just a few nights ago I woke up with this thought: *Was Dr. Schreber afraid of children?* Or the child he once was? Fear is often just beneath the tyrant's fury, a fear that must grow with the trajectory of his flight from himself. At Dachau I went inside a barrack. It was a standard design, similar in many camps. The plan of the camps too was standard, and resembled, so I was told by a German friend, the camp sites designed for the Hitler Youth. This seemed to me significant, not as a clue in an analysis, but more like a gesture that colors and changes a speaker's words.

It is the summer of 1940. After working for nearly a decade on liquid fuel rockets, Wernher von Braun begins to design a missile that can be used in the war. He is part of a team trying to meet certain military specifications. The missile must be carried through railway tunnels. It must cover a range of 275 kilometers and carry a warhead weighing one metric ton. The engineers have determined that the motor of this rocket, a prototype of the

V-2, will need to be fueled by a pump, and now a pump has been made. Von Braun is free to turn his attention to the turbine drive.

When I think of this missile, or of men sleeping in a barrack, hands exposed, lying on top of worn blankets, an image of Himmler's hands comes to me. Those who remember him say that as he conducted a conversation, discussing a plan, for example, or giving a new order, his hands would lie on top of his desk, limp and inert. He did not like to witness the consequences of his commands. His plans were launched toward distant targets and blind to the consequences of flesh.

After a few months, in one of countless orders which mystify him, coming from a nameless source, and with no explanation, but which he must obey, Heinz is transferred from Sachsenhausen to Flossenbürg. The regime at this camp is the same, but here the commandant, unlike Himmler, does not choose to distance himself from the suffering of others. He is instead drawn to it. He will have a man flogged for the slightest infraction of the rules, and then stand to watch as this punishment is inflicted. The man who is flogged is made to call out the number of lashes as he is lashed, creating in him, no doubt, the feeling that he is causing his own pain. As the man's skin bursts open and he cries out in pain, the commandant's eyes grow excited. His face turns red. His hand slips into his trousers, and he begins to handle himself.

Was the commandant in this moment in any way an extension of the Reichsführer, living out a hidden aspect of this man, one who takes pleasure in the pain of others? This explanation must shed some light, except perhaps as it is intended through the category of an inexplicable perversity to put the crimes Himmler committed at a distance from any understanding of ourselves. The Reichsführer's sexuality is so commonplace. He was remarkable only for the extent of his prudery as a young man. Later, like so many men, he has a wife, who dominates him, and a mistress, younger, more docile, adoring, whom he in turn adores. It has been suggested that he takes pleasure in seeing the naked bodies of boys and young men. If he has a sexual fetish it is certainly this, the worship of physical perfection in the male body. And this worship has its sadistic aspects: his efforts to control reproduction, to force SS men to procreate with many women, the kidnapping from occupied countries of children deemed worthy. Under the veneer of his worship, an earlier rage must haunt him. The subject of cruel insults from other boys with hardier bodies, and the torturous methods his father used to raise him, does he not feel rage toward his persecutors, a rage that, in the course of time, enters history? Yet this is an essential part of the picture: he is dulled to rage. So many of his feelings are inaccessible to him. Like the concentration camps he commands, in many ways he remains absent to himself. And in this he is not so different from the civilization that produced him.

Writing this, I have tried to find my own rage. The memory is immediate. I am a child, almost nine years old. I sit on the cold pavement of a winter day in Los Angeles. My grandmother has angered me. There is a terrible injustice. A punishment that has enraged me. As I sit picking blades of grass and arranging them into piles, I am torturing her in my mind. I have tied her up and I am shouting at her. Threatening her. Striking her. I batter her, batter her as if with each blow, each landing of my hand against her flesh, I can force my way into her, I can be inside her, I can grab hold of someone inside her, someone who feels, who feels as I do, who feels the hurt I feel, the wound I feel, who feels pain as I feel pain. I am forcing her to feel what I feel. I am forcing her to know me. And as I strike her, blow after blow, a shudder of weeping is released in me, and I become utterly myself, the weeping in me becoming rage, the rage turning to tears, all the time my heart beating, all the time uttering a soundless, bitter, passionate cry, a cry of vengeance and of love.

Is this what is in the torturer's heart? With each blow of his whip does he want to make the tortured one feel as he himself has felt?

The desire to know and be known is strong in all of us. Many years after the day I imagined myself as my grandmother's torturer I came to understand that, just as I had wanted my grandmother to feel what I had felt, she wanted me to feel as she had felt. Not what she felt as a woman, but what she had felt long ago as a child. Her childhood was lost to her, the feelings no longer remembered. One way or another, through punishment, severity or even ridicule, she could goad me into fury and then tears. I expressed for her all she had held inside for so long.

One day, the commandant at Flossenbürg encounters a victim who will not cry and Heinz is a witness to this meeting. As usual this prisoner must count out the number of blows assigned to him. The beating commences. And the prisoner counts out the numbers. But otherwise he is silent. Except for the numbers, not a cry, not a sound, passes his lips. And this puts the commandant in a rage. He orders the guard to strike harder with the lash; he increases the number of lashes; he orders the prisoner to begin counting from zero again. Finally, the beating shall continue *until the swine starts screaming,* he shouts. And now, when the prisoner's blood is flowing to the ground, he starts to howl. And with this, the commandant's face grows red, and his hands slip into his trousers again.

A connection between violence and sexuality threads its way through many histories. As we sit in the living room together, looking out over the water, Laura's stories move in and out of the world of her family, and of our shared world, its habits, its wars. She is telling me another story about her father, the general. They were living on the missile base. She had been out late baby-sitting. When she returned home the house was dark. She had no key. It was raining hard. She rang. There was no answer. Then she began to pound on the door. Suddenly the door opened. The hallway was dark. She was yanked into this darkness by her father. He was standing naked. Without speaking to her he began to slap her hard across the face, again and again, and did not stop until her mother, appearing in the stairs in a bathrobe, stood between them. *I knew,* she told me, *they had been making love.*

What was the source of his rage? Did it come from childhood, or battle, or both, the battle awakening the panic of an earlier abuse? The training a soldier receives is to wreak his anger on others. Anyone near receives it. I have heard stories of a man waking at night screaming in terror, reaching for a gun hidden under the pillow, and pointing it or even firing at his own family. In a play about Heracles by Euripides, the great warrior, who has just returned from the underworld, thinking that he has vanquished death, is claimed by madness. He believes himself to be in the home of his enemy. But he is in his own home and, finding his own children, mistakes them for the children of his enemy, clubs one to death and then kills the other two with arrows.

But it is not only warriors who wreak vengeance on their own children. Suffering is passed on from parent to child unto many generations. Did I know as a child that my grandmother's unclaimed fury had made its way into my mother's psyche too? With all her will my mother tried not to repeat against her own children the crimes that had battered her. Where my grandmother was tyrannical, my mother was tolerant and gave free reign. Where my grandmother goaded with critical remarks, my mother was encouraging, and even elaborately praising. But, like my grandfather, my mother drank too much. It was a way of life for her. Sooner or later the long nights would come. Every time I returned home, either to live with her or to visit, I prayed she would not drink again, while I braced myself for what I knew to be inevitable. The evening would begin with a few beers at home, followed by an endless tour of several bars. Either I went along and waited in cars, or I waited at home. In the early morning she would return, her eyes wandering like moths in their sockets. We would sit in two chairs opposite each other, as if these were prearranged places, marked out for us on the stage by a powerful but invisible director. She would start by joking with me. She was marvelously witty when she was drunk. All her natural intelligence was released then and allowed to bloom. But this performance was brief. Her humor turned by dark degrees to meanness. What must have daily constricted her, a kind of sea monster, feeding beneath the waters of her consciousness, and strong, would rise up to stop her glee and mine. Then she would strike. If I was not in my chair to receive her words, she would come and get me. What she said was viperous to me, sank like venom into my veins, and burned a path inside me. Even today I can remember very few of the words she used. She said that my laugh was too loud, or ugly. That I was incapable of loving. I am thankful now that, because she was not in her right mind, I knew at least in a part of myself that these accusations were unfounded. Yet they produced a doubt in me, a lingering shadow, the sense that perhaps I deserved whatever suffering befell me, and that shadow lingers.

Even if a feeling has been made secret, even if it has vanished from memory, can it have disappeared altogether? A weapon is lifted with the force of a forgotten memory. The memory has no words, only the insistence of a pain that has turned into fury. A body, tender in its childhood or its nakedness, lies under this weapon. And this body takes up the rage, the pain, the disowned memory with each blow.

1893. *Self-Portrait at Table*. An etching and aquatint, the first in a long series of self-portraits that span the artist's life. A single lamp illuminates her face, the upper part of the body and the table where she sits. Everything else is in darkness. At first glance one thinks of loneliness. But after a moment it is solitude one sees. And a single moment in that solitude, as if one note of music, resonant and deep, played uninterrupted, echoing from every surface, coming to full consciousness in this woman, who in this instant looks out to those who will return her gaze with a face that has taken in and is expressing the music in the air about her.

Solemnly and with a quiet patience, her hands pause over the etching she makes, a form she is bringing into being, the one she recognizes as herself.

Who are we? The answer is not easy. There are so many strands to the story, and one must trace every strand. I begin to suspect each thread goes out infinitely and touches everything, everyone. I read these words from an ancient gnostic text, words that have been lost to us for a long time: *For I am the first and the last.* Though in another account we have heard the beginning of this speech spoken by Jesus, here these words come to us in the voice of the goddess. *I am the honored one and scorned one,* the older text goes on. *I am the whore and the holy one. I am the wife and the virgin. I am the barren one, and many are her sons.* These words take on a new meaning for me, as I remember them now. *I am the silence that is incomprehensible,* the text reads, and ends, *I am the utterance of my name.*

Were you to trace any life, and study even the minute consequences, the effect, for instance, of a three-minute walk over a patch of grass, of words said casually to a stranger who happens to sit nearby in a public place, the range of that life would extend way beyond the territory we imagine it to inhabit. This is of course less difficult to understand when imagining the boundaries of a life such as Heinrich Himmler had.

   After my visit to Dachau, I went to Paris where, in the fourteenth arrondissement, in the Métro station, I met Hélène. She stopped to help me read my map. We found we were going in the same direction, and thus it was on our way there that we began to speak. Something told me she had survived a concentration camp. And she had. She too fell into the circle of Himmler's life and its consequences. Himmler never went to Paris. At the time of the first mass arrests there he was taking a group of high Nazi officials on a tour of Auschwitz. During the tour, by his orders, the prisoners were made to stand at attention for six hours under the hot sun, but that is another story. Under his command, the Gestapo in Paris began to prepare for the mass arrests of Jews.

Paris had fallen to the German armies in July 1940. By September of that year a notice went up in all the neighborhoods. *Avis aux Israélites,* it read. *Notice to Israelites. By the demand of the occupying authorities, Israelites must present themselves, by October 2, without delay, equipped with identification papers, to the office of the Censor, to complete an identity card.* The notice was signed by the mayor and threatened the most severe punishment for the failure to comply. Through this process vital information was recorded about each Jewish family. Names, ages, addresses, occupations, places of work. An index card was made up for each person. And each card was then duplicated and sent to the offices of the Gestapo on Avenue Foch. There, the cards were duplicated several more times so that the names could be filed by several categories, alphabetically by surname, by address, by arrondissement, occupation and nationality. At this point in history, work that would be done by computer now was painstakingly completed by countless men and women. Their labor continued feverishly almost until the hour of the first mass arrests, the *rafles,* two years later.

One can trace every death to an order signed by Himmler, yet these arrests could never have taken place on such a massive scale without this vast system of information. What did they think, those who were enlisted for this work? They were civilians. French. There were of course Nazi collaborators, among them, those who shared the same philosophy, or who simply obeyed and profited from whoever might be in power. But among the men and women who did this work, my suspicion is, there were many who tried to keep from themselves the knowledge of what they did. Of course, the final purpose of their labors was never revealed to those who prepared the machinery of arrest. If a man allowed his imagination to stray in the direction of this purpose, he could no doubt comfort himself with the argument that he was only handling pieces of paper. He could tell himself that matters were simply being set in order. The men and women who manufacture the trigger mechanisms for nuclear bombs do not tell themselves they are making weapons. They say simply that they are metal forgers.

There are many ways we have of standing outside ourselves in ignorance. Those who have learned as children to become strangers to themselves do not find this a difficult task. Habit has made it natural not to feel. To ignore the consequences of what one does in the world becomes ordinary. And this tendency is encouraged by a social structure that makes fragments of real events. One is never allowed to see the effects of what one does. But this ignorance is not entirely passive. For some, blindness becomes a kind of refuge, a way of life that is chosen, even with stubborn volition, and does not yield easily even to visible evidence.

The arrests were accompanied by an elaborate procedure, needed on some level, no doubt, for practical reasons, but also serving another purpose. They garbed this violence in the cloak of legality. A mind separated from the depths of itself cannot easily tell right from wrong. To this mind, the outward signs of law and order signify righteousness. That Himmler had such a mind was not unique in his generation, nor, I suspect, in ours.

In a museum in Paris I found a mimeographed sheet giving instructions to the Parisian police on how to arrest Jews. They must always carry red pencils, the sheet admonished, because all records regarding the arrests of Jews must be written in red. And the instructions went on to specify that, regarding the arrests of Jews, all records must be made in triplicate. Finally, the sheet of instructions included a way to categorize those Jews arrested. I could not make any sense of the categories. I only knew them to be crucial. That they might determine life and death for a woman, or man, or child. And that in the mind that invented these categories they had to have had some hidden significance, standing, like the crudely shaped characters of a medieval play, for shades of feeling, hidden states of being, secret knowledge.

For the most part, the men who designed the first missiles were not interested in weapons so much as flight. In his account of the early work at Peenemünde laboratories, Wernher von Braun explains that the scientists there had discovered a way to fund their research by making rockets appeal to the military. Colonel Dornberger told the other scientists that they could not hope to continue if all they created were experimental rockets. All Wernher von Braun wanted was to design vehicles that would travel to the moon. In the early fifties, in a book he wrote with two other scientists, he speaks of the reasons for such a flight. Yes, he says, curiosity and adventure play a part. But the primary reason is *to increase man's knowledge of the universe.*

To tell a story, or to hear a story told, is not a simple transmission of information. Something else in the telling is given too, so that, once hearing, what one has heard becomes a part of oneself. Hélène and I went to the museum in Paris together. There, among photographs of the first mass arrests and the concentration camp at Drancy, she told me this story. Reading the notice signed by the mayor, she presented herself immediately at the office of the censor. She waited with others, patiently. But when her turn in line came, the censor looked at her carefully. She was blond and had blue eyes. *Are you really Jewish?* he asked her.

The question of who was and who was not Jewish was pivotal to the Nazi mind and much legal controversy hung in the balance of this debate. For a few years, anyone with three Jewish grandparents was considered Jewish. An ancestor who belonged to the faith but was not of Jewish blood would be Jewish. One who did not belong to the faith, but was of Jewish blood, was also Jewish. At the heart of this controversy, I hear the whisper of ambivalence, and perhaps the smallest beginning of compassion. For, to this mind, the one who is not Jewish becomes recognizable as like oneself.

Yes, I am Jewish, she said. *But your mother,* he asked again. *Can you be certain? Yes,* she said. *Ask her, go home and ask her,* he said, putting his stamp away. *But my mother is dead,* she protested. Then, he said, keeping his stamp in the drawer, *Your father. Your father must not be Jewish. Go home and ask him. I know he is Jewish,* Hélène answered. *There is no doubt that he is Jewish. He has always been Jewish, and I am Jewish too.* Then the man was silent, he shook his head. And, looking past her, said, *Perhaps your father was not really your father. Have you thought of that? Perhaps he was not your father?* She was young. *Of course he's my father. How can you say that? Certainly he is my father,* she insisted. *He is Jewish and so am I.* And she demanded that her papers be stamped.

What was in this man's mind as he questioned her? Did he say to himself, Perhaps here is someone I can save? Did he have what Pierre Sauvage has called *a moment of goodness?* What we know as goodness is not a static quality but arrives through a series of choices, some imperceptible, which are continually presented to us.

It is 1941. And Heinrich Himmler pays a visit to the Russian front. He has been put in charge of organizing the *Einsatzgruppen,* moving groups of men who carry out the killing of civilians and partisans. He watches as a deep pit is dug by the captured men and women. Then, suddenly, a young man catches his eye. He is struck by some quality the man possesses. He takes a liking to him. He has the commandant of the *Einsatzgruppen* bring the young man to him. *Who was your father?* he asks. *Your mother? Your grandparents? Do you have at least one grandparent who was not Jewish?* He is trying to save the young man. But he answers no to all the questions. So Himmler, strictly following the letter of the law, watches as the young man is put to death.

The captured men, women and children are ordered to re-move their clothing then. Naked, they stand before the pit they have dug. Some scream. Some attempt escape. The young men in uniform place their rifles against their shoulders and fire into the naked bodies. They do not fall silently. There are cries. There are open wounds. There are faces blown apart. Stomachs opened up. The dying groan. Weep. Flutter. Open their mouths.

There is no photograph of the particular moment when Heinrich Himmler stares into the face of death. What does he look like? Is he pale? He is stricken, the accounts tell us, and more than he thought he would be. He has imagined something quieter, more efficient, like the even rows of numbers, the alphabetical lists of names he likes to put in his files. Something he might be able to understand and contain. But one cannot contain death so easily.

Death with Girl in Her Lap. One of many studies the artist did of death. A girl is drawn, her body dead or almost dead, in that suspended state where the breath is almost gone. There is no movement. No will. The lines the artist has drawn are simple. She has not rendered the natural form of head, arm, buttock, thigh exactly. But all these lines hold the feeling of a body in them. And as my eyes rest on this image, I can feel my own fear of death, and also, the largeness of grief, how grief will not let you remain insulated from your own feelings, or from life itself. It is as if I knew this girl. And death, too, appears to know her, cradling the fragile body with tenderness; she seems to understand the sorrow of dying. Perhaps this figure has taken into herself all the deaths she has witnessed. And in this way, she has become merciful.

Because Himmler finds it so difficult to witness these deaths, the commandant makes an appeal to him. If it is hard for you, he says, think what it must be for these young men who must carry out these executions, day after day. Shaken by what he has seen and heard, Himmler returns to Berlin resolved to ease the pain of these men. He will consult an engineer and set him to work immediately on new designs. Before the year has ended, he presents the *Einsatzgruppen* with a mobile killing truck. Now the young men will not have to witness death day after day. A hose from the exhaust pipe funnels fumes into a chamber built on the bed of a covered truck, which has a red cross painted on its side so its passengers will not be alarmed as they enter it.

To a certain kind of mind, what is hidden away ceases to exist.

Himmler does not like to watch the suffering of his prisoners. In this sense he does not witness the consequences of his own commands. But the mind is like a landscape in which nothing really ever disappears. What seems to have vanished has only transmuted to another form. Not wishing to witness what he has set in motion, still, in a silent part of himself, he must imagine what takes place. So, just as the child is made to live out the unclaimed imagination of the parent, others under Himmler's power were made to bear witness for him. Homosexuals were forced to witness and sometimes take part in the punishment of other homosexuals, Poles of other Poles, Jews of Jews. And as far as possible, the hands of the men of the SS were protected from the touch of death. Other prisoners were required to bury the bodies, or burn them in the ovens.

Hélène was turned in by a Jewish man who was trying, no doubt, to save his own life, and she was put under arrest by another Jewish man, an inmate of the same camp to which she was taken. She was grateful that she herself had not been forced to do harm. But something haunted her. A death that came to stand in place of her own death. As we walked through the streets of Paris she told me this story.

By the time of her arrest she was married and had a young son. Her husband was taken from their apartment during one of the mass arrests that began in July of 1942. Hélène was out at the time with her son. For some time she wandered the streets of Paris. She would sleep at night at the homes of various friends and acquaintances, leaving in the early morning so that she would not arouse suspicion among the neighbors. This was the hardest time, she told me, because there was so little food, even less than she was to have at Drancy. She had no ration card or any way of earning money. Her whole existence was illegal. She had to be as if invisible. She collected scraps from the street. It was on the street that she told me this story, as we walked from the fourth arrondissement to the fifth, crossing the bridge near Notre Dame, making our way toward the Boulevard St. Michel.

Her husband was a citizen of a neutral country and for this reason legally destined for another camp. From this camp he would not be deported. Instead he was taken to the French concentration camp at Drancy. After his arrest, hoping to help him, Hélène managed to take his papers to the Swiss Consulate. But the papers remained there. After her own arrest she was taken with her son to Drancy, where she was reunited with her husband. He told her that her efforts were useless. But still again and again she found ways to smuggle out letters to friends asking them to take her husband's papers from the Swiss Consulate to the camp at Drancy. One of these letters was to save their lives.

After a few months, preparations began to send Hélène and her family to Auschwitz. Along with many other women, she was taken to have her hair cut short, though those consigned to that task decided she should keep her long, blond hair. Still, she was herded along with the others to the train station and packed into the cars. Then, just two hours before the train was scheduled to leave, Hélène, her son and her husband were pulled from the train. Her husband's papers had been brought by the Swiss consul to the camp. The Commandant, by assuming Hélène shared the same nationality with her husband, had made a fortuitous mistake.

But the train had to have a specific number of passengers before it could leave. In Hélène's place the guards brought a young man. She would never forget his face, she told me, or his name. Later she tried to find out whether he had lived or died but could learn nothing.

———

Himmler did not partake in the actual preparations for what he called "the final solution." Nor did he attend the Wannsee Conference where the decision to annihilate millions of human beings was made. He sent his assistant Heydrich. Yet Heydrich, who was there, did not count himself entirely present. He could say that each decision he made was at the bequest of Heinrich Himmler. In this way an odd system of insulation was created. These crimes, these murders of millions, were all carried out in absentia, as if by no one in particular.

This ghostlike quality, the strange absence of a knowing conscience, as if the living creature had abandoned the shell, was spread throughout the entire chain of command. So a French bureaucrat writing a letter in 1942 speaks in detail of the mass arrests that he himself supervised as if he had no other part in these murders except as a kind of spiritless cog in a vast machine whose force compelled him from without. *The German authorities have set aside especially for that purpose enough trains to transport 30,000 Jews,* he writes. *It is therefore necessary that the arrests made should correspond to the capacity of the trains.*

It is August 23, 1943. The first inmates of concentration camp Dora have arrived. Is there some reason why an unusually high percentage of prisoners ordered to work in this camp are homosexuals? They are set to work immediately, working with few tools, often with bare hands, to convert long tunnels carved into the Harz Mountains into a factory for the manufacture of missiles. They work for eighteen hours each day. Six of these hours are set aside for formal procedures, roll calls, official rituals of the camp. For six hours they must try to sleep in the tunnels, on the damp earth, in the same area where the machines, pickaxes, explosions and drills are making a continually deafening noise, twenty-four hours of every day. They are fed very little. They see the daylight only once a week, at the Sunday roll call. The tunnels themselves are illumined with faint light bulbs. The production of missiles have been moved here because the factories at Peenemünde were

bombed. Because the secret work at Peenemünde had been revealed to the Allies by an informer, after the bombing the Reichsführer SS proposed that the factories should be installed in a concentration camp. Here, he argued, security could be more easily
enforced; only the guards had any freedom, and they were subject
to the harsh discipline of the SS. The labor itself could be hidden
under soil of the Harz Mountains.

Memory can be like a long, half-lit tunnel, a tunnel where one is
likely to encounter phantoms of a self, long concealed, no longer
nourished with the force of consciousness, existing in a tortured
state between life and death. In his account of his years at
Peenemünde, Wernher von Braun never mentions concentration
camp Dora. Yet he was seen there more than once by inmates
who remembered him. As the designing engineer, he had to su-
pervise many details of production. Conditions at camp Dora
could not have escaped his attention. Dora did not have its own
crematorium. And so many men and women died in the course of
a day that the bodies waiting to be picked up by trucks and taken
to the ovens of Buchenwald were piled high next to the entrance
to the tunnels.

Perhaps Von Braun told himself that what went on in those tunnels had nothing to do with him. He had not wished for these
events, had not wanted them. The orders came from someone
who had power over him. In the course of this writing I remembered a childhood incident that made me disown myself in the
same way. My best friend, who was my neighbor, had a mean
streak and because of this had a kind of power over the rest of us
who played with her. For a year I left my grandmother's house to
live with my mother again. On my return I had been replaced by
another little girl, and the two of them excluded me. But finally
my chance arrived. My friend had a quarrel with her new friend
and enlisted me in an act of revenge. Together we cornered her at

the back of a yard, pushing her into the garbage cans, yelling nasty words at her, throwing things at her.

My friend led the attack, inventing the strategies and the words which were hurled. With part of myself I knew what it was to be the object of this kind of assault. But I also knew this was the way to regain my place with my friend. Later I disowned my acts, as if I had not committed them. Because I was under the sway of my friend's power, I told myself that what I did was really her doing. And in this way became unreal to myself. It was as if my voice threatening her, my own anger, and my voice calling names, had never existed.

I was told this story by a woman who survived the holocaust. The war had not yet begun. Nor the exiles. Nor the mass arrests. But history was on the point of these events, tipping over, ready to fall into the relentless path of consequences. She was then just a child, playing games in the street. And one day she found herself part of a circle of other children. They had surrounded a little boy and were calling him names because he was Jewish. He was her friend. But she thought if she left this circle, or came to his defense, she herself would lose her standing among the others. Then, suddenly, in an angry voice her mother called her in from the street. As soon as the door shut behind her, her mother began to shout, words incomprehensible to her, and slapped her across the face. *Your father,* her mother finally said, after crying, and in a quieter voice, *was Jewish.* Her father had been dead for three years. Soon after this day her mother too would die. As the danger grew worse her gentile relatives would not harbor her any longer, and she joined the fate of those who tried to live in the margins, as if invisible, as if mere shadows, terrified of a direct glance, of recognition, existing at the unsteady boundary of consciousness.

In disowning the effects we have on others, we disown ourselves. My father watched the suffering of my childhood and did nothing. He was aware of my mother's alcoholism and the state of her mind when she drank. He knew my grandmother to be tyran-

nical. We could speak together of these things almost dispassionately, as if both of us were disinterested witnesses to a fascinating
social drama. But after a day's visit with him, spent at the park, or
riding horses, or at the movies, he would send me back into that
world of suffering we had discussed so dispassionately.

His disinterest in my condition was not heartless. It reflected
the distance he kept from his own experience. One could sense
his suffering but he never expressed it directly. He was absent to a
part of himself. He was closer to tears than many men, but he
never shed those tears. If I cried he would fall into a frightened
silence. And because of this, though I spent a great deal of time
with him, he was always in a certain sense an absent father. Unknowingly I responded in kind, for years, feeling a vaguely defined anger that would neither let me love nor hate him.

My father learned his disinterest under the guise of masculinity.
Boys don't cry. There are whole disciplines, institutions, rubrics
in our culture which serve as categories of denial.

Science is such a category. The torture and death that
Heinrich Himmler found disturbing to witness became acceptable
to him when it fell under this rubric. He liked to watch the
scientific experiments in the concentration camps. And then there
is the rubric of military order. I am looking at a photograph. It
was taken in 1941 in the Ukraine. The men of an *Einsatzgruppen*
are assembled in a group pose. In front of them their rifles rest in
ceremonial order, composed into tripods. They stand straight and
tall. They are clean-shaven and their uniforms are immaculate, *in
apple-pie order,* as we would say in America.

It is not surprising that cleanliness in a profession that sheds
blood would become a compulsion. Blood would evidence guilt
and fear to a mind trying to escape the consequence of its decisions. It is late in the night when Laura tells me one more story.
Her father is about to be sent to Europe, where he will fight in
the Battle of the Bulge and become a general. For weeks her
mother has prepared a party. The guests begin to arrive in formal

dress and sparkling uniforms. The white-gloved junior officers stand to open the doors. Her mother, regal in satin and jewels, starts to descend the staircase. Laura sits on the top stair watching, dressed in her pajamas. Then suddenly a pool of blood appears at her mother's feet, her mother falls to the floor, and almost as quickly, without a word uttered, a junior officer sweeps up the stairs, removes her mother into a waiting car, while another one cleans up the blood. No one tells Laura that her mother has had a miscarriage, and the party continues as if no event had taken place, no small or large death, as if no death were about to take place, nor any blood be spilled.

But the nature of the material world frustrates our efforts to remain free of the suffering of others. The mobile killing van that Himmler summoned into being had some defects. Gas from the exhaust pipes leaked into the cabin where the drivers sat and made them ill. When they went to remove the bodies from the van they were covered with blood and excrement, and their faces bore expressions of anguish. Himmler's engineers fixed the leak, increased the flow of gas so the deaths would be quicker, and built in a drain to collect the bodily fluids that are part of death.

There are times when no engineers can contain death. Over this same landscape through which the mobile killing vans traveled, an invisible cloud would one day spread, and from it would descend a toxic substance that would work its way into the soil and the water, the plants and the bodies of animals, and into human cells, not only in this landscape of the Ukraine, but in the fjords of Norway, the fields of Italy and France, and even here, in the far reaches of California, bringing a death that recalled, more than forty years later, those earlier hidden deaths.

You can see pictures of them. Whole families, whole communities. The fabric on their backs almost worn through. Bodies as if ebbing away before your eyes. Poised on an edge. The cold visible around the thin joints of arms and knees. A bed made in a doorway. Moving then, over time, deeper and deeper into the shadows. Off the streets. Into back rooms, and then to the attics or the cellars. Windows blackened. Given less and less to eat. Moving into smaller and smaller spaces. Sequestered away like forbidden thoughts, or secrets.

Could he have seen in these images of those he had forced into hiding and suffering, into agony and death, an image of the outer reaches of his own consciousness? It is only now that I can begin to see he has become part of them. Those whose fate he sealed. Heinrich Himmler. A part of Jewish history. Remembered by those who fell into the net of his unclaimed life. Claimed as a facet of the wound, part of the tissue of the scar. A mark on the body of our minds, both those of us who know this history and those who do not.

For there is a sense in which we are all witnesses. Hunger, desperation, pain, loneliness, these are all visible in the streets about us. The way of life we live, a life we have never really chosen, forces us to walk past what we see. And out at the edge, beyond what we see or hear, we can feel a greater suffering, cries from a present or past starvation, a present or past torture, cries of those we have never met, coming to us in our dreams, and even if these cries do not survive in our waking knowledge, still, they live on in the part of ourselves we have ceased to know.

I think now of the missile again and how it came into being. Scientific inventions do not spring whole like Athena from the head of Zeus from the analytic implications of scientific discoveries. Technological advance takes shape slowly in the womb of society and is influenced and fed by our shared imagination. What we create thus mirrors the recesses of our own minds, and perhaps also hidden capacities. Television mimics the ability to see in the mind's eye. And the rocket? Perhaps the night flight of the soul, that ability celebrated in witches to send our thoughts as if through the air to those distant from us, to send images of our-

selves, and even our secret feelings, out into an atmosphere beyond ourselves, to see worlds far flung from and strange to us
becomes manifest in a sinister fashion in the missile.

Self-portrait in charcoal. Since the earliest rendering she made of
her own image, much time has passed. The viewer here has
moved closer. Now the artist's head fills the frame. She is much
older in years and her features have taken on that androgyny
which she thought necessary to the work of an artist. Her hair is
white on the paper where the charcoal has not touched it. She is
in profile and facing a definite direction. Her eyes look in that
direction. But they do not focus on anyone or anything. The
portrait is soft, the charcoal rubbed almost gently over the surface,
here light, here dark. Her posture is one not so much of resolution
as resignation. The portrait was drawn just after the First World
War, the war in which her son Peter died. I have seen these eyes in
the faces of those who grieve, eyes that are looking but not focused, seeing perhaps what is no longer visible.

*After the war, German scientists who developed the V-1 and V-2 rocket
immigrate to the United States where they continue to work on rocketry.
Using the Vengeance weapon as a prototype, they develop the first ICBM
missiles.*

On the twenty-third of May 1945, as the war in Europe comes to
an end, Heinrich Himmler is taken prisoner by the Allied command. He has removed the military insignia from his clothing, and
he wears a patch over one eye. Disguised in this manner, and
carrying the identity papers of a man he had condemned to death,
he attempts to cross over the border at Bremervörde. No one at
the checkpoint suspects him of being the Reichsführer SS. But
once under the scrutiny of the guards, all his courage fails him.
Like a trembling schoolboy, he blurts out the truth. Now he will
be taken to a center for interrogation, stripped of his clothing and
searched. He will refuse to wear the uniform of the enemy, so he

will be given a blanket to wrap over his underclothing. Taken to a second center for interrogation, he will be forced to remove this blanket and his underclothes. The interrogators, wishing to make certain he has no poison hidden anywhere, no means by which to end his life and hence avoid giving testimony, will surround his naked body. They will ask him to open his mouth. But just as one of them sees a black capsule wedged between his teeth, he will jerk his head away and swallow. All attempts to save his life will fail. He will not survive to tell his own story. His secrets will die with him.

There were many who lived through those years who did not wish to speak of what they saw or did. None of the German rocket engineers bore witness to what they saw at concentration camp Dora. Common rank and file members of the Nazi Party, those without whose efforts or silent support the machinery could not have gone on, fell almost as a mass into silence. In Berlin and Munich I spoke to many men and women, in my generation or younger, who were the children of soldiers, or party members, or SS men, or generals, or simply believers. Their parents would not speak to them of what had happened. The atmosphere in both cities was as if a pall had been placed over memory. And thus the shared mind of this nation has no roots, no continuous link with what keeps life in a pattern of meaning.

Lately I have come to believe that an as yet undiscovered human need and even a property of matter is the desire for revelation. The truth within us has a way of coming out despite all conscious efforts to conceal it. I have heard stories from those in the generation after the war, all speaking of the same struggle to ferret truth from the silence of their parents so that they themselves could begin to live. One born the year the war ended was never told a word about concentration camps, at home or in school. She began to wake in the early morning hours with nightmares which mirrored down to fine and accurate detail the conditions of the camps. Another woman searching casually through some trunks in the attic of her home found a series of pamphlets, virulently and cruelly anti-Semitic, which had been written by her grandfather, a high Nazi official. Still another pieced together the truth of her father's life, a member of the Gestapo, a man she remembered as playful by contrast to her stern mother. He died in the war. Only over time could she put certain pieces together. How he had had a man working under him beaten. And then, how he had beaten her.

Many of those who survived the holocaust could not bear the memories of what happened to them and, trying to bury the past, they too fell into silence. Others continue to speak as they are able. The manner of speech varies. At an artist's retreat in the Santa Cruz Mountains I met a woman who survived Bergen Belsen and Auschwitz. She inscribes the number eight in many of her paintings. And the number two. This is the story she is telling with those numbers. It was raining the night she arrived with her mother, six brothers and sisters at Auschwitz. It fell very hard, she told me. We were walking in the early evening up a hill brown in the California fall. The path was strewn with yellow leaves illuminated by the sun in its descent. They had endured the long trip from Hungary to Poland, without food or water. They were very tired. Now the sky seemed very black but the platform, lit up with stadium lights, was blinding after the darkness of the train. She would never, she told me, forget the shouting. It is as if she still cannot get the sound out of her ears. The Gestapo gave one shrill order after another, in a language she did not yet understand. They were herded in confusion, blows coming down on them randomly from the guards, past a tall man in a cape. This was Dr. Mengele. He made a single gesture toward all her family and continued it toward her but in a different direction. For days, weeks, months after she had learned what their fate had been she kept walking in the direction of their parting and beyond toward the vanishing point of her vision of them.

There were seven from her family who died there that night. The eighth to die was her father. He was sent to a different camp and died on the day of liberation. Only two lived, she and one brother. The story of one life cannot be told separately from the story of other lives. Who are we? The question is not simple. What we call the self is part of a larger matrix of relationship and society. Had we been born to a different family, in a different time, to a different world, we would not be the same. All the lives that surround us are in us.

On the first day that I met Lenke she asked a question that stays with me still. Why do some inflict on others the suffering they have endured? What is it in a life that makes one choose to do this, or not? It is a question I cannot answer. Not even after several years pondering this question in the light of Heinrich Himmler's soul. Two years after my conversation with Lenke, as if there had been a very long pause in our dialogue, I was given a glimpse in the direction of an answer. Leo told me his story; it sounded back over time, offering not so much solution as response.

The nucleus of every cell in the human body contains the genetic plan for the whole organism.

We sat together in a large and noisy restaurant, light pouring through the windows, the present clamoring for our attention, even as we moved into the past. Leo was nine years old when the war entered his life. He remembers standing in a crowd, he told me, watching as a partisan was flogged and executed by the Germans. *What do you think I felt?* he asked me, the irony detectable in his voice. What he told me fell into his narration as part of a larger picture. The capture, the roughness, the laceration of flesh, the sight of death, all this excited him.

   Violence was not new to him. Through bits and pieces surrounding the central line of his story I came to some idea of what his childhood must have been. His father was a cold man, given to rages over small errors. Leo was beaten often. Such attacks had already forced his older half brother out of the house. It was to this brother that Leo bonded and gave his love.

Leo remembered a party before the war. The room was lively with talk until his older brother arrived. Then a silence fell over everyone. The older men were afraid of this young man, even his father. And to Leo, his brother, with his air of power and command, was a hero. He could scarcely understand the roots of this power, moored in a political system of terror so effective, few even spoke of it. Leo's brother was a young member of Stalin's secret police. Cast into the streets while still a boy, he learned the arts of survival. Eventually he was arrested for assaulting and robbing a man. It was under this circumstance that he offered himself to the NKVD, the forerunner of the KGB, as an interrogator. He learned to torture men and women suspected of treason or of harboring secrets.

He wore high black leather boots and a black leather jacket, which impressed Leo. Leo followed him about, and they would take long walks together, his brother telling him the stories he could tell no one else. How he had tortured a woman. How he had made blood flow from the nipples of her breasts.

Everything he heard from his brother he took into himself. Such love as Leo had for his brother can be a forceful teacher. He did not see his brother often, nor was his intimacy with him great enough to create familiarity. What he had was a continual taste awakening hunger. Never did he know the daily presence of the beloved, or all his imperfections, the real person dwelling behind the mask of the ideal, the shiny and impervious leather. To fill the nearly perpetual absence of his brother he clung to this ideal. An appearance of strength. A certain arrogance in the face of violence, promising an even greater violence. Love always seeks a resting place.

I knew a similar attachment to my sister. Separated when I was six and she was thirteen, the experience of love I knew with her was longing, and over time this bonded me to longing itself. And to the books she brought me to read, the poems she read to me, worlds she pointed me toward.

And the German occupation of the Ukraine? The accident at Chernobyl had taken place just weeks before we met. But long before this event, the same land suffered other wounds. As the Soviet army retreated, they burned crops and killed livestock. Even before the German invasion, the land was charred and black for miles around. Then when the German army came, the executions began. And the deportations. Many were taken away to forced labor camps. Leo was among them.

His father was an agronomist with some knowledge of how to increase crop yields. The whole family was transported to Germany, but at the scientist's camp Leo was transported in another direction. His father watched him go, Leo told me, with no protest, not even the protestation of tears.

What was it like for him in the labor camp to which he was sent? His telling of the past existed in a framework of meaning he had built slowly over the years, and with great pain, forced to this understanding by events that he himself had brought into being, later in his life.

It is a question of passion, he told me. While he was in the camps, he began to worship the uniformed members of the SS and the SA, just as he had loved his brother. Their strength, their ideals, their willingness to do violence, to live for something beyond themselves, the black leather they wore, the way they were clean and polished and tall. He saw those who, like himself, were imprisoned as small and demeaned, caught in the ugliness of survival, lacking any heroism, cowardly, petty. Even now, as he looked back himself with another eye, his disdain for those who suffered persisted in a phantom form, in the timbre of his voice.

The punishment of the guards did not embitter him. In his mind he believed he himself was always justly punished. Once, against the rules, he stole food, honey, while he was working. He did not accept his own hunger as an argument for kindness. He admired the strength with which he was hit. Even the intimacy of the blows gave him a certain pride in himself. Loving the arms that hit him, he could think of this power as his own.

But there were two assaults which he could not forgive. They humiliated him. Now as I write I can see that to him his attackers must have been unworthy of his admiration. He was on a work detail in the neighboring village when a boy his own age slapped him. And later an old woman spat in his face.

This was all he told me of his time of imprisonment. After the liberation, he went into Germany to search for his family. Did he believe that perhaps, even now, something outside of the circle drawn by what he had suffered existed for him? Was there a seed of hope, a wish that made him, thin, weak, on shaking legs, travel the hundreds of miles, sleeping in trains and train stations, to search? He was exhausted, I can imagine, past that edge of weariness in which whatever is real ceases entirely to matter and existence itself is just a gesture, not aimed any longer at outcome, but just a simple expression of what remains and so can seem even brighter. He was making a kind of pilgrimage.

It is in this way, coldness beyond cold, frailty beyond endurance, that sorrow becomes a power. A light begins to shine past the fire of ovens, yet from them, as if stars, or turning leaves, falling and trapped in their fall, nevertheless kept their brilliance, and this brilliance a beacon, like a code, flashes out the precise language of human suffering. Then we know that what we suffer is not going to pass by without meaning.

Self-portrait, 1923. The artist's face is drawn of lines left white on the page which seem as if they were carved out of night. We are very close to her. It is only her face we see. Eye to eye, she looks directly at us. But her eyes are unfocused and weary with that kind of tiredness that has accumulated over so much time we think of it as aging. Her mouth, wide and frank, does not resist gravity any longer. This mouth smiles with an extraordinary subtlety. We can almost laugh with this mouth, drawn with lines which, like all the lines on the lines on the page, resemble scars, or tears in a fabric.

A story is told as much by silence as by speech. Like the white spaces in an etching, such silences render form. But unlike an etching in which the whole is grasped at once, the silence of a story must be understood over time. Leo described to me what his life was like after he found his parents, but he did not describe the moment, or even the day or week, when he found them. Only now as I write these words does the absence of joy in this reunion begin to speak to me. And in the space of this absence I can feel the kind of cold that can extinguish the most intense of fires.

Leo was soon streetwise. His family was near starvation. He worked the black market. Older men buying his goods would ask him for women, and he began to procure for them. He kept his family alive. His father, he told me, never acknowledged his effort. When they moved to America a few years later and Leo reminded him that his work had fed him, his father exclaimed, in a voice of shock and disparagement, *And what you did!*

In 1957, the Soviet Union develops the SS-6, a surface-to-surface missile. It is launched with 32 engines. Failing as a weapon, this device is used to launch the first satellite into space. In 1961, the Soviet Union develops the SS-7. These missiles carry nuclear warheads. They are launched from hardened silos to protect them from attack.

In America he was sent to high school. But he did not know how to be an ordinary boy among boys. He became a street fighter. Together with a group of boys among whom he was the toughest, he would look for something to happen. More than once they devised a trap for homosexual men. They would place the prettiest boy among them on a park bench and wait behind the trees and bushes. Usually a man would pull up in his car and go to sit on the bench next to the boy. When this man made any gesture of seduction, or suggested the boy leave with him, the boys would suddenly appear and, surrounding him, beat him and take his money.

I am thinking of these boys as one after another they forced the weight of their bodies into another man's body and tried to hurt him, to bloody him, to defeat him. I know it is possible to be a stranger to one's feelings. For the years after I was separated from my mother, I forgot that I missed her. My feeling was driven so deep, it was imperceptible, so much a part of me, I would not have called it grief. It is said that when boys or young men attack a man they find effeminate or believe to be homosexual they are trying to put at a distance all traces of homosexuality in themselves. But what does this mean? What is the central passion in this issue of manhood, proven or disproven? In my imagination I witness again the scene that Leo described to me. It is a passionate scene, edged by a love the boys feel for each other, and by something more, by a kind of grief, raging because it is buried so deep inside. Do they rage against this man's body because of what has been withheld from them, held back, like the food of intimacy, imprisoned and guarded in the bodies of older men, in the bodies of fathers? Is it this rage that fires the mettle of what we call manhood?

Yet, are we not all affected by this that is withheld in men? Are we not all forged in the same inferno? It was never said directly, but I know my great-grandfather beat my grandfather, and lectured him, drunkenly, humiliating and shaming him. I am told that as adults they quarreled violently over politics. No one in my family can remember the substance of the disagreement, only the red faces, the angry voices. Now, as I look back to imagine my grandfather passionately reciting the list of those he hated, our black neighbors, the Jews, the Communists, I follow the path of his staring eyes and begin to make out a figure. It is my great-grandfather Colvin, receiving even after his death too indifferently the ardent and raging pleas of his son. And hearing that voice again, I hear an echo from my grandfather's daughter, my mother, whose voice when she had been drinking too much had the same quality, as of the anguish of feeling held back for so long it has become monstrous, the furies inside her unleashed against me.

Leo's telling had a slightly bitter edge, a style which felt like the remnant of an older harshness. He kept looking at me as if to protect himself from any sign of shock in my face. Now he was not certain he would tell me the rest of his story. But he did.

Just after he graduated from high school, the Korean War began. He was drafted, and sent directly to Korea. Was he in combat? Leo shook his head. He was assigned to an intelligence unit. He spoke Russian. And he was directed to interrogate Russian prisoners who were captured behind enemy lines. He told me this story. He was given two men to question. With the first man he made every kind of threat. But he carried nothing out. The man was resolutely silent. And Leo learned nothing from him. He left the room with all his secrets. *You can never,* Leo told me later, *let any man get the better of you.* With the second man he was determined not to fail. He would get him to tell whatever he knew. He made the same threats again, and again met silence. Then, suddenly, using his thumb and finger, he put out the man's eye. And as the man was screaming and bleeding, he told him he would die one way or the other. He was going to be shot. But he had the choice now of seeing his executioners or not, of dying in agony or not. And then the man told him his secrets.

Self-portrait, 1927. She has drawn herself in charcoal again, and in profile. And she still looks out but now her eyes are focused. She is looking at something visible, distant, but perhaps coming slowly closer. Her mouth still turns down, and this must be a characteristic expression because her face is lined in that direction. The form of her face is drawn with soft strokes, blended into the page, as one life blends into another life, or a body into earth. There is something in the quality of her attention, fine lines sketched over her eyebrow. A deeper black circle under her eye. With a resolute, unhappy awareness, she recognizes what is before her.

The life plan of the body is encoded in the DNA molecule, a substance that has the ability to hold information and to replicate itself.

Self-portrait, 1934. As I look now I see in her face that whatever it was she saw before has now arrived. She looks directly at us again and we are even closer to her than before. One finger at the edge of the frame pulls against her eyebrow, against lines drawn there earlier, as if to relieve pain. All the lines lead downward, like rain. Her eyes are open but black, at once impenetrable and infinite. There is a weariness here again, the kind from which one never recovers. And grief? It is that grief I have spoken of earlier, no longer apart from the flesh and bone of her face.

After many years of silence, my mother and I were able to speak of what happened between us and in our family. It was healing for us, to hear and speak the truth, and made for a closeness we had not felt before. Both of us knew we were going to speak before we did.

Before a secret is told one can often feel the weight of it in the atmosphere. Leo gazed at me for a long moment. There was more he wanted to tell me and that I wanted to hear. The rest of his story was everywhere, in the air, in our hands, the traffic on the street, felt. He shook his head again before he began. The war was over, but he had started in a certain direction and now he could not stop. He befriended a young man from the army. This man looked up to him the way he had to his brother. He wanted to teach the younger man what he knew. He had already committed several robberies, and he wanted an accomplice. They went out together, looking for an easy target for the young man to practice on. They found someone who was easy. He was old, and black. Leo showed his friend how to hold his gun, up close to the temple, pointing down. The boy did this. But the old man, terrified, simply ran. As Leo directed him, the younger man held the gun out in front of him to shoot and he pulled the trigger. But the cartridge of the bullet stuck in the chamber. So the man, still alive, kept running. Then, as Leo urged him on, his friend ran after the old man and, jumping on his back, began to hit him on the head with the butt of his pistol. The moment overtook him. Fear, and exhilaration at mastering fear, a deeper rage, all made a fuel for his fury. He hit and hit again and again. He drew blood. Then the man ceased to cry out, ceased to struggle. He lay still. And the younger man kept on hitting, so that the moment of the older man's death was lost in a frenzy of blows. Then finally there was silence. The young man, knowing he had caused a death, stood up shaking and walked away. He was stunned, as if he himself had been beaten. And Leo, who had been calling and shouting to encourage his friend, who had been laughing, he said, so hard he had to hold himself, was silent too. He went to stand by the body of the old man. Blood poured profusely from the wounds on his head. He stared into the face of this dead man. And now in his telling of the story he was crying. He paused. What was it there in that face for him, broken, afraid, shattered, flesh and bone past repair, past any effort, any strength? *I could see,* he told me, *that this man was just like me.*

In 1963 America develops a new missile, the Titan II. It has a larger range, a larger carrying capacity, a new guidance system, and an improved vehicle for re-entry. These missiles are still being deployed.

1938. *Self-portrait.* The artist is once again in profile. But now she faces another direction. The bones of her cheeks, mouth, nose, eyes are still all in shadow. Her eyebrows arch in tired anticipation. She has drawn herself with the simplest of strokes. Charcoal blending softly downward, all the strokes moving downward. This is old age. Not a single line drawn for vanity, or for the sake of pretense, protects us from her age. She is facing toward death.

————

We knew, both Leo and I, that now he was telling me what was most crucial to him. In the telling, some subtle change passed through him. Something unknown was taking shape here, both of us witnesses, both of us part of the event. This that he lived through was what I was seeking to understand. What he saw in the face of the dead man did not leave him. For a long time he was afraid of his own dreams. Every night, the same images returned to him, but images in motion, belonging to a longer narration. He dreamed that he entered a park and began to dig up a grave there. Each night he would plunge his hands in the earth and find the body buried there. But each night the body he found was more and more eroded. This erosion filled him with horror. He could not sleep alone. Every night he would find a different woman to sleep with him. Every night he would drink himself into insensibility. But the images of dreams began to come to him even in his waking hours. And so he began to drink ceaselessly. Finally he could not go on as before. Two months after the death he had witnessed he confessed his part in it.

For many reasons his sentence was light. Both he and his friend were young. They had been soldiers. He knew that, had the man he helped to kill not been black, his sentence would have been longer; or he may himself have been put to death. He said nothing of his years of imprisonment. Except that these years served to quiet the dreams that had haunted him. His wit, his air of toughness, all he had seen make him good at the work he does now with boys who have come into conflict with society, a work which must in some way be intended as restitution.

Yet, as he spoke, I began to see that he believed some part of his soul would never be retrieved. *There is a circle of humanity,* he told me, *and I can feel its warmth. But I am forever outside.*

I made no attempt to soften these words. What he said was true. A silence between us held what had been spoken. Then gradually we began to make small movements. Hands reaching for a key, a cigarette. By a quiet agreement, his story was over, and we were in the present again.

The telling and the hearing of a story is not a simple act. The one who tells must reach down into deeper layers of the self, reviving old feelings, reviewing the past. Whatever is retrieved is reworked into a new form, one that narrates events and gives the listener a path through these events that leads to some fragment of wisdom. The one who hears takes the story in, even to a place not visible or conscious to the mind, yet there. In this inner place a story from another life suffers a subtle change. As it enters the memory of the listener it is augmented by reflection, by other memories, and even the body hearing and responding in the moment of the telling. By such transmissions, consciousness is woven.

Over a year has passed now since I heard Leo's story. In my mind's eye, I see the events of his life as if they were carved out in woodblock prints, like the ones Käthe Kollwitz did. Of all her work, these most resemble Expressionist art. Was it intended that the form be so heavy, as if drawn centuries back into a mute untold history? Her work, and the work of the Expressionist movement, was called degenerate by the Nazis. These images, images of tumultuous inner feelings, or of suffering caused and hidden by social circumstance, were removed from the walls of museums and galleries.

When I was in Munich, a German friend told me that her generation has been deprived of German culture. What existed before the Third Reich was used in Nazi propaganda, and so has become as if dyed with the stain of that history. The artists and writers of the early twentieth century were silenced; they went into exile or perished. The link with the past was broken. Yet, even unremembered, the past never disappears. It exists still and continues under a mantle of silence, invisibly shaping lives.

The DNA molecule is made of long, fine, paired strands. These strands are helically coiled.

What is buried in the past of one generation falls to the next to claim. The children of Nazis and survivors alike have inherited a struggle between silence and speech.

The night I met Hélène at a Métro station in Paris I was returning from dinner with a friend. Ten years older than I, Jewish, French, in 1942, the year before my own birth, Natalie's life was put in danger. She was given false papers and shepherded with other children out of Paris through an underground movement. She lived out the duration of war in the countryside in the home of an ambassador who had diplomatic immunity. A woman who has remained one of her closest friends to this day was with her in this hiding place. The night we had dinner Natalie told me a story about her. This friend, she said, grew up determined to shed her past. She made Natalie promise never to reveal who she was or what had happened to her. She changed her name, denied that she was Jewish and raised her children as gentiles. Then, opening her hands in a characteristic gesture, Natalie smiled at me. The story was to take a gently ironic turn. The past was to return. This summer, she told me, she had held one end of a bridal canopy, what in a Jewish wedding is called a chuppa, at the wedding of her friend's daughter. This girl was marrying the son of an Orthodox rabbi. And her son too, knowing nothing of his mother's past, had gravitated toward Judaism.

In 1975 the SS-19 missile is deployed in the Soviet Union. It carries several warheads, each with a different target. A computer within it controls and detects deviations from its programmed course.

One can find traces of every life in each life. There is a story from my own family history that urges its way onto the page here. Sometime in the eighteenth century three brothers migrated from Scotland to the United States. They came from Aberdeen and bore the name Marks, a name common in that city to Jewish families who had immigrated from Germany to escape the pogroms. Jacob Marks, who descended from these brothers, was my great-great-grandfather. The family story was that he was descended from Huguenots. In our family, only my sister and I speak of the possibility that he could have been Jewish. Jacob married Rosa and they gave birth to a daughter whom they named Sarah. She married Thomas Colvin, and their last son was Ernest Marks Colvin, my grandfather, the same grandfather who would recite to me his furious list of those he hated, including Jews.

Who would my grandfather, I wonder now, have been if he had known his own history. Could he then have seen the shape of his life as part of a larger configuration? Wasn't he without this knowledge like the missile, or the neutron torn away from gravity, the matrix that sustains and makes sense of experience?

In any given cell only a small fraction of the genes are active. Messages to awaken these genes are transmitted by the surrounding cytoplasm, messages from other cells, or from outside substances.

I cannot say for certain what our family history was. I know only that I did gravitate myself toward what seemed missing or lost in me. In my first years of high school I lived alone with my father. He was often gone, at work or staying with his girlfriend. I adopted the family of a school friend, spending hours with them, baby-sitting their younger children, helping with household tasks, sharing meals, spending an evening speaking of art or politics. Then one evening, as I returned home, I saw a strange man standing near my door. He had come to tell me my father was dead, struck by an automobile while he was crossing the street in the light of dusk. I turned for solace and finally shelter to my adopted family. In the short time we lived together, out of my love for them, I took on their gestures, the manner and rhythm of their thought, ways of cooking, cadences, a sprinkling of Yiddish vocabulary. I became in some ways Jewish.

In the late seventies the United States develops a circuitry for the Minuteman rocket which allows for a target to be changed in the midst of flight.

Is there any one of us who can count ourselves outside the circle circumscribed by our common past? Whether or not I was trying to reweave threads severed from my family history, a shared heritage of despair and hope, of destruction and sustenance, was within me. What I received from my adopted family helped me to continue my life. My suffering had been placed, even wordlessly, in a larger stream of suffering, and as if wrapped and held by a culture that had grown up to meet suffering, to retell the tales and place them in a larger context by which all life continues.

L'chayim. Life. Held to even at the worst times. The dream of a better world. The schoolbook, tattered, pages flying loose, gripped in the hands of a young student, his coat open at the shoulder and along the front where the fabric was worn. The ghetto of Slonim. 1938. The Passover cup, fashioned secretly by inmates at Terezin, the Passover plate, the menorah, made at the risk of death from purloined materials. Pictures drawn by those who were there. Despair, the attrition of pain, daily cold, hunger somehow entering the mark of pencil or brush. Butterflies painted by children who all later perished. Stitches made across Lenke's drawings, reminding us of the stitches she sustained in one operation after another, after her liberation, when she was stricken with tuberculosis of the spine. The prisoner forced to pick up discarded clothing of those sent to the gas chambers, who said that among this clothing, as he gathered it, he saw *Stars of David like a drift of yellow flowers.*

As the fertilized egg cell starts to divide, all the daughter cells have identical DNA, but the cells soon cease to look alike, and in a few weeks, a number of different kinds of cells can be recognized in the embryo.

I am thinking again of a child's body. Curled and small. Innocent. The skin soft like velvet to the touch. Eyes open and staring without reserve or calculation, quite simply, into the eyes of who-ever appears in this field of vision. Without secrets. Arms open, ready to receive or give, just in the transpiration of flesh, sharing the sound of the heartbeat, the breath, the warmth of body on body.

In 1977 the Soviet Union puts the SS-NX-17 and SS N-18 into service. These are ballistic missiles to be launched from submarines. In 1978 the United States perfects the underwater launch system of the Tomahawk missile.

I could not, in the end, for some blessed reason, turn away from myself. Not at least in this place. The place of desire. I think now of the small lines etching themselves near the eyes of a woman's face I loved. And how, seeing these lines, I wanted to stroke her face. To lean myself, my body, my skin into her. A part of me unravels as I think of this, and I am taken toward longing, and beyond, into another region, past the walls of this house, or all I can see, stretching farther than the horizon where right now sea and sky blend. It is as if my cells are moving in a larger wave, a wave that takes in every history, every story.

At the end of nine months a multitude of different cells make up the newborn infant's body, including nerve cells, muscle cells, skin cells, reti-nal cells, liver cells, brain cells, cells of the heart that beats, cells of the mouth that opens, cells of the throat that cries . . .

When I think of that young man now, who died in the river near the island of my father's birth, died because he loved another man, I like to imagine his body bathed in the pleasure of that love. To believe that the hands that touched this young man's thighs, his buttocks, his penis, the mouth that felt its way over his body, the man who lay himself between his legs, or over, around his body did this lovingly, and that then the young man felt inside his flesh what radiated from his childlike beauty. Part angel. Bathed in a passionate sweetness. Tasting life at its youngest, most original center, the place of reason, where one is whole again as at birth.

In the last decade the Soviet Union improves its anti-ballistic missiles to make them maneuverable and capable of hovering in midair. The United States continues to develop and test the MX missile, with advanced inertial guidance, capable of delivering 10 pre-armed electronically guided warheads, each with maneuverability, possessing the power and accuracy to penetrate hardened silos. And the Soviet Union begins to design a series of smaller one-warhead mobile missiles, the SS-25, to be driven around by truck, and the SS-X-24, to be drawn on railroad tracks. And the United States develops a new warhead for the Trident missile carrying 14 smaller warheads that can be released in a barrage along a track or a road.

A train is making its way through Germany. All along its route those who are in the cars can look out and see those who are outside the cars. And those who are outside can see those who are inside. Sometimes words are exchanged. Sometimes there is a plea for water. And sometimes, at the risk of life, water is given. Sometimes names are called out, or curses are spoken, under the breath. And sometimes there is only silence.

Who are those on the inside and where are they going? There are rumors. It is best not to ask. There are potatoes to buy with the last of the rations. There is a pot boiling on the stove. And, at any rate, the train has gone; the people have vanished. You did not know them. You will not see them again. Except perhaps in your dreams. But what do those images mean? Images of strangers. Agony that is not yours. A face that does not belong to you. And so in the daylight you try to erase what you have encountered and to forget those tracks that are laid even as if someplace in your body, even as part of yourself.

A STRANGE

LIGHT

V

Like the membranes of all living cells, the membrane of the nerve cell decides what will enter and what will stay out, chooses between what feeds life and what is dangerous.

Under the skin, an old order begins to shift. No one sees. The first signs of change are as imperceptible as the order itself, an order which has been presumed as part of reality, part of the earth upon which one puts a foot, or the step itself, immutable, inarguable. 1893. It is as if two ships, establishing different directions, still unknown to each other, pass in the harbor. On one ship stands Second-Lieutenant Hugh Trenchard. He is just twenty years old. This is his first military assignment. As a member of the Royal Scotch Fusiliers, he is coming to India to maintain the hegemony of the British Empire. His charge is to keep the present order. On another ship, moving through the same waters, Mohandas Gandhi travels away from India and toward South Africa. But this is a circular journey, one which will traverse the mind as well as the earth. Making his way to Cape Town, Gandhi will be forced from the train when he refuses to leave a first-class seat. The seat has been forbidden to those the governing body calls colored. He will spend the night in the railway station and there make a choice, significant, as it will turn out to us all, before he continues his journey.

After learning to separate electrons from atoms, creating, thus, positive ions, scientists discover that as these ions travel at high speeds, releasing their energy to a region known as the positive electrode, a new form of energy is produced.

To sit quietly when faced with aggression may seem unnatural. But it is no more so than to advance into a rain of bullets. A soldier must be drilled over and over to habituate him to advance when his natural bodily desire is to flee. In the words of the Marine Corps *Guidebook,* the purpose of the drill is to instill *automatic response to orders.* It was Frederick the Great who first understood this. He was inspired to invent the Prussian drill by the newly emerging scientific view of the universe as a great machine. The peasants in his army were to be like cogs in the mechanism of official will. The pinnacle of this military tactic was perhaps reached in the First World War. On a single day, July 1, 1916, during the Battle of the Somme, of 110,000 men ordered to emerge from the trenches and march in orderly rows toward the German lines (where machine guns fired from the ramparts) 60,000 were either killed or wounded.

In addition to providing a barrier which protects the cell, the membranes of nerve cells also conduct positive and negative electrical charges along their surfaces.

The drill, however, is just one element among many which to-gether serve to feed a habituated obedience. Not the least among these elements is the experience of danger itself. Whenever any disaster strikes—gunfire, hurricane, or illness—any semblance of order, a regime, a schedule, or a hierarchy of command, is com-forting. The existence of unquestioned orders can create an illu-sion of rationality where there is none. To rise, despite pain and fatigue, and wash your face, clean your teeth, comb your hair, straighten the bedclothes, this seems to keep your world intact.

This energy, known as ionizing radiation, can pass through gas, liquid and even solid matter.

1895. Nearing the turn of the century, Wilhelm Röntgen observes the existence of X rays as they emanate from a glowing cathode tube. In this strange light, the old vision of the world begins to vanish. What an anomalous phenomenon, that matter should produce light. Light that can penetrate hard surfaces and make an image of what lies inside. Yet perhaps this should not be surprising. We who are material beings are always making images of ourselves and try, in this way, to reach the core of our existence.

We live in a lattice of myths. Stories which manifest the meaning of our lives and at the same time define for us the circumference of the imaginal world. What is it we are free to imagine? In the year that X rays are discovered, new images are transgressing old definitions. Just as the boundary between matter and energy begins to blur, so the line between masculine and feminine wavers. Though it is yet to be published, Colette has written her first novel. In its pages, women dress like men, make love with women, celebrate erotic pleasure. Oscar Wilde has written an opera called *Salomé*. A photograph shows him dressed as the heroine, reclining as he reveals a sensuous, rounded belly. The poems he writes make thinly veiled reference to an erotic force between men.

The material origin of human experience and behavior can be located in these rapidly moving changes.

At the end of the First World War, looking backward, it is common to make an idyll of what came before, and to presume that the war itself brought about the end of an old order. But that order was already shifting. One can almost see them, great phantom audiences, filling the theatre. Stylishly dressed, they radiate the ebullience of fashion and class, laughing, applauding, delighting in Wilde's merciless wit, as his lines expose the hypocrisy of Victorian marriage and morals. *The Importance of Being Earnest* opens early in 1895. But despite its astonishing success it is soon to close. Change is never without interruption. In May of the same year, Wilde will be put on trial for homosexuality. In passing sentence the judge announces that he shares *a common sense of indignation at the nature of these charges.*

Soon it is discovered that this radiation has profound implications for all living organisms, including the human body.

In this case, what is called common sense is part of an intricate structure of propriety in the course of disintegration. But this does not make society more amenable to Wilde's vision. The bearer of an augury is often punished. One has only to think of Cassandra. Her punishment was to be unheard. This may seem mild. Unless you understand how such a high, insinuating song can wreak havoc on the singer when it is not heard.

Cassandra was thought mad. Under certain circumstances, madness can come from prophetic overtones, half-heard memories, or dreams that captivate the inner voice. In 1893, the year Hugh Trenchard sailed for India and two years before Oscar Wilde's imprisonment began, another man, who for his own reasons would become famous, bound himself into captivity because of certain dreams he had which assaulted his idea of what was proper. He was Daniel Paul Schreber, son of the pedagogue Dr. Daniel Gottlieb Moritz Schreber.

The doctor's son dreamed that he wanted to be a woman, in his words, *succumbing to intercourse.* For these dreams he incarcerated himself in a psychiatric clinic at Leipzig. One cannot help but suspect that he followed the same course his father would have taken for him. And perhaps also he was following the sense of justice which he himself delivered as chief judge in the high court of Dresden.

One wonders then, are all those who judge homosexuality afraid of their own dreams? The suggestion has been made that Heinrich Himmler, who put his own nephew to death for a homosexual transgression, possessed a hidden homosexuality himself. But I am troubled by this explanation, which, in the end, seems to be no explanation at all. Is there anyone who does not, at least in imagination, transgress the boundaries of sexual identity? Rather, as I enter the atmosphere of Daniel Schreber's vigilance, I sense that the world he lived in and its conventions are like a house of cards balanced on the maintenance of silence about a secret life of both mind and body which, if spoken, might make the whole structure collapse. For to imagine homosexuality would be to imagine the entirety of this secret life and through these images call to consciousness the full force of its being: a territory as dense and obscure as matter once was to the conventional mind but nonetheless physically present, and alive.

The slight negative charge maintained by all the body's cells exists because the interior substances of the cell hold slightly more negative ions than the fluid outside.

It is 1896. Second-Lieutenant Hugh Trenchard is one of ten thousand British officers stationed in India. Here as head of a platoon in the Punjab, he is rediscovering a sense of purpose. Though one day far into the future he will play a crucial role in history's decision to make civilians a principal target of warfare, he has come to India shaken, uncertain who he is or what he should make of his life. It was a terrible shame to weather. There was no warning, not even a hint, until the sudden summons home from school. His father, a barrister, had made a bad investment. The bankruptcy was complete. He stood before the family estate he would have inherited while all that was inside was disgorged. His father's desk, the dining chairs, the silver, even his own butterfly collection and the rifle with which he had shot his first bird, the prized kingfisher, all put up for public auction. The shame had shattered him. But now the vigor, respect, discipline of a new life surround him. His identity is finally secure. This is where he belongs.

Character and the eventual shape a life assumes cannot be understood in isolation from the social circumstances which surround a life. Even the body falls very early under the influence of convention. Gender, notions of propriety, the requirements of class can be said to create a second body that, almost like a suit of clothes, exists as an outer layer to the natural body of birth.

I am looking at one of the many photographs taken of Hugh Trenchard during his celebrated military career. Posed with a group of soldiers and statesmen just after the First World War, his face leaps out from the crowd. It is his eyes which are most animate. They are, as the common saying goes, on fire. And yet, at the same time, about and around his body, large in relation to his small head, there is a kind of torpor, a strange stubbornness, the slight suggestion of a body pulled in two directions.

Subtle though they are, there are indications of an inner conflict in his earliest years. He is, for instance, just nine years old when he succeeds in shooting a bird in flight. Yet he is not entirely happy. This bird he has killed—the brilliantly colored kingfisher—is his favorite. And there is this, too: his love for butterflies. Is it because in the sunlight, leaping through the air, these creatures mirror the flames in his eyes? And does he feel an equal anguish when, taking possession of each trophy, he stills the dazzling wings?

These are not perhaps remarkable crises in the life of a boy of his class in late Victorian England. The delicacy of childhood must lead to manhood. Boys born to this circumstance will be schooled to master their surroundings, through ceremonies of hunting and riding. What will shape this boy and lead him to play his part in history belongs not so much to the realm of the extraordinary as to that unremarkable background through which a whole class of Englishmen will inherit dominion over a steadily growing portion of the earth.

He is proud of his ancestry. Raoul de Trenchard, the knight who fought on the winning side in the Battle of Hastings. And that other Trenchard who was a member of Parliament under Charles I, and the other who served as Secretary of State under William II. For several generations the men in his family have been soldiers and lawyers. Is there any question then that he will be one too? The unbrokenness of the line must be comforting. His father, a respected barrister, has an office in the same street in Taunton where his great-grandfather practiced, the common law he practices now going back to the Norman invasion, the legal language he uses back to the Roman Empire. When Henry Trenchard goes to court he wears the robe and wig that generations of English barristers before him have worn.

Through splitting or fission, the ionization of cells leads to a chain of microscopic events, which one may witness in the end as death by cancer, or the birth of a deformed child.

I am picturing Hugh then as he sits in the back of the courtroom to watch his father at work. He is looking at the white curls of his father's wig. Counting them. Because the proceedings are dull. One man after another stands to speak but he scarcely knows what they are saying or cares.

In fact, his father hardly seems to care himself. Like that other lawyer who practiced in the vale of Taunton, the fictional lawyer of Dickens's *Bleak House,* Henry Trenchard is not passionate about the distinction between right and wrong. He is so well connected to the stream of things. Why trouble safe waters? The order of the cosmos is known and he is fortunate to occupy the place in it he does.

But safety is not compelling to a boy, full of energy and high spirits. Perhaps one day when his parents are out he tries on his father's wig and robe. Dressed like this, he may spend a few moments looking at himself in the mirror. Yet the clothes do not fit. The robe is too hot; it is long and trips his feet and the wig falls over his eyes. He is soon tired of this game. His thoughts are drawn outdoors. That exploding glimmer of color in the sunlight. The brightness that amazes his eyes. He is almost dancing as he leaves the darkened rooms and starts into the green world surrounding the house. Though he will not go far into that country. He is still his father's son.

Tradition gives one the feeling that life is predictable. Yet, in a period of rapid change, tradition can be like a plank of wood, once part of a bridge extending over the water, but now connected to nothing, an illusion of solidity moving randomly in the rushing stream. The turn of the century was a time of transformation in more than one part of the world.

Hugh Trenchard was just thirteen years old in 1888 when Mohandas Gandhi, then nineteen, first set foot on English soil. In that year he traveled to London to study English law. In my mind, while Hugh plays in the gardens of his father's estate, I am imagining Gandhi in one of his rented rooms, standing before the mirror, taking ten minutes (as he tells us he did in his autobiography) to comb his hair properly. He is wearing the dark suit he bought on Bond Street, his bowler hat and his silk tie.

Does the image he sees of himself shining back from the mirror fascinate him? He donned his first English clothes, a white flannel suit, in order to make the trip from Bombay to Southampton. Aside from a few months spent in Bombay to prepare for this trip, he has spent his whole life in rural Indian villages. In his family home there were no mirrors. Now he has learned to sit on a chair in the English manner and take his meals at a table, using knife and fork instead of his hands. And he is studying ballroom dancing, elocution, as well as English history, culture, law. He is becoming, in his own description, more English than an Englishman.

Is he suddenly giddy then, if even for a moment, on encountering this new self? It would be perhaps akin to Oscar Wilde seeing himself in the mirror as Salomé, a woman from another culture, another century. Yet the costume, strange as it is, brings forth qualities within him he somehow always sensed were there, though he may not have named them.

Is it the same now with Gandhi? The self he has taken on is more familiar than we might suppose, the unmistakable manifestation of a submerged identity, one among many possible men within him whose outlines have become clear and recognizable at last. After all, English customs have been making inroads into Indian life since even before 1858 when India became part of the British Empire. He is here to study law because an old family friend, a man of the Brahman caste, advised the family that only by becoming an English barrister could he hope to win the position his father had once held as *dewan,* or governor, of his province.

The ironies of an intermingled culture have followed him to London. An indifferent student who, like Hugh Trenchard, preferred action to words, he never learned Sanskrit sufficiently to be able to study the Bhagavad Gita. But here in an English translation by William Arnold, entitled *Celestial Song,* he is reading the Gita for the first time.

As he looks at his image in the glass, is he thinking of the transience of life? How one self, one identity, can so easily supplant another? It is what Krishna says to Arjuna, urging him into battle. *Worn out garments are shed by the body: Worn out bodies are shed by the dweller within the body. New bodies are donned by the dweller like garments.* Even his name, Gandhi, meaning *grocer* after the trade of his great-grandfather in his native tongue of Gujarati, came to him through English custom. Before the British bureaucracy demanded this usage, Indians did not use surnames.

And there is also this. His mother's tolerance. The devotion with which she has always fasted and followed the rules of ahimsa, never to kill any living being, and yet at the same time, the passion with which her children were taught a respect for other religions, such as the Muslim faith practiced by many in Gandhi's own village. A certain tolerance for difference has been part of his birthright. And the transformation he observes in the mirror must, at one and the same time, deepen and be graced by this tolerance.

Unlike other cells, the charge of the nerve cell does not remain stable. If a nerve is stimulated, the polarities inside and outside the cell reverse.

Many years into the future when Gandhi will lead a famous movement against Britain's domination of India, he will teach his followers to hate oppression but never the oppressor. Will it be easier for him to summon compassion for the English because he himself once inhabited an English body? Between himself and other Englishmen he must have found certain similarities. Far-fetched as it may seem, one can even see some resemblance between Gandhi and Hugh Trenchard. There is the poor academic record they share, though both are sons of professional men, the Gandhi family caste in India being roughly equivalent to the Trenchard's class in Great Britain. Both young men begin life with no inheritance. Both sons are told what profession they must follow by their families. Just as Hugh Trenchard experienced some conflict over shooting a bird, Gandhi is conflicted about the practice of ahimsa, the vow never to harm a living being. He has experimented with eating meat. But, realizing that to continue this practice he must lie to his parents, he has stopped. Above all other ethics, he believes most passionately in honesty. And this too he shares with Trenchard, who will one day be known as a bluntly truthful man, and as a child takes the family motto, *Know thyself,* to heart. And there is this too. It can be seen in the photographs that remain of both men. A certain fire in the eyes.

Thinking about Hugh Trenchard as a young man, the question came to me, where did this fire go? There were, of course, the pranks. The public schools were famous for them. Hugh's brother blew up the fountain in front of his school. Hugh himself helped a group of boys put a donkey in the headmaster's bed. But, faced with his studies, the life goes out of him. His family has already given up the idea that he might become a barrister like his father. The only alternative then is the military, and when one day, passing Harrods, Hugh tells his father he would like to own a department store, his parents, horrified by the prospect of a son in trade, rush him into a school designed to help him prepare for the examinations he will need to pass in order to become an officer. But even here there are books, lessons, charts he must memorize. Faced with this task, he is flaccid. Though his father's bankruptcy increases the urgency of his need to train for a profession, this event only seems to make him a duller student. He is animated only at games.

I can see him now on the playing field. He is captain of the rugby team, his favorite sport. The ball moves as quickly as any thought. There is nothing predictable about it. His wits are quick now, and his mind, enlivened, moves like liquid through his arms, his legs. Sunlight, shadow, leaves turning at the edge of the field, cold air are not apart from his body. Here the invisible heaviness which before muffled all his movements has disappeared. In a split second he has kicked the ball through the goal and hears his own voice, shouting.

But if he has succeeded in escaping the discourse of law, another more subtle argument, the common law of gender, possesses him. Even his wildness is trapped in this form. And the net which catches him is large. How a man should look. What he might say or admit to feeling. How he should stand or walk, gesture. What games he should play. And to what end. Since the Olympic games in ancient Greece, sports have been used to make boys into soldiers. On the battlefield in World War I, in the struggle he will one day join, soldiers will kick a soccer ball toward the enemy line. It is during a spell of training in Scotland with the Kincardine artillery that Hugh learns how much like a sport battle is. Now he applies himself to his studies and finally passes the necessary tests. Within a year he is in India.

Cricket, tennis, squash, field hockey, golf, polo—India at the turn of the century is dotted with English playing fields. Even in the Himalayas at 11,000 feet, the British have built a golf course, the most highly prized golf bag being an elephant's penis, provided the trophy has been shot by its owner.

Hugh Trenchard has organized a polo team in his regiment and won the Viceroy's gold medal in the All-India Rifle Club. He is happy in India. During a four-month leave he wanders through mountains, waking each day to the songs of strange birds. It is as if the colors, sights, sounds have washed his senses; he says he feels born again. Yet still something is missing. He has not been sent here only to play. He wants to see fire.

Every regiment is sent on a tour of duty to the Khyber Pass. But because of a fall from a horse during a steeplechase, he has missed his regiment's expedition against the Afridi tribesmen. And he is disappointed, having nearly given up hope that he will ever do battle, when suddenly hope comes from an unexpected direction. A smoldering conflict between Dutch and British settlers in South Africa has escalated. The Boer Republic has demanded the removal of British troops and the British have refused. On October 11, 1899, the Boer Republic declares war on England.

It is 1900, the year Heinrich Himmler is born to a German schoolmaster in Bavaria, and Oscar Wilde, destitute and forgotten in a hotel in Paris, dies. The Boer War has been raging for several months. Captain Hugh Trenchard is among the soldiers posted there. Yet still he has not entered battle. He has been assigned to a backwater, as an aide to an ailing major at a rest camp. And this he cannot abide. Breaking rank, he jumps aboard a supply train headed for Johannesburg, where he will rejoin the Royal Scots Fusiliers in the thick of the fighting.

Now his skill at polo serves him well. That light in his eyes, the streak of rebelliousness, a certain ingenuity under pressure, qualities lying quiescent in his heart, will come into being at last. He has organized a cavalry of unruly Australians and soon finds himself galloping over the wild lands in pursuit of a Boer encampment. Does he think at this moment about death? But death seems impossible now. His body is quick with life. He is about to see his first fire. It is no wonder he does not pause as he approaches the farmhouse. Boer families are supposed to have been taken off the land, moved into concentration camps. He cannot afford any second thoughts. This is just one mansion in the larger house of the Empire. Quickly he leads a patrol to the building and, dismounting, moves around a wall and toward the door. Then it happens. A sudden flash, a report sounding even after he is stricken. Wounded, he pitches forward and falls.

Before 1943 radioactive elements existed only in traces, in a few rare places on the planet, where, for instance, hundreds of thousands of years ago a spontaneous chain reaction occurred.

Is it possible? The hands lifting the stretcher that carry Hugh Trenchard from battlefield to ambulance to hospital, can they be delicately brown, the hue of Indian skin, the hands perhaps, even, of Mohandas Gandhi himself? For he is there, somewhere in the same war, leading an ambulance corps of eleven hundred Indians who attend to many different battle fronts. At this time in his life Gandhi feels a loyalty to the British. He has recently garnered experience as a nurse, volunteering a few hours a week in a hospital for indentured laborers. His first offer to organize an ambulance corps among Indians is refused. But after heavy casualties the British reconsider. Gandhi hopes that this show of service will convince the Empire of the worthiness of its Indian subjects in South Africa.

Meanwhile, though his wounds are nearly fatal, Trenchard is to survive. Lying on a table, nearly unconscious, except for the vague sounds of voices that permeate the anesthesia of shock, he hears those who attend him discuss his death. Later he will insist that he was never afraid. He never doubted that he would live. He is that kind of soldier, often heroic in battle, who believes himself to be invincible.

I have some insight into this kind of bravado. During a recent attack of a chronic illness, I had many dreams of my own death, and woke more than once with the sensations of dying. In the daylight I felt no fear. It was only in the middle of the night that I experienced panic. The mind can forget what the body, defined by each breath, subject to the heart beating, does not.

1901. Is it a bright day? Trenchard's biographer does not tell us. But one might imagine that the snow blazes with light. Trenchard is on a toboggan hurtling on a downward course, once again approaching a sharp curve at high speed. He makes no effort to slow his progress. All day he has sped the same course, and each time, approaching the curve, he has been flung from the toboggan forward into the snow.

At the urging of his nurse, he has come to Switzerland to convalesce in the mountain air. He has survived his wounds but, one lung removed, lame, one leg paralyzed, he cannot return to battle. Feeling beaten, the sight of the toboggan lifts his spirits. Here is a challenge, even despite his injuries, he can engage. As he slides into the curve he is thrown once more, and this time, because of the trajectory of his flight, he bounces off the embankment and falls a second time. The others on the slope rush to his aid. But he surprises everyone, even himself. He rises and begins to walk, now without aid, without a limp, the movement of his left leg mysteriously restored.

Was a delicate nerve revitalized, a misplaced disc manipulated by this fortuitous accident? Whatever the cause, this recovery burnishes the image he has of himself as invincible. Like a phoenix risen from the flames, he has regained his health.

It is just as well. He is a man who abides neither weakness nor fear. He tells anyone who will listen, *I hate sick people.* And when several years into the future he will command the Allied bombing operations, he will ridicule the pilots who wish to wear parachutes. In part a reaction to his mother's many illnesses, nevertheless, the thinking is not his alone. It is part of military philosophy. The soldier enters a territory which exists between life and death with the desire for victory not only over the enemy but also over his own fear. Whether or not he conquers that fear reflects on his manhood. The Greek word for courage in battle, used often in the *Iliad,* is *andreia,* a word that should more accurately be translated as *virility* or *manliness.* Throughout the battle of Troy men are *unmanned* by fear. It is a curious habit of mind that can imagine a man unmanned by the nature of his own feelings.

It is 1903. Daniel Schreber, released from years of incarceration, publishes an account of the life of his mind in this time. His *Memoirs* describe a fantastic process of transformation. He believes himself to have become a woman. In the beginning this development alarms him. He writes that he is being unmanned; his penis is vanishing; breasts grow. Voices assault him: *fancy a person who was a Senatspräsident allowing himself to be f_ _ _ _ _.* Trying to prove his virility, he fights with the male attendants. Finally he accepts his fate: he is the last human being on earth, and this is why he must be a woman, to deliver by divine impregnation a virgin birth. Dressing in ribbons and jewelry, he announces, *I have wholeheartedly inscribed the cultivation of femininity on my banner.*

In the same year two other events held so far apart in the imagination, it is as if they take place in different worlds, intersect in time. In October a small group of women interested in women's suffrage gather at the home of Emmeline Pankhurst in Manchester, for the purpose, in Mrs. Pankhurst's words, *of organization.* Out of this meeting the Women's Social and Political Union is formed. Two months later, on December 14 of the same year, Wilbur

Wright attempts a sustained flight with an airplane powered by an engine. Though he fails, in just three days his brother Orville will succeed. He will fly first for twelve seconds and then for nearly a minute.

As I contemplate these events in proximity, a certain electricity ignites between them, a spark that might perhaps illuminate what was before obscure, and now only very slowly delineates against a larger background. In the haze I can just make out an outline of Blériot's plane that will land, in 1909, on the cliffs of Dover, after the first crossing of the Channel.

But 1909 has not yet arrived. Though a new age of mechanical heroism is dawning, this is still 1903, the age of the horse, and Hugh Trenchard is back in the saddle again. Through a series of victorious tennis matches he has strived to convince the army of his prowess. Finally, circumventing bureaucracy, he re-enlists. Once more in Africa, for three months he virtually lives on his horse. Yet he lacks his earlier stamina. The old pathway of the bullet which destroyed his lung still bleeds. At the end of a day's trek he is known to faint and must be carried bodily from his horse. *Under the spur of such a will,* his biographer writes, Trenchard's body *becomes acclimatized to pain.*

The metaphor is unerring. Language conceals history, and ideas which on the surface may have vanished persist in habitual images. In this case to think of Trenchard's body under the spur of his will is to recall the image of the knight and his steed. In this iconography the horse is a symbol of the animal instincts of the rider. And the knight mounting his horse becomes *logos* in a state of mastery over matter.

Certainly anyone who has ever been ill can understand the appeal of this idea. To conquer the wayward body, its pain, its fatigue, with reason. It is an old habit, deeply engendered. In the field, Trenchard would not let his thoughts wander near the terrain of desire for a soft bed or a cup of tea. One can win this battle temporarily by evading the experience of flesh and focusing the mind elsewhere. But there is also a strange bliss to be discovered through surrender to physical limitation. After grieving the initial loss of control, one senses that another, more subtle grief has gone. The return of the body to consciousness has assuaged a loss so deep it had become familiar.

Does this explain the passionate love of the soldier for his horse? Warm and breathing beneath him, the animal reminds him of what he has perhaps forgotten. The body of the horse is like the body of a woman for him. In the heat of the ride, the horse draws the language of a lover from him. Klaus Theweileit records these endearments uttered in memories of dreams by the officers of the Freikorps: *How warm you are, how full of life, how sweet your breathing.*

It is 1905. Dressed in full military regalia, and emanating the strange beauty of power, Wilhelm II, Kaiser of Germany, rides a white horse through the streets of Tangier. The parade has ceremonial significance. Moroccan tribesmen line the pathway of his advance. He is followed by a retinue of German officers who are dressed just as he is dressed.

The Kaiser is here to pledge support for Moroccan independence. He has not traveled all this way, though, for the benefit of the Moroccans alone. He is trying to prevent Britain and France from gaining more territory. One can almost imagine them, the nation-states, moving like ritual dancers in an increasingly clear direction, as they seek more land in Africa, Asia and the New World. The Kaiser has fallen behind. Bit by bit parts of the globe are being claimed. Britain colors on her maps in red all the territories she has colonized. In the last decade four million square miles have turned crimson through her efforts. Competing with Britain since the turn of the century, Germany has expanded her navy. The other European nations have followed suit. They have begun an arms race.

It is 1907. Hoping to reach an agreement on arms reduction, a second international peace conference convenes at The Hague.

But the participants fail to reach any agreement on this subject. They do, however, agree to modify the rules of war. Among the rules to be changed is a principle adopted just eight years earlier at the first peace conference prohibiting the dropping of projectiles and explosives from flying machines. Now that decision will be reversed. Without bombardment, it is argued, the aircraft would have no means of defense. The bombardment of undefended places, however, is still to be prohibited.

It will be many years before this second prohibition is removed but when it is, the bombardment of undefended places will gradually fade into a background of normalcy. With the passage of time certain ideas, including military strategies, begin to seem as if they have always existed. In this way they move outside the confines of doubt. Repetition of certain events, the duplication of the same choice, the founding of institutions and then buildings and then landmarks based on this choice accrue around an idea and give it the illusory sense of natural law.

A few years ago I traveled to Germany, hoping during that journey to visit Nordhausen, and whatever remains of concentration camp Dora, in the Harz Mountains, where the V-2 rockets were produced. But illness kept me from this visit. Yet in the first-class compartment of a train traveling from Freiburg, where I had been recuperating, to the airport at Frankfurt, I had an unexpected interview. Unable to sit up for long periods, I was stretched out over three seats when an older woman appeared, dressed with a certain flair, her face bright with expectation, as she stood in the doorway waiting for her seat. When a friend explained to her in German that I was ill, she insisted that I remain as I was. She suggested I put my feet in her lap. Telling me that her granddaughter had also been ill and liked to have her feet massaged, she stroked my feet. She told us she was a widow. Her husband had been dead for two years. But she was not unhappy. She believed in happiness and cheerfulness. She had the manner of a great actress, entertaining and charming. Her husband, she told us proudly, was the designer of Hitler's most famous airplane, one that dropped countless bombs over Britain. From this statement, she moved, without a pause, but also without the hurried pace of one who wishes to avoid a certain topic, to the professions of her sons. The fabric of her life was as if uninterrupted by any questions.

Writing of the past in the present tense, as if it were unraveling now, one knows all along what the future will be and this produces an odd tension. I know that one day Major Hugh Trenchard will raise his voice against the prohibition of bombing undefended places. But he himself does not know this. In 1907, the year of the conference, he is still in Africa. At this date he has not even become interested in airplanes. This is, however, the year he becomes commandant of British regiments in southern Nigeria.

I am imagining him as he sits majestically still on his horse while he watches over the construction of the playing fields he has ordered. Does he switch back and forth on this animal trained for the quick turns of sport? I doubt the Ibo warriors summoned for this task understand its purpose. Trenchard will offer trophies for soccer, tennis, golf and, of course, polo. He takes these games seriously. Some years into the future he will recommend that Royal Air Force pilots be encouraged to engage in winter sports. He believes sport teaches manliness and team spirit. He is not alone in his belief. The use of sport to prepare young men for battle is an old tradition.

The agony of athletes at the first Olympic games was never far from the agony of the warrior. And the crown of glory belonged to both.

Glory. This is a word with many meanings, shaded by the wounds of battle, brushed by the wings of angels in their flight toward heaven. What is glorious is what is praised. But it is also that radiance surrounding a holy presence. And to go to glory means to die.

In this word one can begin to make out the limits of a field; it is here that a soldier faces death. What brings him glory is his courage, his virility. But there, just over the boundary, in a more female territory that begins at the edge of the field, a different landscape begins. It is the terrain of shame and I have been there. This is the shame that accompanies bodily weakness. So ingrained is this response to bodily failure in our learning that in moments of trembling or faintness shame can even precede, by hardly perceptible degrees, the awareness of frailty itself. Skirting the edge of the battlefield, this is the terrain of submission.

Trenchard, whose mother suffered from prolonged illness, has an open disdain for sickness, either in himself or others. He rarely admits to weakness of any kind. He presses himself and his regiment past the point of exhaustion, marching hundreds of miles in extreme heat through the jungle, urging his men to ignore their fear of poison arrows or full powder charges at close range.

Yet what makes a man a soldier is not only the ability to face hardship and danger but his willingness to inflict these on others as well. There are, for instance, Ibo tribespeople in the territory Trenchard commands who are resisting British rule. As commandant of the region he makes the decision to set the recalcitrant villages on fire.

I am thinking of him now at the site of one of these purgations. As he watches this community of homes go up in flames, is he thinking of the loss of his own birthplace? Yet there is a certain freedom in loss. And the idea that he caused this blaze must embolden him. He stands watching transfixed as the fire roars through all that has been standing before his eyes, transforming the old structures to empty space. Now that he is the master of it, this swift change excites him. The air is cleansed. What once existed, unquestioned substance, has dissolved before his eyes. Everything seems possible now.

Yes, of course, there is the suffering he sees on the faces of the Ibo whose village has been destroyed. But he is above this pain.

He can see the longer view. The necessity of a British presence here. The righteousness of the judgment. After all, the Ibo because of their superstitions have been murdering twins just after birth, and they punish the mother who bore them. He is then, he reasons, bringing rationality to this world and, at the same time, protecting the women and children.

Looking back over a life, certain seemingly small events later take on the aura of prescience, as if pointing to what will come. One story of Trenchard's military ingenuity under pressure can be read as a strange augury of a future as obscure to the present as the eventual fate of flying machines still is. Trenchard is marching through the Nigerian jungle when unexpectedly he meets with a force of Ibo warriors that far outnumber his own troops. Facing hand-to-hand combat with only fifty surviving soldiers against hundreds of Ibo, he orders his artillery officer to set off fireworks carried to signal other columns. As the star shells burst into red petals of light in the sky, the Ibo warriors, terrified and confused, retreat.

Had Hugh Trenchard known anything of Ibo cosmology, he might have turned at this moment of victory to see if any other pattern of events shadowed his path. For as the Nigerian writer Chinua Achebe has written, in the Ibo way of thinking, *nothing stands alone*. There is always another thing standing beside it.

Isn't it possible that for every event somewhere a double, inverted, mocking or answering, giving depth and perspective, exists as day does for night, summer for winter? Perhaps historians who search for sequence and causation miss the delicate dance in which events brush by, nod to and circle one another? For in the same year and on the same continent, as if mirroring Trenchard's fireworks, an illumination of an entirely different kind is taking place. Mohandas Gandhi, still following his loyalty to the British Empire, has once again organized an ambulance corps, this time to accompany British soldiers in Natal. A conflict has broken out between the Zulu and the British administrators of Natal who have annexed their land. Gandhi is dismayed with what he sees; his loyalty is strained past the breaking point. The British attempt to control what they call a rebellion through public floggings and hangings. Gandhi's corps tends mostly to the Zulu, whose festering wounds have been neglected by a European medical corps. The British have fired indiscriminately in villages, wounding men, women and children alike, many times attacking even those Zulu friendly to the Empire.

This brutality precipitates a crisis in Gandhi. The old order through which he had organized his perceptions is being challenged. But it is through this crisis that he begins to see and finally commit his life in the direction of a larger principle. In this way an insight which has been unnamed but still growing for years comes finally into being, as if made visible by an inner burst of light, set off by an event that punctured the veil of an old unknowing. It is in this time that Gandhi accepts the gravity of his undertaking. Believing that abstinence will help him focus his energy on his work, he takes a vow of celibacy. He begins to pray daily, and this habit sharpens his awareness of an inner voice from which he will henceforth accept guidance. Listening to his inner voice, he perceives the first configuration of what will soon be named *Satyagraha,* the principle of standing by the truth, by which he will lead his life.

But there is more in this history that does not immediately meet the eyes. Looking back, as I do now, on that point of illumination, I begin to wonder if Gandhi's revelation was fed not only by the injustices he witnessed but because he witnessed them as a nurse. I can make out his image now. He is bending over the body of a Zulu man whose wound has been untended for days and is now so infected that a sweetly sour odor surrounds the two. The wounded man is feverish. If he had any words of English they have faded now in the extremity of pain. This couple has no common language except the look in the wounded man's eye when, from time to time, he returns to what we call consciousness and focuses his gaze on the man who tends him.

Is it that time has blurred the form, or have two men fused in some mysterious way, for they appear, one bending over the other, almost as one seamless curve, breathing together, the boundary between them erased? Does nurse join patient or patient blend with nurse? One cannot tell. The entire atmosphere has softened. All around them boundaries appear to be dissolving.

They can hardly know that at this date, somewhere to the north, the blurred edges of a projected beam of alpha particles discovered on a piece of photographic paper points to the dissolution of the boundary between matter and energy. As Ernest Rutherford notes, *The atoms of matter must be the seat of intense electrical forces.*

Yet, though news of this has not yet been broadcast to the world, the two who are dissolving must have some sense of it. Phenomena exist long before they are observed by scientists. They can be felt. Outside the scope of vision, they continue, vivid and uncompromised, except perhaps by the silent wish to be known. So it is that, looking even further backward through time, one finds that Walt Whitman, nursing wounded men during the Civil War, senses the same fusion. Images of suffering, wounds, stumps of amputated limbs enter his dreams, the course of his daily thoughts, even his silences.

And turning to look just a few years into the future, after the First World War has begun, one can see a young German stretcher-bearer. The man he is carrying has a gaping wound in his stomach. Just as the stretcher-bearer begins to find the cries of the man unbearable, the man himself calls out that he can no longer bear his pain. The stretcher-bearer stops and, laying the stretcher down, begins to stroke the wounded man all over his body, as if he were a mother, moved now not only past the boundaries of separation but also beyond any circumscribed idea of self. The voices of dying and wounded men will never leave him. Later, in his most vulnerable moments, these voices will haunt him as nightmare and hallucination.

This fusion does not stop at some imagined borderline be-

tween mind and body but enters also into flesh and bone. Looking still further into the future, one can see a nurse leaving a field
hospital in Vietnam. She has just cleaned the wounds of a man
burned over most of his body. Each time his image returns to her
mind, even hours later, she retches. The odor of a green bacterial
slime covering the wounds she dressed, mingled with the smell of
napalm, will linger in her nostrils for nearly a year.

In this world of frailty at the edge of the battlefield the line between *I* and *not I* has a dangerous tremor. But it, too, like the
phenomenon of the laboratory, has existed all along, everywhere,
and at all times. Only in this world is it suddenly made more
visible. With a simple shift in focus, the bounded self appears to
blend with others. Dualities fade. And those things we take to be
opposite can be seen on closer view to be mingled. One might
take any pair as an example. But my mind, at this moment, is
resting on Mohandas Gandhi and Hugh Trenchard. Could they
have existed without each other? Gandhi educated in England,
raised in a country colonized by the British Empire. Trenchard
shaped from an early age to the purposes of that Empire. An
Empire which in a curious way began to shape itself like a dominating and possessive lover around Gandhi's homeland calling it
the jewel in the crown.

At a certain angle, the gem cannot be distinguished from the
setting. How alike from this vantage point are Trenchard and
Gandhi! Both leaders. Both courageous, alike even in their asceti-
cism. Yet here in the midst of this sameness, were we to shift our
point of view just slightly, a kind of shimmer begins to appear,
changing alternately from dark to light, from similarity to difference again. For there is a dimension in one that is not in the
other. Gandhi longs for a certain state of mind. He has tasted it
more than once, even occasionally dwelled in it. It is not the
warrior's state of mind. It exists more in a world traditionally
considered female: the world of reception, stillness, surrender.
Did Gandhi suspect that this bliss might be discovered in and

through the pathways of desire? This is not a question I can answer here, except to note that I am amazed by the persistence of
paradox. I am beginning to fathom the wisdom of the Ibo way of
thinking. Nothing stands alone. Each person on earth is accompanied by another, the *chi,* who belongs to the spirit world. And this
world is not so distant as we in our cosmology imagine it to be.
Dichotomies, such as life and death, are, for the Ibo, impossible.
Life moves into death which moves into life. Nor is the geography
of death remarkably different from life. The two worlds are continuous and the *chi* transport themselves back and forth with ease.

It is a movement the culture of Trenchard has forgotten. A movement of which I, too, growing up in postwar years in California,
knew little. Until I was sixteen, when the death of my father gave
me my first entry into the terrain between life and death. It was
his death above all that made me feel unprotected in the world. I
felt him, even if silently and without effect, as an ally. So in the
shadowy aftermath of death, a shadow self was born to me,
stricken with grief and rage. The vast order of life had somehow
excluded me, placed me shaking at its edges, a provisional, unli-
censed player. Yet the hinterland of death has its own power, and
soon I began to recognize that forbidden, unspoken knowledge in
the rare others I encountered who had it also.

What is it that breaks open? There is a kind of radiance surrounding this passage. In the proximity to death, extraordinary
capacities are revealed. The sensual world grows more vivid. Life,
even in the ordinary conjugations of events, is enlarged. The
stretcher-bearer, who will later become famous as a music teacher,
listens with a different part of himself to the voices of the
wounded and dying as they cry for help. He begins to understand
that the human voice has a far wider range than he had ever
known before. This singing near the edge of death travels far
beyond even the capability of celebrated singers, and at the same
time passes outside the limits circumscribed by gender. In the
moment of crisis, social sanction dissolves. Men sing like women.

And to hear this truly is to pass into an undiscovered country. Sensual perception becomes an event of transmutation.

But we are still in 1907. The First World War has not yet begun. That is seven years off into the future. The European nations are not entirely ready yet to experience a continuity with other selves and other worlds. If there is a wave that travels through us all as we ourselves travel through time and space, we sometimes keep this motion from consciousness. Is it fear that keeps us so disjointed? In the year of Gandhi's return to South Africa from Natal the government breaks a promise to the Indian community. Jan Smuts (who will one day be President) introduces legislation requiring all Asians in South Africa to register. Identification once again is required. Free movement is restricted. Following the principle of Satyagraha, Gandhi will be among those who will protest this policy through passive resistance.

Satyagraha. Gandhi translates the second part of the word, *graha,* as *firmness.* But it can also mean *grasping.* To grasp the truth is a delicate gesture, like taking a hand in greeting. A lightness of touch is needed if one is to feel the presence of another being. This is very different from another meaning, which is to *seize,* and *grip,* as in *wrest power from the grasp of* or *to grasp a woman by her waist.* In this other life of the word, the power of dominion over India had been *grasped* by the British Empire. And Africa is in the process of being *grasped.*

To imagine the whole shape of this gesture, one must take a few steps back. At the beginning of the century, somewhere near the Niger River, English troops thrust outward in every direction. They are warning away the French and the Germans, claiming for themselves alone this territory of two hundred and fifty tribes who speak nearly four hundred languages. Through these rough, frenetic gestures the British claim to own a space they now call Nigeria.

Though outwardly the quality of this movement appears powerful, if not brutal, inwardly, as I imagine myself voyaging inside the body of the British Empire, the experience of this grasping motion is above all one of desperate hunger. The raid on resources and avarice for trade, long associated with this movement, is visibly present. But beneath that another kind of hunger can be felt too, in another, more subtle dimension, perhaps almost forgotten. It is a hunger I can see on the faces of European visitors to the tribal exhibit which was part of the Paris World Exposition of 1900. A rare desire haunts the outward expressions of curiosity, wonder, derision shown by the men, women and children who press themselves against the barbed wire, getting as close as they can to Africa: the people of another color, the reassembled village huts, the instruments, clothing, dance, fire. Is something here to draw them? Something within these strange people from this strange place? Slowly at first, and then with a burst almost of revelation, the images made by these strangers begin to emerge in European painting and sculpture. Silently and surely they will continue to work their way to the core where finally they will reshape the very idea of beauty in European art.

1907. Why is it we linger so long at this date? A kind of hiatus occurs here. As if the breath were held. It is what I imagine the painter doing, Pablo Picasso, in the late spring of the year, as he stares transfixed at the African art in the *Musée d'Ethnographie du Trocadéro*. From this encounter, from even this very moment, for he uses the word *suddenly,* he understands why he is a painter. The masks he is looking into, he realizes, are magical. They possess real power. They are *weapons* to use against the dangers of life.

But there is another weapon on the horizon. Imitating at least one aspect, Blériot's famous flight across the English Channel, let us make another leap in space and time now. It is 1909. Staring in a direction that he calls *the future,* the poet F. T. Marinetti is transfixed by what he calls *this intoxicating spectacle,* the performance of this machine that defies gravity. *We strong Futurists,* he writes, *have felt ourselves suddenly detached from women, who have suddenly become too earthly*. In his love of flight, Marinetti joins a long tradition, and one that will extend into the future. In just three decades Il Duce himself, dressed in the costume of an aviator, will appear in the pages of a Futurist magazine.

In the year my daughter was born, 1968, I photographed her posed next to a newspaper that showed the first footstep on the moon. Is the cherished dream to reach the stars also part of a desire, as Marinetti writes, to *abandon the earth?* Flight is an ancient symbol of release from earthly limitation. But it is also a symbol of new possibility, opened as the mind is freed from certain restraints. One speaks thus of a flight of the imagination.

The Futurist thought of himself as a victorious hero, who claimed as part of his victory both women and the earth as his possessions. But the life of the mind is never solitary. In 1909, the year of Blériot's flight, women cause the social imagination to shift in another direction. Insisting on the right of petition, they force their way into the House of Commons, where they are arrested. Once in prison, some of these women embark on the first hunger strikes. Are they aware, these women who struggle for constitutional rights, that Gandhi is visiting London? He has come for the same purpose. To argue for liberation, he must convince the British Parliament that the South African constitution, which this Parliament legislates, ought to respect the rights of its Asian citizens.

This vision of such a possible future eludes the Houses of Parliament. Gandhi's arguments, and the arguments of women, are made in vain. But in this year another future, the future of the flying machines, does begin to make a claim on their minds. Lord Montagu vividly describes the possibility of a raid on London by a fleet of airships: a destroyed capital, post office, telephone exchange, and even Parliament itself. In a debate in the House of Commons it is suggested that aerial bombardment might be used in the future to terrorize civilians. As the argument continues, it becomes a probability. Something must be done. What was unimaginable becomes certitude. Britain must develop the capacity for such bombardment, as a defensive measure.

Is the path to the present inevitable? So it would seem only later, looking back over a chain of events. Yet at each moment of every life a series of other choices can be felt hovering, even singing a cacophonous chorus of advice, over every decision. It is 1910. Trenchard's life is once again thrown off its course. He will need to find a new direction. By the measure of the Empire he serves, he has done well in Africa. With his last expedition he has added 8,000 square miles to the official maps of British territory. To the best of his ability, he has carried out the order of the governor of Nigeria: *Give me roads, good broad straight roads straight through the jungles . . . then we'll be able to let in the light.*

What was it like then to witness the transformation wrought by this construction? A geometric idea of precision suddenly imposed on a landscape, lived on and in for centuries. The land itself like a body submitted to military discipline. Or like a mind, tutored along certain acceptable pathways, so that finally all that lies outside certain avenues of thought begins to assume an air of unreality.

The land of course is still there. Only now it has receded into the background. It is what you see in your peripheral vision as you speed down the highway. The complexity of it, the intricate presence of it, has been reduced now to a single word, *jungle*. If once you breathed its breath or slept surrounded by its dark or wakened with its light, you no longer remember. You tell yourself life has improved. The jungle is in the past. To enter it is to stray from the path, or to be pulled down into some unknown depth. It is an exotic place, intriguing but also unpredictable, uncontrolled, threatening the well-paved order of existence.

Yet even the most carefully governed lives become unpredictable. By 1910 Trenchard has fallen seriously ill. He must return to London with an abscess of the liver. His heart flutters at the least exertion. His legs buckle under him. Yet because he will not rest enough, the time of his convalescence is extended.

According to Trenchard's biographer, he had *mapped and tamed the forest*. Yet some things eluded him. In his reports on the features of Nigeria it is doubtful that he included any of the Ibo stories, so plentiful in the region. Had he known the famous tale of the man who wrestled with his *chi,* he might have been a better patient. For the Ibo, the *chi* who accompanies each being is different than the self, and sometimes at odds. In this story, the wrestler, like Major Trenchard or the British Empire, is invincible. He has wrestled all his tribesmen, all his countrymen, all the animals. And still no one defeats him. Looking for a better match, he crosses into the spirit world. And there he wrestles all the spirits, once again defeating every possible opponent. Still unsatisfied, he cries out, *Is there no one else?* Everyone begs him to leave but he will not listen. Finally a thin, frail-looking man appears ready to do battle with him. It is his own *chi.* Laughing, the wrestler begins as if to crush this weak foe, but his *chi* lifts him easily with one hand and, dashing him to the ground, destroys him.

It is still 1910. Through a labyrinthine route, shaped by a complexity of ideas and events, the continent of Africa has become the proving ground for European and American masculinity. In this way the image of Teddy Roosevelt, rifle in hand, posed against the supine body of an elephant, resembles an icon. Like the gold-embossed likeness of a saint, it is to be studied and imitated. In this year, descending from the train at Oak Park, Illinois, Roosevelt is hoisted onto the shoulders of admiring men and taken through streets filled with cheering crowds. Among those who carry him are Anson Hemingway and his grandson Ernest, now eleven years old. Ernest wears his khaki suit, modeled after the clothes Teddy wears on his safaris. He will wear the same suit whenever he goes to visit his favorite room in Chicago's Museum of Natural History: the Hall of African Mammals.

What is it that draws him here to gaze at these strange, huge creatures, standing absolutely still against painted backdrops of the veldt, lit up, and staring implacably from glass eyes? Will it be the same force that draws him later, as a just grown young man, to enlist with the ambulance corps in the First World War? He will be wounded in this war, and come home to write about this wounding, and the war, and battle. In one book a young man is injured in the leg. The leg heals but his life is forever changed. In another, the hero is emasculated in battle, but this wound never heals. It informs the voice of the novel, and, in a sense too, the voice of a generation, disillusioned, trusting no belief or purpose. But that voice belongs to a future we have not yet reached.

In this round of the telling, it is still four years before the Great War. Yet the subject of the loss of manhood is present even now. This is, however, a topic of conversation over which one lowers one's voice or uses veiled reference. Does this derive from a Victorian reticence about sexual matters, or is there something more here too? A kind of force field of fear, as if a direct approach might bring danger or collapse. For the topic of masculine strength which dominates the shared imagination does not have to be mentioned. Rather the ground of this obsession is as if a part of the natural foundation of existence. Metaphors of manly performance permeate language. But, like the image of Teddy Roosevelt's big stick, they are used naively. As we move forward in time, is this obsession perhaps beginning to be at least partly visible?

In the following year, 1911, Sigmund Freud publishes his analysis of Daniel Paul Schreber. Unable to meet with his subject, Freud reads *The Memoirs of a Neurotic*. In these pages he learns that Judge Schreber believes himself to have been castrated, first by the director of the clinic and then by God.

Beneath these interpretations Freud discovers what he calls a father complex. It is a complex that runs through many illnesses, he says. The subject suffers an erotic love for his father but he cannot admit this even to himself. Freud fails to notice the remarkable similarity between the tortures Schreber imagines and the famous child-rearing methods of Dr. Schreber, the judge's father.

Nor does he see the judge's case as symbolic of any social condition. Through his study of Daniel Paul Schreber, he elucidates the condition known as paranoia, a classic pathology, engraved forever as part of a universal human condition, a pitfall in the private life of the psyche. In this way, the figure of the Senatspräsident, displaying what he calls his voluptuous femininity, dressed in necklaces and lace, moving languorously about the rooms of the Sonnestein clinic, enters our imagination as an emblem of insanity, a wild and curious exception to the normal development of masculinity.

But here, in the present, after the two world wars have already occurred, and in another frame of mind entirely, I ask, is it possible, dreams, irrational thoughts, the ravings of lunatics, can these be auguries of a shared future we have not yet considered? Viewed in a certain cast of light, and over the divide of time, the effeminate madman is an odd double for the masculine warrior, a lithe and sensuous shadow stepping as if suddenly from behind a mirror.

Thinking now about the Ibo story of the wrestler, I begin to wonder if *chi* is not something like what we have learned to call the unconscious. But there is more, isn't there, in this telling? Another world, the world of spirits, not in the least immaterial, for the Ibo world of spirits is not like our heaven. It is a world equally material and, at the same time, existing beside us. Only in some unexplained way, what is unconscious in us grows more powerful in this neighboring world and waits to meet us.

I have read of, and more recently had some direct experience with, cultures in which a man or woman who sees what others do not see, or who moves across and beyond the boundaries of gender, is understood to have a kind of power. This is the one who will learn how to travel back and forth from the next world to this one, who can forge an access to the spirits and bring back their knowledge.

Could this explain why certain lines of poetry seem to foretell the future? *Yet each man kills the thing he loves,* Oscar Wilde wrote in *The Ballad of Reading Gaol* during his imprisonment for homosexuality. Perhaps at times a wider scope of vision appears to one who has wandered outside powerful social proscriptions.

1911. In the same year that Sigmund Freud publishes his famous case study of paranoia, Ernest Rutherford delivers a significant paper to the Manchester Literary and Philosophical Society. Here, he explains his theory that the mass of the atom is concentrated in a nucleus. The thought first comes to him as a fleeting half image glimpsed out of the corner of his eye. Something phantasmagorical, and hardly possible in reality.

An experiment with alpha particles has eluded perfection. Unaccountably, stray particles cloud the results. All attempts to control this have failed. Where did they come from? Was it possible that the scintillation of these particles could be created by aiming them at a metal surface? The thought seems absurd. The atom, being a void within a void, would not impede the passage of these particles. They should pass through metal as easily as a bullet passes through tissue paper. But something, a sudden electrifying turn of mind, pointing in an uncertain direction, leads him to construct the experiment anyway. Contrary to every known model, the particles are reflected back at ninety degrees and even sharper angles. Rutherford's conclusion is accepted: the nucleus of the atom exists. But this conclusion is just a beginning. It has upset the established laws, and an older idea of the nature of space must yield now to another kind of void.

In the same year still, as if existing in another world and wholly unrelated to Rutherford's work in the laboratory, which has to date yielded no weapons, Lieutenant Myron S. Crissy of the United States Army drops a live bomb on an experimental target in San Francisco from a biplane designed by the Wright brothers. In the following year, 1912, in Great Britain, both the Royal Flying Corps and the Naval Flying Corps are officially instituted. The German Aviation Experimental Establishment is founded at Berlin-Adershof, and the French *Service de l'Aéronautique de la Marine* is formed. The age of flight has begun.

The moment nearly eludes Hugh Trenchard. After a slow convalescence, he has aged. His face bears an unhealthy pallor and he is thinner. The War Office assigns him to a peacetime regiment in Londonderry. To entertain himself he builds another polo team. But he is bored. He longs for Africa. In this life, he is a shadow of his former self, clocking time until retirement. Trying to regain the old ground, he applies to the Egyptian Army, the International Gendarmerie in Macedonia, the British mounted defense forces in South Africa, Australia, New Zealand, but without success. Nearing middle age, he is too old.

It is still 1912. Can the approach of the Great War be felt even as a tremor in the earth is felt by an animal before an earthquake? The mood is not one of regret and apprehension. Instead, on both sides of what will become a great divide one senses a restless boredom. Ernst Jünger, who is to become a famous German soldier in the approaching war, feels this restlessness. Just seventeen and finding the comfortable bourgeois world of his elders suffocating, he longs for Africa too. Carrying a guidebook to this mysterious continent which he imagines to be full of excitement for him, he sets off for Verdun, where he plans to join the Foreign Legion. But his career as a soldier is temporarily halted. Jünger's father, a successful German businessman, arranges with the German Foreign Office for the prompt return of his son.

Jünger must be a boy in his father's house for two more years. The passage, however, is inevitable. Childhood ends. One must move on. One has a life. The body ages. And then, before one suspects it even approaching, middle age begins. An old way of life loses its vitality, becomes even impossible. At these moments of change, one reaches out, even if unknowingly, for some slight shift in perspective.

Is it perhaps then a new point of view hovering like a faint scent of fresh air from other rooms in a mansion whose windows and doors will open to different worlds that draw these two men, Trenchard and Jünger, one British, one German, one younger, one older, toward a common course? I can feel it now as I write. For months now, in the presence of this other possibility, language itself has grown past certain confined chambers and moves even now with the suggestion of joy.

One suspects that in these crucial, incipient years a similar impulse is shared by a whole culture. Rutherford is not alone in his discoveries. Einstein has already put forward the theory that a sphere in motion takes on the shape of an ellipse, that time and space are part of a continuum and cannot be considered separately. That there are no straight lines. And gravity is simply a curve in the continuum. That light travels in discrete units. Now in 1912, observing the relationship between orbiting electrons and lines of spectral light, Niels Bohr discovers discontinuities in the subatomic world. Mechanistic physics cannot account for events here either. Bohr is happy with this discovery. He has begun to find the logic of the old physics stifling.

Habits of thought. One can sense the invisible lines drawn at the frontier. What lies beyond is ignored. Unfathomable. Or perhaps noticed with alarm. And then interrogated and sent hurriedly in another direction. But one grows bored. It is as if the organism, the body itself, deprived of its own infinite complexity, falls into despair.

Is this then the promise the air holds for Hugh Trenchard, a change in perspective? In 1912, Captain Lorraine, an old friend from Nigeria, writes him. *You've no idea what you're missing.* He has joined the Royal Flying Corps. *Come and see men crawling like ants.*

According to his biographer, Trenchard will be thrilled by his first flight. I can imagine it now. It is an experience new to the world. It can hardly be put into words. The body is quickly part of the body of the plane. The speed over ground like a great rush of blood. You lift, at first imperceptibly, until you know suddenly you are gliding just over the ground, and then, in a swift arc, you rise. The white rocky edge of a mountain is just below you. You can almost touch it. You feel like laughing. You are as if born again. Air rushes through the engine, the cockpit, over and under the wings. In your new body, everything is air.

But Trenchard nearly misses his departure. He is thirty-nine. At forty he will be disqualified. He must fly alone and pass the examinations in four weeks. The question is contrary to history but still I cannot help but wonder what would have happened had he missed his chance? The effect is of a film being rolled backward. He is pulled down out of the sky, perhaps even out of his uniform, propelled into a different life. Is it possible? Does he fulfill his childhood dream to become the manager of Harrods department store? Others who would have been under his military command are also affected. Some die earlier. Many rise from the grave and move back into life, as if nothing unusual had transpired.

And in the inner landscape of his mind? Earthbound, does he move now on a path unaided by machines toward a change in perspective of another kind? His father is dying. His friend Captain Lorraine perishes in an accident. He himself is aging. Somewhere in the quieter recesses of his consciousness does he hear a different music, one that plays even in his own earthbound body? Listening, does he stop for a moment? It is as if he were at the edge of a field. One he walks past every day. But now, under the sharpening shadow of this sound, he is held by what he sees. What he knows is like what the aviator knows. It cannot be easily spoken. The outline of a yellow flower is more distinct to him. He is caught by the way the grass moves in the breeze. But though what he comprehends can be felt in these details, there is more. It is not just the flower and the grass, it is also himself. He is perhaps discovering a different relationship to gravity in the motion of his own cells. And it is this he recognizes in the field.

He thought he knew himself. He was made of hard masculinity. Tough at the core and steady. This fluttering substance, the soft almost wavering quality, that which might melt, give way, or undulate as it passed, this belonged to the female body and it was utterly strange that he should find it in himself. Unbefitting his manliness. And yet. Yet something unknown had opened if even for a second and this was intriguing. Might he go further in this direction?

But of course this is only fantasy. Though he has a rebellious streak, Trenchard is a traditional man. In this he resembles Ernst Jünger, who will soon be among his enemies on the battlefield. They are cut from a mold cast by the social body. Their advances through life are as if already guided by the unwritten laws of society.

There is of course a mystery to life and its wanderings, a momentary hesitation, a sudden turn. Nothing is predictable. The war that is coming is not here yet. But there are forces which shape this particular field. I can see them. They are arranged like tin armies who wait and watch over the lives of boys who will become soldiers. How can one fail to be impressed? The uniforms themselves are splendid. Shiny gold buttons. Sometimes a plume on the hat. A red brim. Bits of braid at the shoulders, the fringe falling over an arm, swaying with each step. Ribbons arranged in neat rows across the chest. A sword that hangs ceremoniously at the side in a radiant silver scabbard, embossed with fantastically curled filigree in a serpentine line.

If the meaning of these adornments is just beyond the understanding of a child's mind, still he recognizes the tone, the gesture, the feel of significance. Already he wants to be a soldier. He has learned to salute, and his father, drawing himself to his full height, stands still for him and salutes him back. Then they laugh, or his father winks at him. He loves the sound of his father's voice when he tells his war stories.

I am thinking of Douglas MacArthur, growing up in the shadow of his father's uniform. The stories he heard since birth. His father's heroic siege in the Civil War. The dash with which he ignored orders, faced danger, won the battle.

The romance of heroism can pull a child's mind with all the force of a wave drawing a swimmer out to sea. I know this from experience. Looking into a future which, of course, from this vantage point I already know as memory, there will be one world war followed decades later by another. I will be born in the midst of this second war. Douglas MacArthur will be a famous general. My father is not a soldier. Even so, at the age of two I will put on my sister's WAC uniform, several sizes too big. It is because the family is laughing that I am crying in the photograph. I will spend hours copying the drawings of Japanese fliers in combat with Americans that my sister and her friends, six years older than I, have become so adept at making. The fierce expressions on the faces of the enemy pilots. Golden energy emitted in jagged streaks from the fuselage of the airplanes. This is a world I long to enter, to be initiated into. Spencer Tracy, Gregory Peck, Audie Murphy, all in brown or blue uniforms. The newsreels of soldiers landing on the beach, crawling on their bellies, as I do, following my sister and her friends, whether or not I am wanted. And then of course there is the poster. It covers the closet door of the wood-paneled attic which is a bedroom for the boys across the street. On it is a famous photograph showing a team of men who strain mightily to raise an American flag. It has become a permanent fixture in my mind, and mixed somehow with the whispered story of a man down the street, shell-shocked, unhealed, who shot himself in an attic room.

Masculinity and the requirements of gender have a way of surrounding a life. Family history, the traditions of class, military training are as if at the edge of an invisible army that is sequestered in the background, blending in so well, it can hardly be seen. To become a man according to society's idea of manhood seems to be an act of nature.

The fledgling boy must be weaned from the softer habits of his infancy. He must stop running to bury his head in the lap of his mother. He must not whimper. He is after all his father's son, isn't he? When his father slaps him hard on the back, he comes to welcome this blow. Yes, there are pleasures he relinquishes. But, over time, deprivation, discomfort, even pain become part of his patrimony.

I know what the gradual slide into a different, less pleasured body can be. A daily level of pain slips into the background and ceases to be registered as anything but the presence of oneself. If pleasure, not even intense pleasure but the natural pleasure of the body in a state of ease, returns, this can be alarming. I have had such moments. One feels nearly off balance, intoxicated, as if one more moment might break the entire structure of existence apart.

Gradually, then, as the growing boy looks into the mirror a motionless, harder face, a poker face, becomes his face. He knows no other. And now he begins to take pride in the taut body, the rigid spine, fists held up in the correct position, feet thick and steady. He has achieved an exceptional mastery over himself.

I am looking at the Marine Corps training manual. It explains that in the drill men in a unit are trained to march as one. To illustrate distance and file, one photograph of the same man is repeated across the page. His uniform is properly pressed and buttoned, his posture, musculature all fixed in a state of military perfection. He has achieved what John F. Lucy, soon to be a recruit in the First World War, calls *a rigidity of limb*. One must stare long and hard at this photograph to grasp the strangeness. The first and most powerful impression of this image is familiarity. You know this man, or the essence of his character; in your mind you see him step off these pages and out of uniform.

Can you see it there in the square, the impassive expression? Just a glimpse of an earlier history, a training that has gone on perhaps since childhood?

In my mind I place a photograph of Oscar Wilde dressed as Salomé, displaying his folds of sensuous flesh, next to this image of the well-disciplined soldier as he repeats himself across the page. Wilde of course rebels. Let us move back in time for a moment again to the turn of the century. One can see it in his body. He is called a lotus-eater. Pleasure-seeker. No wonder the Marquess of Queensberry is up in arms that his son, Lord Alfred Douglas, has become Wilde's lover. This lithe body. Those rhythmic, undulating movements. That pouting, sensuous mouth. The eyelids half closed as if in rapture. It would be disgusting to this man, famous for inventing the rules of fisticuffs, who is himself a model of Victorian manliness.

And on this note, let us return to 1912. Oscar Wilde has been dead for over a decade. The Marquess himself is fading. We are following a younger man through history now, though he is equally manly. In fact, the inner territory of his body, trained like the body of the Marquess to be impenetrable, has become dull and lifeless. Trenchard is stifled. Even suffocated. The air is too close. He needs space. And it is perhaps in this mood that he longs for Africa, or dreams of entering the cockpit of an airplane.

This is of course what he does. It is the obvious move. Everything in his background points him in this direction. How difficult it is to change a way of life, especially if it is successful. One thread pulled undoes a whole weave. It would not be simply a uniform taken off but a different bed to lie in, changed pathways through the mind, the nerves as they spread like streams and rivulets different, perhaps the whole body transformed, not the same language spoken, even the tone in the voices you hear every day altered, and how do you interpret the nuances? That his father is dying, his friend has died, his body is aging makes him more cautious. Yes, a change is needed. But let's not be impetuous. Let us stay within certain boundaries. There has already been so much loss. One must stand one's ground. He passes all the tests. Some just barely but the instruction has been rapid and scant. He is taken into the Royal Flying Corps.

Is he still thrilled by the ascent? He has always felt himself to be invincible. He is stolid, laconic. Yet there is a certain gleam to his eyes in some of the photographs which suggests perhaps he feels like a god in the air. Valleys, mountains, whole cities, the temptations of Salomé slip away as if they were nothing. But now, rising into the air with him, I feel certain he sequesters even in the darkest regions of his body another secret joy, lifting his hands from the wheel, throwing back his head, feeling even for an instant like a butterfly lifted by the wind. He submits to the sensation of floating. Yes, Major Trenchard is impeccably male. But even the most militantly masculine of men, the Futurist Marinetti, glancingly voices this feeling, a *blossoming, azured* flight, before he weds this image to *a raised foot. On the march.*

It is 1913. Minor movements of exception do not make the plot deviate from its course. In the spring of this year a series of experiments is carried out by the Royal Flying Corps. Several two-pound bags of flour wrapped in tissue paper are dropped from heights of 200, and then 500, and then 1,800 feet to see if they will hit the targets they are aimed at. At the same time, from an airship named *Beta,* a plumb line is suspended to determine when the plane is vertically over the target. After the bomb is released, the distance by which it has missed its mark is recorded. When the plumb line fails to record accurate measurements, the construction of a bombsight begins.

The waging of war calls for an accurate aim. Homer tells us how Patroclus drew Achilles's borrowed chariot next to Thestor in his chariot and, from one moving station to another, thrust a well-aimed spear into the boy, plucking him out of life. All day, in the same battle where he would later meet his own death, he pinned one man after another with this skill.

Such a clearsighted aim can also describe a movement of the mind. Satyagraha. To perceive the truth. How is it an idea takes form and then moves unerringly to the heart? In 1913, Mohandas Gandhi, still in South Africa, reconsiders an earlier principle. In the early spring, while pilots in Britain are trying to hit their targets, a decision handed down by the Cape Supreme Court brings about a change in Gandhi's thinking. Until this date the movement for Indian rights was restricted to men. Gandhi felt it unmanly to ask women to join this struggle fraught with conflict and hence suffering. But now the Cape Court has refused to honor Hindu, Muslim or Parsi marriages. Only Christian unions will be officially recognized. Seeing that this decision affects both men and women alike, Gandhi reverses the old policy. Now women, along with the poor, will make up the largest portion of the rank and file of the Satyagraha movement.

Over the ensuing years, in his own way Gandhi will continue to be an advocate for the improvement of women's lives. Yet he will also continue to believe in the preservation of Hindu culture. The two aims will not be easy to reconcile. *It is good to swim in the waters of tradition but to sink in them is suicide,* he says. The current is nearly impossible to negotiate. Though in the end he realizes he has learned much from his wife, Kasturbai, he is not a woman. He has been raised as a man. Still, his empathy, and perhaps even his whole being, leans farther and farther away from the traditional mandates of his own sex.

I am looking at a photograph of Gandhi taken in 1913. For seven years now he has put aside the clothes of an English gentleman that he learned to wear in London. Now he is dressed in traditional Indian clothing, a silk dhoti flowing down to his knees, and a skirt. He has shaven off the mustache that can be seen in earlier photographs and this makes him look younger and nearly feminine.

The notion that men of other cultures, especially those with a darker hue of skin, are less masculine than Englishmen is common in the British Empire at this date. It has been a sore point with Indian men. Some, in the movement working for Indian independence, have suggested that Indian men ought to eat meat. "Behold the mighty Englishman/he rules the Indian small/Because being a meateater/He is five cubits tall," has become a popular verse in India. But dominance is not what Gandhi seeks now. That an Indian laborer once removed his turban in Gandhi's presence, a form of tribute Indian men are supposed to pay to Englishmen, troubled him deeply. He refuses to dress as an Englishman any longer.

But beneath the outer layer of the change in his appearance, another more subtle process ensues. He is shedding not only the clothing of colonists but the last vestiges of that frame of mind which belongs to Empire. Body and soul he is transforming, eschewing any form of aggression. For several years now he has been celibate. He has given up a sexuality that in him had been dominating and at times almost violently grasping. Still, he appears to be more sensual; his lips more full, his whole being delicately, readily present; he has a stunning, almost androgynous beauty. He is walking miles every day now and this makes him strong. But the boundaries that define him have softened. And he is entirely unhidden, almost translucent.

It is one year before the Great War. The heat of it can be felt, approaching. Reports have arrived in England that describe the growth of a German air force. Trenchard is promoted to lieutenant colonel, second in command of the Central Flying School. He is thinking along the lines of strategy. A training maneuver has convinced him of the value of airplanes used to watch the movements of enemy troops. The airplane, he says, will transform the battlefield.

———

The twenty-eighth of June 1914. Looking back, one feels it could have been any event. The nations are already armed and aligned. The assassination of the heir to the Austrian throne, Archduke Francis Ferdinand, simply accelerates what has already begun. But those who are there at this moment have difficulty seeing into the future. Phantom shapes obscure their vision. On the horizon they see other wars, other times. By now Francis Ferdinand is just a figurehead. But the feel and force of monarchy linger. And on the battlefield the ghosts of kings' armies clash.

This is often the way one moves into the future. For what you begin to see, there is no ready language. If you were to remain silent, listen, perhaps in response you might be able to move in a new way. Glide into it slowly, aware of every slight difference, skin and cells intelligent, reading. But trained as you are in certain regimens, chances are you proceed directly according to the old patterns, trying again what was tried before.

Though they have finally grasped the significance of the aerial view, that the battlefield has changed fundamentally has not yet occurred to the generals. How did this happen? No one willed it to be so. The rifles used now have a longer range. Men in an advancing file no longer have a chance to rush their opponents if they can be sighted and shot at a thousand yards. And now the machine gun seals this possibility forever. Even lingering back out of the range of these guns, soldiers are targets for artillery, shells which fly over their heads, demolishing everyone, everything in a wide radius, leaving a depression in the earth into which, advancing or retreating, one stumbles, even falling at times into now dismembered flesh. They could not foresee this.

Nor the length of the line. Conscription swells the armies. So many more can be brought by rail than by foot or on horseback. So they must dig trenches and the trenches do not stop growing until they run continuously across France and Belgium, from the sea to the Swiss border. The land around is scorched. Nothing lives. Not even, as Wilfred Owen writes home to his mother, an insect. Only the men and the rats, on either side of what is called *no man's land,* in trenches, shelling opposing armies. At certain places the trenches thicken, like the keloid scars of those who survived Hiroshima, making by their profusion even minor movement impossible.

Attempt after attempt to advance fails. Europe convulsed in battle is now in a state of paralysis. All motion, forward or back, is constricted to a matter of yards. Ordered by their officers to move into the field, men move out of their trenches into a perilous sky, thickened with metal. They are quickly stopped. Death answered by death, the bodies lie everywhere unburied around them.

One reaches an impasse. Every effort fails. At the periphery of vision, the first signs of despair appear. There is no way out. Except perhaps a kind of grace, coming as if unbidden, in the instant when a descent has reached its nadir. The philosopher Simone Weil suggests that at this moment to taste the sweetness of defeat one must surrender. All effort ceases. Something softens in the field. One begins then, in the light of this changed focus, to see a different outline, moving just there, a dot on the horizon. And then suddenly the whole picture has changed. And it is by grace alone that one moves into a new landscape.

But, of course, there is no surrender here. There is instead a certitude. There will be a victory. Kitchener, who won in South Africa and the Sudan, will win again. If the war is already extending past the earliest predictions, the generals are launching an attack that will turn the tide. On the eve of this battle, the commander of Allied forces on the Western Front, General Haig, records in his diary, *The wire has never been so well cut nor the artillery preparation so thorough.* Writing to his wife, he confides, *I feel that every step in my plan has been taken with divine help.*

———

This is his plan. He still believes in the cavalry. To protect their advance, it will be necessary to silence the enemy guns. Preparations are undertaken. A town built to house and feed the hundreds of thousands of soldiers. A medical station established. The trenches have already been dug. They are improved, with more barbed wire, further lines of trenches behind the front, shellproof dugouts to compete with the enemy's trenches, which have been fortified for over a year. Shells will be aimed at enemy artillery and machines. This barrage will cut the barbed wire protecting their trenches. Hundreds of guns are set up at sites as far as possible from enemy counterfire all along the fifteen-mile front. Placed in advance of these sites, observers will direct the fire of the guns. At a depth of six feet telephone lines are laid between gun site and observation post. Nearby fighter squadrons are readied to take command of the air.

Hugh Trenchard is there. It is June 1916. We have leaped precipitously over two years. In this period Trenchard has argued for the use of airplanes, fitted with machine guns and bombs. First he is in charge of training pilots and readying airplanes. Then he moves to France to command the first wing of airplanes, and finally he is made general officer commanding the Royal Flying Corps. He is a brigadier general now. His airplanes have machine guns. One week before the planned advance, he directs the flight of a makeshift bomber, escorted by fighter planes, as it drops a phosphorous bomb on a German balloon. His biographer tells us there is a huge explosion of the most impressive fireworks; everything blows into the air. He does not tell us the fate of the German soldier suspended from the balloon. Does he slip by rope safely to the ground? Does he attempt the fall unaided? Or does he, like Icarus, perish in the flames?

One cannot fault the biographer for failing to notice his passing. So many have already died. We are now nearly two years into a war which was supposed to be over in six months, as everyone

said, in the naive beginning, *by Christmas*. That a war which seems
to stretch out forever should speed by so quickly in narration is
strange. Is it the monotony? It is not easy after all to distinguish
one event from another in this territory. The landscape is mono-
chromatic—graduating shades of charred darkness cover everything. Even the red of blood disappears as it dries. The cadavers of
men and horses lying out in the sun sometimes for months blend
in, except for their odor, with the rutted wreckage of earth. The
dark rats which eat everything—cadavers, wounded men, supplies, tablecloths, operation orders—are matted with mud. The
lice too blend in with everything that is earth-colored and cannot
be seen. Everyone here is in and of the mud; the water in the
trenches rises at least to the calves, more often to the knees, or
waist high. Feet, always cold and wet, become infected. Must be
amputated. Day after day one sees nothing but two mud walls,
running as if infinitely and in an endless labyrinth, and the sky.
The sky alone, in those moments when it is silent, recalls one to
other possibilities.

Is there something then that I am missing here, an absence
that truncates my narrative? I could tell you that in 1914 British
naval fliers carried out four bombing attacks in German territory,
the last against the zeppelin sheds at Cuxhaven on Christmas Day.
I know this will be of interest to a future generation. But now, on
this page, in this paragraph, starting this sentence, I find myself
knee deep, waist deep, in the mud of a trench. And what am I
doing here? Because after all I am a woman. I am not cast in a
soldierly mold. My childhood interest in uniforms and battles,
being inappropriate, has waned. Yet even so, I must confess that
there is something familiar here. Something I recognize. The feet
for instance. Cold. Wet. What they feel like. I have some sense of
this. Numb. You forget they exist. Except when you walk, the
ground has become oddly removed, and distant as a friend who
suddenly grows aloof. Your whole body, also cold, partakes of this
numbness. Yes, there is danger. But the danger, oddly unreal as
the feel of your own skin, comes to you only in brutal flashes in

which you are taken as if into a nightmare self, a demonic, terror-ized twin.

And now, as I speak, settling my gaze, and sinking more deeply into the atmosphere of this place, I begin to realize I am not the only woman here. She is, in fact, everywhere. Her great telluric body stretches the whole length of the trenches. That man who has to be removed now because he is trembling continually and weeping is possessed by her. At night, surreptitiously, she enters the dreams of even the most hardened soldiers, making them cry out with unwilled fear. And she is there in the throes of that horse whose whole body quivers, whose mouth arches open, whose eyes roll back and fog, who freezes then into a motionless motion.

She was there in the countryside before the shelling began, teasing the soldier who had fallen asleep under that apple tree just coming into blossom. She will be there in November with the lieutenant as the hole he is hiding in caves in over him, the weight of his tin hat pressing his chin into his chest, the soft earth yielding slightly to his struggles, slowly settling around him so that the movements of his ribs are more and more restricted, and the voices of the others recede. And she is there of course on July 1, at the start of the Battle of the Somme when the first lines of men advance in a slow, evenly spaced order toward the German trenches.

It is not as they had expected. The barbed wire in front of the German trenches has not been well cut. The German artillery positions have not been destroyed. Even the officers are confused. This new battle is foreign to them. Some of them, called up after years of inaction, veterans of the South African war, refer to these French fields as *kopjes,* though the terrain is entirely different. Whole lines of men are cut down by the machine guns as if a scythe had been run over a field of grass. The morale is broken. Wounded or frightened men cling to their officers' knees as they wade through the mud and the fallen, trying to lead their regiments forward. But where are their regiments? Can this be? Only two men still stand past the barbed wire? Is it wise now to retreat? But to where? The sky full of explosion is opaque. The ground seems to roll and change its shape. The noise is deafening. Mingling with the burst of shells and the infinitely mindless report of the machine guns, one can hear the moans and occasional shrieks of the wounded. The drill formation has completely collapsed. No one is marching in synchronized step. No one is marching. The cavalry never breaks through.

It is a species of death. The general's plans belonged to an ancient tradition. As early as the Battle of Thermopylae, the cavalry have been the elite among soldiers, a symbol of all that is noble in battle. The splendid uniforms, feathered hats, gleaming weapons will be retired now. It is not easy to relinquish such glory. For a moment, the battlefield will be stripped of meaning. The loss is spiritual, unequivocal. Lance and sword ready, skillfully mounted, they wait in the wings for weeks. When they are finally called to battle they are easily defeated. An entire squadron of Indian cavalry shot down in one charge. Three thousand South African cavalrymen reduced to eight hundred in just six days.

I am thinking again about the nature of change. The old soldier cherishes tradition. Yet this is a paradox of history. The same passion for war creates new and ingenious weapons, each of which changes war forever. Everything is mechanized. Soldiers arrive by train. So that they can synchronize their movements precisely, and still hold up a rifle, the wristwatch is invented. A whole army is provided with form letters to send home, the first in existence. And in the midst of the battle a new armored creature arrives, cumbersome and heavy, pulling itself by caterpillar tracks over the rough land, blindly spewing bullets in its path.

The purpose of the cavalry, to ram through a line of defense, will be carried out by tanks now. And, yes, the men who operate the tanks are valorous. But their pursuit lacks the dignity of the soldier on horseback. Confined to a narrow, hellish space, the temperature rising above 110 degrees from the heat of the engine, blistering spent shell cases rolling about them, trying to hear each other over the roar of the engine, the artillery, unable to see anything in the darkness inside. It would be like a feverish body. Racked, heroic in a certain way but not inspiring.

Still the animating ardor of the cavalry has not entirely vanished. It is into the air then that this spirit flies, heavenward but not to heaven, ready to live another life. Men on both sides of the line understand this transformation. Trenchard has exchanged his polo horse for a Sopwith. And if Ernst Jünger, his young enemy, stifled in his longing for Africa, miraculously carries on the heroic tradition in the trenches of the Somme, another young German soldier, Hermann Göring, leaves those trenches before the great battle even begins, and by his own route reaches the air. Had he been born a generation earlier he certainly would have ridden a horse into battle. The man he most admired as a child, not his father, but his mother's lover, was a cavalry officer. Following the footsteps of this man, Göring is a brilliant cadet in the military academy. In the first few days of the war he does his best to emulate a past now quickly vanishing. He steals four horses from the retreating French. And the next day formulates a daring plan to ride into the center of a French occupied village to bodily steal the French commanding officer. But the plan fails. And soon his regiment moves to the trenches.

Here, he is disillusioned with the boring mud of the Somme. Is it possible then that this disillusionment might spread to war itself, and that, given a few more months in the trenches, he might turn his life in a different direction? But chance removes him from this ground. Stricken with rheumatic fever, he is sent to a hospital in Freiburg. And as he begins to get well, he discovers the flying school that is stationed there.

It is as if the spirit of the cavalry had risen like a phoenix from the flames. Far from disillusioned now, he is thrilled. He refuses to return to the front with his old battalion. Soon he will fly a white Fokker G7 over the same terrain.

He is a dashing figure in his leather, his goggles, a striped scarf wrapped about his neck, staring implacably from the cockpit of his airplane. He has a reputation for bravery. Beginning as a camera-observer, in order to get the best shots he grips the side of the cockpit with his legs and ankles and leans into the air as the airplane swoops over its target. He is known as the flying trapezist. It is not long before he becomes a pilot. Over the course of the war he will be wounded, seriously, and return to battle, shooting down fifteen enemy aircraft. He earns Germany's highest medal: Pour le Mérite. And like the other fliers, Von Richthofen, Lowenhardt, Udet, Hawker, Rickenbacker, he becomes a public idol. Now *he* is the object of cameras. His picture posed in front of his airplane is published in the newspapers; feted, paraded, he enters a pantheon of military heroes.

The balloonist, who shared the air with him, is not so celebrated. Is it the shape of the balloon, rounded and womblike? This balloon is not brightly colored like its ancestors. It is a military shade and blends in with the battlefield. Still, there is a feeling of whimsy that cannot be denied. One wants to laugh in its presence, as one does with a butterfly or a cloud. It does not, like the airplane, move in any purposeful direction, but wafts above the battle, almost like a decoration. Must not the balloonist, then, partake somewhat of this mood? The tiny figures beneath him scurry about small as ants. He is not without feeling for them, but at this height he cannot really make out the different colors and markings of the uniform. A certain orientation thus eludes him. To be sure, he knows where the enemy territory is. He will be able to report correctly the movements of British troops. But for the moment he catches himself smiling. A heavy piece of artillery has fallen over and sinks into the mud. A line of men summoned by bugle arises and then scurries quickly backward. How can he ever explain this smile in his report? There is no necessity. For in this instant he ceases to exist. He explodes, along with the balloon, into a spectacular show of light.

———

Yet, uncelebrated as he is, the balloonist, dying this way, suddenly, violently, in the course of battle, still shares a certain bond with all other men at arms, even the famous fliers. It is a bond that stretches across enemy lines, especially among airmen. They read about each other in the press and learn to recognize one another by numbers painted on the planes they fly. They admire one another's exploits. Göring is one of the fliers who is singled out by the British. He himself knows Trenchard. And between the wars the two men will write each other, confiding a mutual respect.

At the thought of this friendship my mind is brought back to a story I read from the life of a boy in a German military academy. It begins with the loneliness of a boy who is isolated from his family. He longs for touch, for intimacies, but he has not yet been accepted by the other boys. He is still a pledge, raw, uninitiated. Then one day when, under the pressure of a beating from his teachers, he has informed on another boy, he is surrounded by his fellow students. They lead him to a table where he is laid on his stomach and beaten by all of them at once with leather thongs. Just before he feels he will disintegrate, the boys cease their attack. As he rises slowly and with difficulty to his feet again, he is given a handshake by the eldest boy. This is the sign that from now on he will be welcome among them.

This acceptance is soon followed by a second rite of initiation. As part of his graduation to a full-fledged cadet, whatever baby teeth still remain in his mouth are now pulled out by the academy's dentist. By these two ordeals, he is taken into the social body of masculinity.

And what a tyrannical body this is. Here on the ground again you can just make out this figure, standing booted and erect in the trenches, watching every move, vigilant lest there be a moment of cowardice, of shirking, of female weakness. One might imagine the woman in the trench simply disappearing beneath this harsh and penetrating gaze. But what a surprise. She is not as submissive as the Victorian mind suggests. How could one predict this? She puts up a fight. She is, in fact, fiercely, unremittingly present. So, to paraphrase Richard Aldington's novel that will soon be written about this war, the would-be military hero is amazed and disturbed to discover how his body will not obey him. At the sight and sound of flying shrapnel, bullets, explosions, his flesh shrinks, his head ducks, his whole body cowers, even though he rails at himself, calling himself *coward, poltroon, sissy.*

Not the idea of death but a wall of flame, not the abstract notion of sacrifice but the bodily knowledge that just under your foot, as you take your next step, there may be a mine. Contrary to all your training, your body bends over as if to protect what is vital, your hands spring to catch your body as it falls, your eyes shut, as something flies into your face.

You are caught then between these two, forced into a no-man's-land between the social body and the body you were born with which is too much like a woman's body. If you turn in one direction you betray the honor of your gender. You are, as Homer said, unmanned. But your body of birth will not obey. Refuses movement. Produces paralysis. Becomes as immobile as the trenches themselves, the body frozen, as Elaine Showalter writes, in *a silent complaint* against masculinity. There is a word for it. It is called *shell shock.*

But your mind will not admit its complaint. You cannot put what you are feeling into words. You were among the bravest, after all. You went into battle believing yourself invincible. Bullets veered from their course as you advanced. Shellfire cannot break through the invisible shield of your confidence. You are cloaked by tradition and discipline. Then the unthinkable happens. A shell nearly misses you, or it gives you a slight wound, or the man standing next to you, your friend, has half his face blown away. And your shield is broken, the cloak rent to shreds. Something in your body suddenly knows death with an unmitigated certainty. And you simply cannot move your legs. Your head aches violently. You can no longer remember who you are, or at least the last two years have vanished. The last day you remember is the day before you enlisted.

At one moment you were home, eating a family dinner. You are especially fond for some reason of your mother and father or your girlfriend or the still green pasture just outside of town. And then, inexplicably, you are here, at the special wing of the hospital, it is explained to you, designed for your kind of case. You are questioned. After a while you learn that those who do not answer the questions correctly are shot. For your loss of memory you are given an injection of sodium amytal. When your head still hurts you are given a lumbar puncture. If you are a German soldier you are given shock treatment. And you are returned to the front. If you come back in the same condition, weeping, disabled, the level of shock is increased. Soon the treatment you receive competes with your terror of the front. And you learn there are some who do not survive these treatments.

But perhaps it does not happen exactly like this. You are not shell-shocked. You are seriously wounded. You didn't believe this possible, but now it has happened to you. Despite all your training you cry out for help. There are no stretcher-bearers here. The other men are instructed to leave you. You know this. But the pain, the loss of blood, makes you panic. Hour upon hour you wait. The pain settles deep into you, becomes you. You are not the man you once were. You are simply a man in pain. Someone appears quickly and then leaves, without uttering a word to you. You find you are longing for a word. Just a kind word. A moment of compassion. The bandages, the hospital, cease to matter. What you want even more than water, even more than the cessation of pain, is this small measure of kindness in a voice, a look. Finally a doctor comes. He administers morphia, applies a bandage. You will have to stay where you are for the night. But you are all right now. The doctor has listened. Someone has cared. Attended. Divine compassion has flowed over you.

Of course for many no one comes. It is impossible to retrieve all the wounded. The dead can go on unattended for days. There is pain that is unending and unanswerable. I have been near the edge of the circumstance. You are compelled finally to admit there is no reason for it. You have been caught in history. No effort will save you. Your once soft thigh against the stinging cold of the ice grows hard as the earth is hard. Tenderness and touch exist in a foreign country, forever inaccessible now. The unspent life still in you already eases into the charred remains of the field. Even practical reason, order, consequence, have left you. You do not cry out any longer. Silence no longer wounds you. You do not make plans or imagine a rescue. And then suddenly, there is no explaining why, you have not summoned this, but still, you are being held, held as if by ghostly arms and soothed by an invisible compassion.

Because there is a compassion here in the field where no one is standing. It is almost as if stray bits of energy belonging to souls that have passed, souls that have suffered as these men suffer now, linger, drawn by the memory of a shared ordeal. There are unseen forces. Charted in no laboratory as yet. Ghostlike presences. What a surprise then as I stare into the veils of space to discover among the others the shade of an outline I recognize, wandering empathetically along the trenches. Can it be Oscar Wilde?

One would not have guessed he knew anything of this ordeal. Unless you were to follow him into Reading Gaol, and to the several cells in the other prisons he occupied for two years. There was the senseless labor. Carrying heavy weights up and down a ramp for hours every day. The constant cold. Damp setting into his bones. The bed with no mattress. The thin gruel of a diet. The steadily wasting body. The floggings. Withheld food. Absence of light. A view of nothing but gray prison walls. The bucket, overflowing, filled with his own defecation, giving the air a sickening odor. No wonder the warden predicted that after this imprisonment his life would not last long.

But if Wilde's spirit is anywhere in this region of suffering, it is not visible. At this particular moment in history the idea of such a presence on a battlefield is too absurd to imagine. No matter that some of the soldiers fall in love, become lovers. This fact hardly affects the popular image of the warrior. Even Wilde's former lover, Lord Alfred, blames the defeat of British armies in Europe on the vice he once practiced with Wilde. And Rupert Brooke, heroic voice of his age, soon to die on his way to the battlefield, sees the war as a chance to slough off the demoralizing influence of feminism and *hermaphroditism*.

The look we cast back then must be softened, as it falls on any single man, by this sense of the social body. General Trenchard is caught up in a national mood. When he tries to discourage his pilots from wearing parachutes (which he takes as a sign of weakness), he is perhaps a modicum more extreme in his approach than is common in these crucial years of change. But certainly he is not without feeling for his men. The war was not his doing. An onerous duty has fallen to those who have to carry it out, especially the commanders.

It is with this in mind that General Trenchard speaks of the discipline and fortitude required of the officer who must order his men into death, who does not let his reluctance sway him from what is necessary. When he is criticized for incurring too many casualties after the 60th Squadron suffers heavy losses, his biographer tells us a *less resolute commander might have changed his course*. But this is a quality for which he has been decorated. He does not change his course. Instead, pleading with London for more men, more planes, he enlarges the formations of escorting bombers.

With so much death, he thinks, of course, about morale. In one month half the squadron has been killed or wounded. When his men wake in the morning, will they be daunted at the breakfast table by the sight of three more empty places? No seat must remain empty. The conversation would be desultory. Grow almost to a halt. In the back of everyone's mind would be more than one death. And so replacements are always in the wings, ready to sit at the table. Instead of brooding then over friends who have gone forever, his men are taken up with welcoming newcomers and making them comfortable.

After the war's end, in the year of the Spanish influenza, another side of Trenchard's existence will emerge briefly, barely seen in its fluttering, transitory existence. Trenchard is among those stricken with illness, and because as usual he does not rest as his doctor orders, he veers precariously toward death. He has contracted pneumonia. It is then that Mrs. Boyle, the widow of a friend, arrives. He had called her earlier, but she was still in France. She comes still wearing her Red Cross uniform. Over several days as she nurses him, he lapses frequently into a restless sleep. And in that sleep another self, long sequestered, begins to speak. Telling her, but not telling her, confessing, but not hearing his own confession, a half-coherent speech expresses a terrible grief over all the men he has ordered into death.

She will take this grief with her, a memory, her private prize. Because now, she tells herself, she knows the real man. And though in a few months' time she will be his wife, out of kindness she will never speak of it with him. The confession, then, remains a secret except in her mind, and if this second self has a place in the world, it is with her.

Who among these two selves is the real self, the one who makes decisions by day, or the other, who cries out at night?

I am reminded that nothing stands alone. Everything has something standing beside it. And the two are really one. Watching the wind blow through the field, it is as if two winds are blowing, each from a different direction. But after a moment, from a longer view, one can see that it is the same wind bending and turning its trajectory.

Is Trenchard accompanied on the battlefield by another softer and sorrowing self? This is not a question that can be answered. Sorrow and fear are thick in the atmosphere. But they must be avoided. Softness is all about; the softness of wounds, of deteriorating flesh, of the dead, and it cannot be abided. Grief must run to hardness, fury and cold calculation, for the clear line of motion in its planned trajectory can be lost in this wavering ocean of decay.

And unless victory is wrought from this pain, it will all seem senseless, stupid, debased.

It is a moving part of the tale. Achilles stands crying high on a hill. His battle cry is inspired by the death of his friend Patroclus. He has no armor. The lame god, god of injury and suffering, will forge it for him overnight. But just his presence here, the rage in his voice, the uncanny bareness of him without his armor, frightens the Trojan warriors and lends hope to the Achaeans. There is a shift in the battlefield clear as a shift in a symphony when the melody moves from one instrument to another. In this moment the Greeks succeed in winning Patroclus's body back.

When the body returns, Achilles washes it and wraps it. But it is not enough to have the body back. Before Patroclus's body goes into the ground, Achilles will return to battle, in his new armor. A life must be claimed for this life, the life of the slayer, Hector. And that is not all. This is Achilles's glory. Should he die, death will not have the last word. Troy will fall. Long after his death, the name *Achilles* will be pronounced with awe.

The response, though, is not always the same. *Achilles* is the abstract form, the golden, unchanging standard against which the real, the living, are measured. The real do not always conform. Even in the *Iliad,* men whimper and tremble. Captain Arthur Agius, 3rd Battalion, Royal Fusiliers, 56th Division, is shell-shocked on the first day of the Battle of the Somme. He huddles in a corner, his face to the wall. Though it makes him ashamed, he cannot stop crying. His legs will not support him. He has not been injured. But he has witnessed the death of several friends. His young subaltern, newly out, disappears in an explosion. *So many gone,* he will say later, before his squadron even reaches their own trench. They are treading on the dead.

Of course, soldiers are trained for another response. On the first day of the Battle of the Somme, Private Ernest Deighton, 8th Battalion, King's Own Yorkshire Light Infantry, 8th Division, finds himself within twenty-five or thirty yards of the German trenches. But as he enters the space through which he must make his advance he finds the air is thick with machine-gun fire. A bullet strikes his friend, Clem Cummington. The wound is in his friend's chest and is fatal. His friend is dead immediately. Private Deighton himself is wounded in the shoulder. But the sight of his friend's death makes him wild. He advances just to the edge of a German dugout; looking directly at the men, and cursing them, he drops a Mills bomb in their midst. Turning from the explosion, he encounters another German soldier face to face, and thrusts his bayonet into this man, killing him. This is exactly what he has been taught to do.

A friend dies. Standing perhaps just in front of you. Or behind you. The wound gaping and spurting blood. The body suddenly not the one you knew, the life drained out, hardening quickly. You cannot stay there beside your friend trying, though you know it is useless, to stanch the blood. You cannot place your hand on the brow, and shudder as if the passage of his soul had made its way through your body too, the shuddering making a wail inside you, as you find yourself held at the edge of death, not dying yourself, but the full force of it rocking your body. You cannot. That is against all orders. It has been repeated again and again. Leave him. Leave the body. Continue your advance.

And all this must go on in the fog of battle. You are frightened of fear. But you are also disoriented. What should you do now? Where is the enemy? Where is your own trench? Where is the commanding officer? If these pages are thick with death, think of the battlefield. Corpses in different stages of decay, the slowly dying, moments of death exist around you everywhere. Who are you? You are perhaps among the living, but can you be certain?

It is of course understandable that the generals must be kept from battle. They cannot direct the movements of troops in this fog. They must have an overview. Both sides are so evenly matched. Strategy is crucial. It is 1917. The Battle of the Somme has failed. The French lose badly in the Nivelle offensive. Troops are in mutiny. If they are to stop the tide of death that threatens to sweep over and engulf them, they must think clearly now. Certainly there is some way to wrest control of fate. One must remain cool in the presence of this tide. Unmoved, the generals scrutinize the field for a point of weakness, a plan of attack.

It would be then like looking at the meadow, the field and forest around it, as a pattern; one that, a few decades into the future, might appear on a green screen in bright metallic colors, the repeated Y's representing grass, the X's standing for trees, mathematical coordinates creating dimension, an illusion of perspective, the diminishing background indicating a long view.

But there is more. Another element in the formula, entering like a stray particle perhaps predicted but not yet part of the equation. Since September 1915 German zeppelins have dropped fire bombs over London. At the Dolphin Pub on Red Lion Street seventeen men perish when the building collapses over them. Civilians are still dying. A wave of shock spreads over the screen. Something ephemeral, immeasurable. The spirit is daunted. And a certain boundary passed.

One can easily follow the train of logic. In its own fashion it is inexorable. The losses on the battlefield after all are massive. War is not what it was before. It is a perspective common to both sides of the battle. *Modern warfare is total* . . . Captain Peter Strasser, head of the German Navy's Airship Division, writes. *A soldier cannot function at the front without the factory worker, the farmer.* He is writing to his mother. *What we do is repugnant to us too but necessary.* There is an odd courage in the logic; it is of course military courage: one must sacrifice lives to save lives. He addresses his mother. *I know you understand what I say. My men are brave and honorable. Their cause is holy, and how can they sin while doing their duty?* Does his mother accept his logic?

Or does she absent herself from the dialogue? Certain thoughts move to the periphery of her consciousness. It is an old habit of mind, shared by many women. Like the wife of the SS guard who, as she heard rumors of what, in the course of his day, her husband did, slept apart from him for a while but, with the erosion of time, returned. It has almost the feeling of a mass, this wave of convention and memory, making it seemingly impossible at certain moments to take a step. Does she put his letter in the drawer with all the other letters from her children? And the most recent photographs? When she writes in response it is then perhaps as if she never read his letter. She simply sends her good wishes, asking after him as she usually does, hinting that he should be careful to eat and rest as well as he can.

It is June 1917. The women's suffrage bill condoned by an overwhelming majority finally passes out of committee in the House of Commons. Women have, after all, joined the war effort as equals. They have worked in munitions factories, coal yards, driven vans, carried messages at the front, even joined the land army. If there was a moment of doubt within the suffrage movement, a second thought that shadowed participation, early on in the war, this thought is gone now. The women who resist the war are in a minority faction, a voice repudiated, disowned by the rest.

Second thoughts, weak and wavering as they are, musings, ponderous reflections can be costly in a time of war. Particularly in the modern age. Everything moves so swiftly. A new technology must be noticed, and put to use quickly, if victory is to be won. One month earlier, Jan Smuts, now a general, arrives in London from South Africa to serve on the Imperial War Cabinet. He has come in time to witness an aerial attack on London. He grasps the implications of this new kind of warfare immediately. Civilians are terrorized by the attack, and this undermines the morale of the nation. The destruction of cities, he predicts, will soon become one of *the principal operations of war.*

In his homeland, South Africa, he is a distinguished statesman. His arrival in England is thus a significant social occasion. A banquet is held at the Savoy Hotel to celebrate his presence. Of course I was not there that night. But I have some idea. Seated at the side of my grandmother, I've attended banquets which were faded, less regal replicas of this one. A white linen tablecloth is spread over a long, long table. The finest bone china and heavy silver gleam in their rows. Bowls of cut flowers are spaced regularly three feet apart. Place cards, perhaps in white with embossed gold writing, announce each name. Men in black tie and tails, women in evening gowns, various silks, some sequins, in small embroidered shoes, flowers at their wrists, move familiarly into their seats and hardly look as cups of cold consommé are served from the left. A dessert, *French* perhaps and sweet, not entirely eaten, lies wrapped by the discarded linen. The host stands. Slowly the conversation makes a descent and then disappears.

Lord Selborne is proud to introduce Lieutenant General Jan Christian Smuts, South African statesman and soldier. General Smuts is proud to be here. He is an elegant and graceful speaker. Distinguished. The women imagine him in bed. We are all part of one race, he says. Cambridge bred, he knows his audience. The unity of the white race is essential. He peruses the table, taking in everyone, stopping only at a boundary placed discreetly at the service door. The white man's task is to civilize Africa. Are there electric lights? Are the windows blacked out? The style of his speech connotes a certain largess. Years of education and tradition lie behind the vision that unfolds before him. A possible future. The white presence in Africa. Of course, it makes one smile, he says, that missionaries once took Africans as wives. We know better now. A strict separation is necessary. Separate regions. Separate houses. Separate governing principles. One cannot apply the same rules to this different race. Are the buttons on his shirt made of bone? Is the shirt perhaps hand-stitched? Does he casually finger the polished wood of the rostrum as he talks? The African mind is closer to an animal mind. One can teach only the simplest Christian morality. Once the white man is secure in South Africa, the white race can move north and civilize the whole continent. This is what he sees in the future.

I am of course in that future now, straining to listen back over the decades to this voice from a time before I was born. My mother is just five years old. My father is seven. As I cock my ear in the direction of the childhood of my parents, I can hear the faintest breath of a tone. It is low and pleasingly masculine like the voice of a doctor or a scientist, calm and assured.

As a child, I lost the power of my voice for several years. It was shyness. In between my voice and the other voices there was a vast gulf. The ease with which they participated in the ebb and flow of conversation was a mystery to me. I spoke seldom, and in a barely audible tone. After my parents' divorce and my banishment to my grandmother's house, the right of speech was no longer mine. I believed somehow I would be tolerated only in stillness.

Many years after the Great War has ended, a stretcher-bearer in that war, whose name was Alfred Wolfsohn, will be famous for his knowledge of how to enlarge and enrich the capacity of the human voice. From what he hears in the voices of the dying, he understands that the power, the tone, the range of the voice reflect the life of the soul. This voice expands as the soul traverses its full range through life and death, fear of death, grief and joy. Conversely, as the human capacity for sound grows, a knowledge of heretofore hidden realms of being comes into consciousness.

Was Cassandra's voice made beautiful by the power of prophecy? Or was it instead distorted by the bitter taste of denial? The chorus, as written by Aeschylus, tells her, *You make music that is a mixture/ ugly cries of terror and high-pitched melodies.* Perhaps the music grew ugly because no one heard. She was ridiculed. The terrible anguish of her vision was hers alone to bear. The less her warnings were heeded the more insistent she became. The silent reproval that met her voice threatened to close her throat. So, trying to force her voice past this closing, she let out strange shrieks, sounds perhaps not dissimilar to the sounds of those horrified and shocked on the battlefield by sights they had not predicted. Is it in such a voice that one should deliver the lines Euripides wrote for Cassandra, *Only a madman depopulates and plunders cities. . . . He who does so creates a desert in which he'll perish*? Can such words be said calmly when the speaker herself is part of the plunder?

But we are in 1917. And our speaker is calm. He is used to being heard. It is no surprise then that on July 11 the Prime Minister appoints him as the only member besides himself to sit on a committee convened to study the war in the air. Smuts works prodigiously and well. The report the committee issues bears his name. One cannot tell the story of strategic bombing without invoking it now. The Smuts Report. His vision has become part of history.

Does he always enhance his predictions with a rosy glow? He promises that the bombing of cities will bring about a swifter cessation of this war, and then a lasting peace. If one has any doubts, these visions are nudged toward plausibility by a healthy aureole of optimism which is as if his birthright. Everything, he believes, has always turned out all right in the end.

There is none of this finesse in General Trenchard's appearance. The many photographs taken of him at different stations along his rise to eminence show a man with blunt ruddy features, thick, large and somewhat ill at ease, his eyes alive with excitement but betraying no humor. His voice is said to be gruff. He is laconic when he speaks, either too brusque or difficult to follow, as if the place in the universe he occupies cannot easily be communicated. His rise to power is not smooth. He makes enemies. Loses his temper. Maneuvers clumsily.

The provenance of this graceless state is not hard to imagine. Early in life he lost his footing in the social world. The ground of the middle class is always tenuous; this ground collapsed for him with his father's bankruptcy. Besides the loss of the family home, there was the humiliation of poverty. He was kept at school only through the generosity of the schoolmaster. One cannot help but suspect that this loss of financial power made a sad comment to the boy on his father's manhood.

I know it is impossible. Chinua Achebe, the Nigerian writer, descended from the Ibo, was not yet born when Hugh Trenchard was an administrator in Nigeria. This passage from Achebe's novel *Things Fall Apart* describes an Ibo man, not an Englishman. Still the resemblance is haunting. As a boy, the Ibo man was disturbed to learn that the word the village used for his father, *agbala,* had two meanings. The first meaning was *man with no title.* But it also meant *woman. His whole life was dominated by fear,* Achebe writes of his hero, an undaunted warrior and wrestler . . . *the fear of himself lest he should be found to resemble his father.*

Many years have passed since General Trenchard was a boy. He is forty-four years old now, as the war enters its last year. But old terrors felt earlier in life can return with a new force later. I myself have felt the cold chill of middle age at my back. You begin to think of time. The leaves inevitably turn color. The blaze is even past its peak. Winter is near. If once you thought you were impervious, you are shocked to discover that time does not stop for you either. So over the raw persistence of its advance you attempt to lay some structure of meaning. Perhaps you are aging, but nevertheless you are making an ascent. Your achievements accumulate. Each year you advance even higher. If shadows of former selves lie shed about you, still your name is followed by grander and greater titles.

There are of course those who amaze us with a different path. Life is embedded with meaning for them. But it is not dependent on social recognition. The meaning lies somewhere deeper, untouched by the worldly eventuation of success or loss.

The year is still 1917. Gandhi has taken up the cause of the mill workers in Ahmedabad, who seek a small but crucial increment in their modest wages. When the mill owners refuse to speak with them, they go on strike. Gandhi meets with them every day to encourage them. They assemble under a babul tree where he speaks to them of Satyagraha and joins them in prayer. The mill owners do not relent easily. As time passes, the strikers begin to lose heart. They and their families have had little or nothing to eat for weeks.

Is it because he feels at one with those who are starving that Gandhi begins his fast? In certain states of mind, meditation, trance and other moments difficult to name, the world appears to come into the self. The sight of a tree at the edge of the field, its leaves brightly yellow, its branches swaying slightly in the breeze, is suddenly inside your skin. You are not so much inhabited as aware. All along it has been like this. The movement of the tree, the joy, the suffering of the world is your own. *Unbidden and all by themselves,* he will write later of the pledge he makes, *the words came to my lips.* It is March 15 and he is standing under the tree when he promises he will not touch food until the strike is settled.

Hearing this, Anasuyabeha, the sister of a mill owner who has joined the workers, begins to weep. The workers themselves call out that it is they who should fast. No, Gandhi tells them, the fast is his to undertake.

It is not a simple matter for him. This will be the first of seventeen fasts he will undertake as part of his practice of Satyagraha. The fast must always be the last resort. And it must never be used to manipulate or exert power over others. Because of this he has some misgivings. The mill owners are friends. It is wrong to use force of any kind. He does not want them to capitulate simply because of their concern for him. Partaking in a fast, one must never be attached to the outcome. What arrives as a consequence cannot be predicted. Such an attachment would rob the fast of inner joy.

This is not a familiar approach to those who have learned to measure strength by outward signs. A man with no title. In the simplest of clothes. Whose manner is hardly commanding. Whose stature is small. Whose voice is strangely light, filled almost as if with air, a lilt, cajoling the listener through no willfulness except a quality of being able to laugh at some shared but forgotten, even ineluctable joke. Yet, and this is the mystery, despite this lightness that comes no doubt from detachment, the voice moves into you; smoothly a veil is parted, and someone inside you is revealed, immersed, merging, indistinguishable from your own secret suffering and the suffering you witness.

Can you really believe such a moment? Has it happened or is it just a part of your imagination? In any case miles and miles away another history continues. The heavy artillery is still in place, aligned on each side of the trenches. In countless cities throughout Europe factories work day and night to make shells which will burst, catch on fire, stun and maim flesh, bone.

In December 1917, Hugh Trenchard is named Chief of Staff of what will become the newly Independent Royal Air Force. But his command will not last long. The story will take another turn. Another smaller conflict moves in tandem with this great war. Trenchard will share his command with the Secretary of State for the Air Force, Lord Rothermere. The two men dislike each other. Trenchard is rude and blunt in his manner. There are even those who say he is arrogant and full of pride. On his part, he believes the Minister of Air is evasive and incompetent. Both men resign. The outcome is irreversible. A fall from power. Coming into the final year of the war, Trenchard has lost his place in the order of events.

For weeks he sits on a park bench. He is despondent, confused. He wants to think in solitude. He dresses in civilian clothes, staring for hours into the freshly budding trees of Green Park. What direction his life should take now is unclear to him.

Among the posts he has been offered is the command of long-range bombing in France. Could it be that at this moment, surrounded by the silent trees, he hears some faint echo of Cassandra's cry, *The agony, agony of the city utterly ruined*? But even if he does, his waking mind is taken up with more practical problems. There are not enough airplanes, not enough pilots to assist in battle and to bomb German cities at the same time. So much weighs in the balance. There has been a revolution in Russia. The Germans will withdraw troops now from the east and advance on the Western Front. Even more airplanes will be needed to attend the battlefield. Will it help the war to bomb cities?

If this is a pivotal juncture in his life, what is his mood? I cannot imagine him thinking of inner joy. He would no doubt feel such a thought to be indulgent. I have no difficulty entering this state of mind. I am thinking of my grandmother. I can imagine her in April 1917, cleaning house. She carried out her daily work with a vengeance. She did not become an actress as she had dreamed. She did what was expected of her, her duty. Her joy was not in the doing but in the achievement.

It can be dangerous to live for experience itself. One might wander too far outside the predictable structures, confining as they are. No, Trenchard is not thinking of the insecurities of his childhood now, or even of his own aging body. Yet all that is oddly present in the nakedness he feels out of uniform. Just as strangers do not recognize him, he does not recognize himself. His body is amorphous. He cannot delineate himself, draw the boundaries properly. It is as if he has been given another body, another skin, strangely familiar, an earlier self, too frail, too revealed, unnerving.

Private choices, embedded as they are in habitual response, are never isolated from the social atmosphere which surrounds them. In 1917 the British nation is forged into one body pledged to discipline and duty. There is thus a kind of public outcry over Trenchard's temporary stillness. In the park he overhears a naval officer, who does not recognize him out of uniform, suggest that he should be shot for desertion. Is it shame that propels him in a certain direction? I can imagine him standing up from the park bench for the last time. When he steps into his apartment he goes directly to his closet. He removes the civilian jacket he has worn for days. As the familiar epaulets fall into place over his shoulders does he feel that his life has meaning once more? Within hours he calls the Home Office. Despite his misgivings about the usefulness of the tactic, he accepts the command of long-range bombing.

It is then through an odd series of events mixing family and national history that Hugh Trenchard finds himself at the apex of history. He cannot know the distant consequences of what he does. Even the practical questions he once had are silenced now. As a soldier his duty is to serve. His task now is to prove the usefulness of long-range bombing. Given the strategic considerations, the logic is obvious. There is no way to inflict efficacious damage on factories and railways with so few planes and so few bombs and without a means to hit the targets more accurately.

Does he hesitate before the only logical conclusion? His body tired beyond saying, I can imagine the slightest tremor of a wish passing before him. If there were any way out he might take it. But the tremor is imperceptible. Only the tangle of it all appears to him. All those dead bodies on either side. Has he gotten used to it, the dismemberment, the various colors of blood? And there is the other entanglement too, accruing as it has over so many years, all the coats with insignia he has worn, a history stretching back as far as he can remember, back several generations, past even his imagination. There is only one choice.

Let it burn. The whole apparatus. Let his soldiers fly over those cities and drop their bombs. Let the cities disappear. Let there be empty space where once a way of life, a machinery of war, stood. This idea breathes life into his exhausted body once more. He will spread his raids over many cities, so that no one in any city will feel safe. It is clear what must be done. We must try, he says, *to crush the spirit of the German people*.

If there is no joy in taking this course, the joy will be in the outcome. It is 1918. He is collecting evidence of success. By August he has dropped hundreds of tons of bombs over Cologne, Bonn, Kohlberg, Wiesbaden, Mainz, Mannheim, Stuttgart, Rheims, Metz, Saarbrücken. The new Minister of Air, Lord Weir, tells him not to be too scrupulous about the accuracy of his aim. To prove moral and physical damage, he takes photographs showing the bombs falling. As part of his case, he has retrieved a letter from a German citizen. *One feels as if one were no longer a human being,* the anonymous man writes. *One air raid after another.* Trenchard's campaign of terror is working . . . *one is daily, hourly prepared for the worst.*

For each event in history there are many possible narrations. General Trenchard is shaping the long-range bombing of Germany into an argument. The bombings slow the German offensive, he says. They are helping to turn the tide of the war. And the tide *is* turning. The steadily accruing attrition of hunger and short supplies caused by the Allied blockade of Germany is having an effect. It has been a year since America declared war, and now her armies are fighting in France. The troops are fresh and well armed. In the summer of 1918 they succeed in stopping the German advance on Paris. German troops retreat from Belleau Wood and Château-Thierry.

I talked to a soldier who fought in the battles of Belleau Wood and Château-Thierry. He was twenty-two years old when he fought in those battles. Now, nearly a century had passed since his birth.

The process of narration that creates an order of events can hardly be separated over time from the events themselves. Tom told me his story in studied manner. He began as he slowly climbed the stairs, wearing the faded Marine Corps hat he had worn in battle, by singing "The Halls of Montezuma" in a voice high and cracking with age. Spoken with an eloquence that belongs to an earlier age, each word he uttered carried a stentorian significance. *I was born the middle child in a family of thirteen children on an isolated farm of illiterate parents in 1895. My people were an obscure people.*

His parents grew up in the South just after the Civil War. It was the period of reconstruction. Northern troops occupied the region. Because the schools still taught a Southern perspective on the war, the troops had closed them. And that was why his parents never learned to read. It was as if they had been placed outside the stream of history. A story was being told, and they were not in it. *I have no idea what got me interested in the world,* he said.

As chance would have it, though he never graduated high school, Tom, a bright child interested in learning, was chosen to attend Mississippi College as part of a program for poor but intelligent children. He became a servant for the college president's family, and in turn they gave him a home and paid for his education. His hunger for a larger world, though, was not satisfied. A few days after his graduation he boarded a train for New Orleans, a city he had heard of all his life but never seen. It was on this trip, while walking on the banks of the Mississippi, that he saw a Marine Corps recruiting station. America had already entered the war. His entire graduating class planned to enter officers' training school in the next month. But he did not want to wait. The recruiting officer promised him that if he signed up immediately he would be on a train to Norfolk, Virginia, in two hours, and on a ship to France within the week.

The story of his experience in the war, told over the years, on so many occasions, had taken on a formal structure, so that what I heard now was like the recitation of an old legend, handed down over generations. He went into the war without training. While he was at the top of the mast of the battleship *Henderson,* the ship was torpedoed by a German submarine. He would not leave the mast until he was ordered to do so. He spent the night in a lifeboat at sea. *The most dreadful night of my life,* he said, though it was excitement and not fear which threaded through his telling. He was thrilled, he told me, to be on a large ship, to land on foreign soil, to meet soldiers from New Zealand and Australia. And in a conspiratorial tone, as if imparting forbidden knowledge, he told me that the busiest road in France was the one between Toul and Brest. Toul was where the soldiers convened, and Brest was a prostitute town.

He never fired a gun in the war. He was not trained to do so, and though he never said he was glad he had not caused another man's death, the relief was evident in his voice. When I asked him if he was afraid standing on the mast, he said, no, he thought he was just half crazy. But though he would not admit to fear, his pride was not a pride in masculine prowess. When he said, *We fought the Germans,* he was quick to add that the German armies were poorly armed and worn out from years of battle, whereas the American troops were well armed and fresh. He meant something else when he told me, *I had more experience in life in that war than I had had in all my twenty-two years.*

What moved him to cherish this year of his life was that during these months he felt his place in history. He was part of the Battle of Belleau Wood and the American advance on Château-Thierry. It was here that Pershing finally proved to the French commander of Allied forces, General Foch, that an independent American army could help to turn the tide of the war. It was in these battles that the German advance on Paris was first stopped. Did I know, he asked me, about these battles? *They are a part of the public record,* he said.

He knew nothing, he told me, of why the war was fought. Even today the causes mystify him. There was no great justice he was trying to defend. No righteousness, except the righteousness of a young man called and answering the call with his life. He could imagine playing a part in history now, because he had done so. But he could not imagine deciding what the course of history ought to be.

The shape he gave to his story had long been etched in his mind. When I asked him what it was like to be under fire, he repeated a story he had already told me more than once: how he would feed ammunition to the machine gunner and then step away because the machine gun became a target. He had asked me to stop him if he repeated himself. He knew his short-term memory was failing. But because I hoped that some new insight might come to the surface, I let him tell me this story again. It was as if he were caught in an eddy of consciousness. He went on repeating the same story over and over, pausing at the end just briefly, only to begin again. It was with the fifth telling that a different version appeared. Once, just after he had fed the ammunition into the machine gun, he stepped back as he had been taught to do, and then the machine gun and the gunner were hit by a shell. One moment the gunner was there in front of his eyes, and in the next, after the burst of the shell, the noise, the fire, he had vanished. No trace of him was left to bury. His body was dispersed by the blast in pieces too small to recognize. Tom still remembered his name.

Once while I was staying in a small pensione in Greece, the father of the owner woke a family of British tourists at dawn to tell them his war stories. He remained dressed throughout the day in his old uniform, saber at his side. He had fought in the war with the Turks, a history now dim to the rest of us who could barely grasp the outlines of his glory. We laughed at his constant telling. But now I am hearing the repetition of the old warrior in a new way. Is there perhaps a silent hope, buried along with inadmissible memories, that perhaps some fragment of what has been censored from the official story will be restored? And the pain and shock of that memory woven thus into a fabric of meaning, shared in the common arena of knowledge?

Tom hesitated. The death of this man he had come to know in battle was unattached to his narrative, and floated as if part of a sea of all that is incomprehensible in life. Blinking, he returned to the plot. He was injured. A minor wound to the head. And damage to his heart from the strain and shock of battle that is still with him. His story, though, did not center on this injury. It was only that this disability conferred on him another honorific moment. A detachment of wounded men was sent home on a large passenger liner that had been used to bring Woodrow Wilson to France. This was a crowning moment in his telling, and confirmed his place in a history that from now on would give his life meaning.

But there are others for whom the same war takes meaning away from life. The story breaks apart. Images pried loose from any structure of significance surround them like a host of demons. They themselves begin to resemble the half-dead monsters which haunt them. *Drooping tongues from jars that slob their relish/ Baring teeth that leer like skulls' teeth wicked.* The poet Wilfred Owen describes ex-soldiers caught in perpetual horror. *Always they must see things and hear them/ Batter of guns and shatter of flying muscles.* Everything they see recalls the war. *Sunlight seems a blood smear; night comes blood-black; dawn breaks open like a wound. . . .*

I have some understanding of shell shock. Limbs numb. Disorientation. Loss of memory. These are the physical symptoms of the chronic disease I have. In the fifth year of writing this book I met a man who had been shell-shocked in the Vietnam War. I asked him to tell me his story, and he tried. But he had lost the capacity to make a meaning from the events of his life. He had difficulty speaking at all. It was as if his will had collapsed, or some connection between speech and the central spine of his existence had eroded. Whatever he said floated oddly away from him and into the room, unfinished, unanchored. The manner of his telling told me more than what he said. He was not fully present in the telling of his own history, but more disturbing than this absence was his visible and always failing effort to enter his own life.

He was drafted at eighteen and served two years in Germany. His return to civilian life was not successful. He was young. His father, a laconic man who worked for the Union Carbide Company at Oak Ridge, convinced him to re-enlist. His father had fought in World War II, and his uncle was a career officer in the army. The choice seemed natural. Later, he would serve under his uncle in Vietnam.

The war was not what he imagined. He was constantly under fire, even at the base camp. Shells exploded next to him. He saw the bodies of men he knew fly apart, detached, aimless. Everyone smoked weed. He too acquired the habit. He wanted to leave the army as a conscientious objector. But he was sent to an army psychiatrist and threatened with dishonorable discharge. Then he simply ceased to care. Some new officer would show up who had seen no action and start giving orders, he said. He has never been the same since. He flies off the handle with anyone in authority. His mind doesn't seem to work well. He can't hold down a job, or even at times put two and two together. He is one of the homeless.

I began to suspect his lassitude concealed a state of paralysis, not of the body, but of the soul. He was as if suspended in the past, disbelieving the old values, yet unable to act on his own beliefs.

He was not raised to speak about his feelings or his thoughts. His father spoke little to him, and of an interior life, not at all. Now, what he experienced in the war has sunk into an even deeper silence than his father's.

Once a nerve cell has been excited, reversing its charge, a chain reaction is created carrying the impulse from nerve cell to nerve cell until the impulse ends in movement.

I have two photographs of my father as a child. The first photograph, the one my cousin sent me, is the one taken before the

Great War. He is a baby. He leans forward and away from my grandfather, who holds him. You can see that my grandfather's desolate mood has entered his body, but the cast of his face at this moment seems transitory. His face still bears an infant innocence, an openness. In the second photograph, taken sometime in the midst of the war, he sits without his father on the steps of a house, his arm around his dog. He is cloyingly dressed in a sunsuit with a sailor collar, and he holds a flower. But the expression on his face is not a child's. His father's sorrow has become his own. When was it then that another expression, an uncomfortable smile, was layered over this face?

It is late in the day on November 10, 1918, when Hugh Trenchard, seated at his desk, receives a memo from the commanding officer of an Italian squadron stationed nearby. He has heard the rumor that a cease-fire has been arranged. Even now pilots under Trenchard's command are dropping bombs over the valley of the Moselle. Trenchard waits through the night for their return. All the pilots return safely and by morning the rumor is confirmed.

The war is over. Thirty-seven million have been wounded. Nine million have died. On the day of the Armistice, the parents of Wilfred Owen are informed that he died two weeks earlier. Other deaths, partial or invisible, the death of a state of mind, of a way of life, are slower to emerge. The land is ravaged. Bodies are disabled. Memories are entrenched. And if slowly a certain configuration begins to unravel, it does not vanish entirely but instead remains, like the ghost of a previous painting, lying just beneath the surface, giving all the colors a different cast.

There are those who do not lay down their arms easily. On the day of the Armistice Hermann Göring, who has replaced Von Richthofen as commanding officer of the Flying Circus, has been ordered to fly his squadron to Strasbourg where he is to hand his airplanes over to the French. But on the day of the Armistice he disobeys this order. Sending just a few pilots to Strasbourg, he flies with the rest of the squadron to Germany where they destroy their planes on landing.

From each fragmentation of the atom as many as eighty possible products are formed, each releasing ionizing radiation. The violence of this process also causes chemicals in the air or water nearby to absorb energy, change their substance and become radioactive.

Among those who accept the end of the war, it continues in another form. The stories have already begun to be told. Now a transmutation will occur through language. On the day of the Armistice, Ernest Hemingway writes home from a hospital in Milan, *I did come very close to the big adventure.* He encloses an illustration of the medals he has received from the Italian army for his service in the medical corps. Over the next years he will embellish the story of his part in the war, expanding the image of his heroism. Ernst Jünger, one of fourteen infantrymen to have received the *Pour le mérite,* will continue for five years in military service, until he retires to write about the war. Through his novel, he will construct a mythic soldier, larger, stronger than life, with *keen bloodthirsty nerves.* Other lives are set now on an almost predictable course. George Patton has been awarded both the Distinguished Service Cross and the Distinguished Service Medal. He returns home a colonel. Douglas MacArthur has been made a general. Are they swept along by history or do they make history? But the question perhaps arises from a certain frame of mind which is itself fixed to events as they have been remembered. For, in a different light, one can begin to perceive the edges of one shared movement in what we have called the private and the public worlds, one motion shaping and shaped by all that exists.

All nerve cells have the same structure: a cell body holding the nucleus, dendrites which receive connections from other nerve cells, axons which connect to dendrites or cell bodies of other nerve cells.

It is January 1919. The demobilization of British soldiers proceeds slowly. Several mutinies have broken out. General Trenchard complains that he is tired. He thinks of resigning from service. But he is needed. He is assigned to control a rebellion on the docks at Portsmouth. Does he remember his encounter with the Ibo warriors, the fireworks that sent them fleeing? Or is he thinking of his campaign of terror against German cities? He plans another dramatic explosion of light. First he cuts the electrical current to the enormous shed where the men are assembled. Then he appears in the shed with several men carrying rifles where, at his signal the men throw back the bolts of their rifles, and electricity is restored, shedding a glaring light on the mutineers. The tactic is successful.

It is April 1919. Alpha particles colliding with nitrogen have produced strange scintillations. Ernest Rutherford succeeds in determining that these are hydrogen atoms. Atoms of nitrogen have been split. This disintegration will allow scientists to study the inner recesses of the atomic world. In the summer of the same year Enrico Fermi, just eighteen years old, and still a student, spends his vacation months in Rome reading books and papers on the latest discoveries in theoretical physics. He takes his bibliography from Ernest Rutherford's paper on radioactive substances.

For each newly created radioactive chemical, it will take hundreds of thousands of years to return to a normal state. Until that time, the process of fragmentation, and release of toxicity, will continue.

Is there perhaps a long silence in the year following the war, a period in which particles still fall quietly to earth, leaving the shape of the outcome as yet unclear? It is early in the year 1919. Winston Churchill, recently made Secretary of State for War and Air, decides to keep the Royal Air Force as an independent branch of the service. He looks for a commander. A report crosses his desk detailing the mutiny at Portsmouth. Churchill is impressed with General Trenchard's performance. He asks him to take command of the Royal Air Force once again.

Almost immediately an opportunity to prove the usefulness of the Royal Air Force presents itself. In Somaliland a mullah and his men have successfully resisted British attempts to control them throughout the war. Now Trenchard sends his pilots to bomb the mullah. The mullah is forced into retreat, and when he reaches Abyssinia, he is killed. Calculating the cost of this victory to be merely £77,000, Trenchard argues that bomber squadrons are the best means of pacification. The Royal Air Force is stationed in Egypt, to police Iraq and protect Britain's sea route to India and the Far East.

At the synapse where the axon of one cell joins the dendrite or body of another the reversal of electrical charge leads to the release of a chemical substance, called a neurotransmitter.

It is in the same year, on October 15 in Vienna, that Sigmund Freud appears before a commission investigating the treatment of soldiers with electric shock. There is a scandal. Shell-shocked men returning more than once from the trenches for treatment received increasingly strong electrical currents. Some suffered permanent damage. Others died. Freud is sympathetic to Professor Wagner-Jauregg, who supervised this treatment. The professor, he reasons, cannot have intended to inflict damage. There was a war. The situation was demanding. Still, he argues that if *war neurotics* were malingerers, as the professor diagnosed, their malingering was unconscious. And unconscious feelings are beyond conscious control. Psychoanalysis, he suggests, would have been a better way to return them to the trenches.

It is 1921. General Trenchard's bombers, attacking an Iraqi encampment, fire with machine guns on the families of tribesmen who in their fear flee into the lake. There is a national scandal. Churchill writes Trenchard that *to fire willfully on women and children is a disgraceful act*. He urges Trenchard to court-martial the pilots responsible. But Trenchard, who believes that *the luxury of a conscience has no place in the army,* defends the pilots. They were carrying out *to the letter* a course of action defined for them by civilian administrators. He disciplines them lightly.

Radioactive substances, depending on the type of particle released, can pass through skin, or be taken into the body with air, food, or water, or through an open wound, entering the blood stream, the lymph system, or they may be incorporated into bone and tissue, remaining there for a few hours, or a lifetime.

The attack on the Iraqi tribesmen reminds me, of course, of an incident which occurred during the Vietnam War, the attack at My Lai. I remember looking at the photographs. Small children, infants lying face down, flesh ribboned open and bloody. The terrified face of a young woman about to be raped and the un-speakable pain of her mother beside her. The sergeant who led this attack was prosecuted. But there were many other incidents that never came to trial. And perhaps a pattern that was never exposed drifts even now into the future we occupy.

It is still 1921. Mohandas Gandhi, now called the Mahatma, or Great Soul, has adopted still another style of clothing. It is as if progressively over time he has stripped away one layer after an-other. Now he wears only the loincloth of an Indian peasant. This is made of the homespun cloth called *khadi,* now part of the campaign for independence that includes a boycott of British cloth and the revival of spinning among peasants who cannot make a living off the land. Chest bare, thin arms and legs uncov-ered, one can see him spin his thread with a simple hand tool every day for half an hour. He calls it a sacrament.

Once this chemical touches the membrane of another cell that membrane becomes six hundred more times permeable to a substance that changes the charge of the interior cell from negative to positive.

It is 1924. If the psyche that was once impenetrable opens now, there is, at the same time, a hardening. A structure felt momentarily as fragile, even coming apart, is grasped suddenly with a new tenacity. Ernst Jünger publishes *Storm of Steel*, depicting himself *as a wandering knight, who has broken many a lance, born by the desire to kill*. If the story he once told in his wartime journals was saturated with second thoughts, complexities, traces short of pure strength, these have vanished now. At the same time, the *knight's illusions have melted away in sarcastic laughter*. Violence transcends every earthly concern. And around and about these lines, emerging as if from the same telling of the story, another voice can be heard. A young corporal in the army begins to speak about a betrayal of Germany's pride and strength. Hermann Göring is listening. What he hears begins to shape the direction of his future life.

Exposing cells to the microscopic explosions of ionizing radiation can cause cell death, or cell radiation. It can make the cell unable to replace itself, or stop reproducing itself.

I can imagine it. All the fortitude of your being, even your own desire to survive, moves with a certain rhythm. The march. You have nearly died. You have witnessed death. Your ears are still ringing with the sound of shells. You can scarcely describe this sound. No one who was not there understands it. The march has stopped. Your foot is in midair. Suddenly the world is swirling about you in a different direction. You strain at the boundaries of language to find the words, a story, a plausible order.

There are neural pathways which carry impulses inward to the central nervous system and pathways which carry impulses outward determining response. Impulses leading inward carry knowledge everywhere in the nervous system about everything that affects the body.

It is an irony of history that the symptoms of shell shock resemble in many ways the symptoms of radiation sickness. Lassitude. Confusion. Sometimes a tremor. Forgetfulness. Did I not have an illness which affects the immune system, as does radiation, and causes its own kind of shock, I would not have noticed the similarity. I visited a doctor near Freiburg, the small city in the Black Forest where Göring was sent when he was recovering from rheumatic fever, and where he learned to fly. One afternoon on the arm of a friend I took a walk in the village cemetery near our rented rooms. There were many young and recent deaths. The doctor told us it was cancer and leukemia, the result, she believed, of fallout from nuclear tests that had drifted in the direction of Freiburg. The stones told their own somber story, names, ages, sometimes a line of poetry.

Am I imagining this? So much of the land, the fields, have a strange flatness now. You notice it where it is not so. Out of time. Quaint. Picturesque. From a past I know was far from perfect. Still, there is something almost palpable in the fields outside Freiburg, children playing in the newly mown grass, pines at the edge, dark beginnings of a forest.

Cellular damage from radiation manifests as damage to a particular organ of the body. If radionuclides lodge in the bone they can cause damage to the bone marrow, resulting in bone cancer or leukemia.

There is something we long for that is not here. A life knitted together by a vast and intricate meaning, implicated in the movements of our hands, tongues, eyes as they pass over the momentary landscape. It is 1925. It is the year that Gandhi will spend touring the Indian countryside. Passing on the practice of spinning cloth by hand, he will teach even the most remote villagers the virtues of a direct relationship with nature and an autonomous economy. He explains his Constructive Programme. The notions of frugality and prayer are old ideas. But there is also a newer concept, the principle of equality with untouchables and with women.

This knowledge, interpreted by the central nervous system, and evaluated according to memory, old habits, present postures, attitudes, is transformed and sent back to the periphery as decision, commanding how the body will respond.

Is he carried along in a stream, not entirely of his own making? Other lives mingled with his? Other stories he has heard? Some he imagines. He depicts an India before the British Empire, filled with spinning wheels. It is an illusionary past he creates. A vision of the future inscribed as if into memory. Except that there must be some memory, some intimation, drawing the image to him. He can envision then a whole cloth never before woven, a justice that has not been seen before, an equality which perhaps always existed, except that it was silent and still.

If these particles lodge in the lungs they can cause respiratory diseases. General exposure can be experienced as stress to a hereditary weakness. Individual breakdown from exposure occurs at the most vulnerable points. The young are especially affected.

It is 1926. The advent of speech takes many courses. At times an old story must peel away so that a new telling can begin. Hemingway's war stories, having been embellished with added bullets and wounds, suddenly cease. *I distrust all frank and simple people,* he writes in his first novel, *especially when their stories hold together.* This is the voice of the generation after the war, trusting nothing, pared down, nearly flat, with an ironic cadence, a world weariness seeking excitement. But it is not a voice that affects Enrico Fermi, who has just been made professor of theoretical physics at the University of Rome. He needs no stimulation. He is about to explore a new world. He will try to disassemble the nucleus of the atom.

The flow of knowledge within the nervous system is not simple. It does not travel back and forth so much as in a circle, simultaneously, mutually.

Sensation evokes movement which evokes new sensation which modifies movement, creating one conscious experience.

In Britain, other experiments of a different nature are occurring. It is 1927. Under General Trenchard's command the Royal Air Force has succeeded in launching a pilotless missile. It has a range of two hundred miles and has landed within five miles of its target.

If radiation damage occurs in the sperm or ovum, this affects procreation, causing defects, stillbirths, or the inability to conceive.

It is 1928. General Trenchard is finally retiring from service. He leaves for the future command what he calls his *last will and testament*. He regrets that the plans for a guided missile are not being carried out. The future will lie, he says, in this direction. Air attacks, in crushing enemy morale, will be decisive. In the next war both sides will bomb without scruple those targets they find most effective. He urges the government to accept this fact and to prepare to meet and deliver these attacks, which will be inevitable.

The human nervous system, containing countless nerve cells, intricate pathways, possibilities for response, feeling, knowledge, has evolved gradually over a million years of subtle augmentations and changes.

The circle of time drawn in this telling returns. There will be a next war. Bombings. The Bomb. Small explosions invisible in the air. In tissue, blood, bone. Inevitable and yet can there be an unraveling in the telling and another story that begins to reweave the strands, new on the loom once more? Are there earlier voices, older than the stories we have heard—shock and cry of war dismembered—interior language of the cell, standing stone of history, oddly familiar in our hands, making us lean toward what we have not yet perceived?

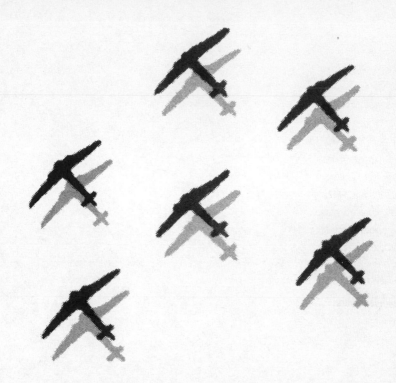

NOTES TOWARD
A SKETCH
FOR A WORK
IN PROGRESS

VI

IF

she had lived, what would she have done with the rest of her life? What would she have painted? And would she have gone on singing as she worked?

August 1990
My thought is to weave a journal into the pages of the sixth chapter. Here I will record notes about the process of writing this chapter and the book.

I ask this last question because Charlotte was singing all the time that she painted and wrote her great work, *Life or Theatre?* Marita Guenther told me this when I went to visit her in the South of France, two years ago. And how did Marita, who never knew Charlotte, know this intimate detail of her life? That is another story which perhaps I will tell later.

August
What I am seeking is the effect of a work in progress, a work that still continues off the page, and is only completed in the imagination.

My own fascination with Charlotte Salomon began over ten years ago. A thick book reproducing her major work, *Life or The-*

atre? *A Play with Music,* was displayed in the window of a bookstore in my neighborhood. On the cover of this book was a painting of the face of a young woman. As she stared into the eyes of the viewer, her presence was extraordinary. This was a self-portrait in the tradition of Rembrandt, worthy of Käthe Kollwitz, penetrating, frank, evoking at one and the same time a feeling of intimacy and the desire for an equally clear knowledge of oneself.

August
So the chapter will include traces of my own process in telling these stories.

When I opened the book I discovered that this "play" consisted of a series of paintings, 769 in number, which depicted the story of the painter's life. Words written on the paintings, together with an accompanying text, made the work like a play, with a plot, dialogue, drama. At certain points, Charlotte even indicates music to be played or hummed with it.

August
This last section of the book should be like a sketch for a painting. And not only the journal, but the text too should have, in places, this slightly unfinished quality.

I found the form innovative and exciting, but in the end what truly drew me was the simple fact that she had created this work to save her life.

August
I want the boundaries of the book to be opened, letting in the atmosphere of contemporary events.

Her story begins with a suicide. In 1913, a year before the First World War began, her aunt Charlotte, after whom she was

named, jumped into a river in Berlin and drowned. This death
was one in a long chain reaction of suicides in her mother's family. In *Life or Theatre?* Charlotte traces the pattern back to her
mother's uncle who killed himself. After this there were cousins,
then her aunt Charlotte, then her own mother, and finally, almost
in her presence, her grandmother committed suicide. She tells the
story so she will not repeat this cycle of destruction.

August
*There is so much that is extraordinary happening around us at such
an intense pace. The end of the Cold War. And the beginning perhaps of
another war in the Middle East.*

Why is it I find this so compelling, Charlotte's effort to see
herself and her family history honestly, and yet, at the same time,
to render what she sees into art? What she has made is a beautiful
mirror, but also a self-image that is not static, that lives in the
imagination of the viewer, opening up new possibilities to the
mind.

August
*Events are happening more quickly now than we can absorb them.
Borders are changing so rapidly, a map made today will no longer be
accurate tomorrow.*

At the end of this long book about many kinds of denial, I
want to write about testimony. About bearing witness to events in
such a way that they become lucid, their inner life revealed. When
light is shed in this way, can it not change the course of events? I
find Charlotte's story especially pertinent now because she addresses the question of self-destruction. I have come to believe
that our shared movement toward nuclear war is a movement
toward mass suicide.

August
For months I have been saving clippings from the newspapers. There is a story, for instance, of the collapse of discipline in the People's Army of East Germany. The newspapers describe it as an identity crisis.

Perhaps there is something within us as a social body that wishes to die. Or perhaps there is a dimension of ourselves that must be sacrificed if we are to go on living. It is not so much that I expect an answer. It is instead simply the desire to turn and look in that direction.

August
The identity crisis they are talking about is probably one of national boundaries. But of course there are other identities placed in jeopardy now, such as the identity of the warrior.

And there is this also: Charlotte was a civilian who was trapped by the violence of public life, as we are all trapped and held hostage by nuclear weapons now. Her private troubles are depicted against a background of dramatic historical events. Her story is simultaneously a story about war and about a family.

August
Without the Cold War, warriors are not so necessary any more.

Charlotte was born in Berlin between the First and the Second World Wars.

August
One's identity can be threatened by any change, even a change for the better. I notice it in my own process. The longer certain words remain on the page, the less I want to alter the text.

Charlotte's family was Jewish, well assimilated into the German middle class. Is it only in her memory or was it true of the atmosphere of her grandparents' home that all traces of Jewishness were effaced? In Charlotte's depiction her grandparents' home has a feeling which is almost international now among people of a class.

August

Met with Shirley Kaufman, who is visiting from Israel. She showed me a poem she wrote recently. I found it very moving. Images of the holocaust mingled, ending with a river of salt. It begins with a story a man told her. A survivor. His first sexual experience. At Bergen Belsen. A stolen moment with himself, touching himself, all the time looking over his shoulder.

Charlotte's mother Franziska was beautiful, charming and "popular." Her younger sister, the first Charlotte, felt diminished in her presence. I know something of jealousy among sisters. My mother loved my sister more than she did me. She told me once it was simply a matter of closeness. They had spent more years together before the family diaspora. From the ages of six to eight and then from nine to eleven, I was with my grandparents. I did not add the years up then, nor did I ask if seven years were not enough to form a bond between mother and daughter. I simply shrugged off her explanation as a reality I had long ago accepted.

August

Shirley is worried about the possibility of war. Might Israel be pushed by the United States into using nuclear weapons against Iraq?

When my mother and father divorced, I was sent to my grandmother's house, and my sister was sent to live with my great-aunt, my grandmother's sister, who lived six hundred miles away. Years later she held these miles against me. And something else, I suspect, came between us. My grandmother, who was the matriarch of the family, chose me as *her* favorite. Then I was blond and my sister dark in a culture that worships blondness and fears darkness. And in the years that I was married, she was a lesbian, marginal, marked with shame, only half visible.

August
When we first met, Shirley was living in California, and in another marriage, with three children. But she fell in love with another man, a teacher, critic and an Israeli. She left her marriage and her life here to move to Israel. I remember how much I admired the courage it must have required to make that change.

The feeling of not being acceptable or loved cuts deeply into the psyche, often leaving an unhealable wound. And what is played out in families is also played out in the schoolyard. Certain children are favored among their peers. Others excluded. Himmler never forgot the years when he was rejected in this way.

August
Now, twenty years later, we are drinking tea in the house of Shirley's daughter, who is a mother now, and my friend too. "It is not what you would think it is, the Middle East," Shirley says. The hostilities are predictable, but everywhere there are pockets of contradiction. She tells me about her friendship with a Lebanese poet. Because no mail passes directly between Jerusalem and Beirut they correspond through her daughters' addresses in the United States. He is a German scholar too, and has translated Trakl and the Bible into Arabic.

Of course patterns of exclusion continue past school years. There is no saying where they begin or end. In the family, or in society at large. Jews. Homosexuals. A darker color of skin, hair. A different accent. Clothes or shoes that are not fine enough. All these prejudices accumulate in an intricate lattice of meaning and injury.

September
Language as both bond and division. Lenke telling me that in Swe-
den she and Nelly Sachs studied Kabbala together in German. Lenke had
learned German in Auschwitz.

Charlotte's mother was not the same after her sister jumped to
her death. But the effect on her was not immediately visible.
Except that she insisted to her parents that she be allowed to
become a nurse and tend to soldiers wounded in the war. Finally,
after much pleading, they relented but only on the condition that
she stay away from the front.

September
There are so many stories I heard in the course of the writing that I
would like to include in the book. But one cannot tell everything. The
urgency of testimony, of bearing witness. A crowd pressing, like passen-
gers, pushing to board a train already filled to capacity.

It was in a hospital in Berlin that Charlotte's mother met her
future husband, Charlotte's father. He was a doctor. In one painting Charlotte depicts the two of them hovering over the body of a
man who has a severe wound. It looks as if either his genitals or
his intestines have been injured.

September
Even in the retelling of one story, so many details have had to be left
out. And others are given a new prominence. That is, I give them a
prominence. And then the book itself, moving with its own life, makes
certain choices which I must obey.

Just after Charlotte's parents are married, her father is called
away to the front. Franziska's parents want her to stay on with
them. But she refuses. She goes to live in the apartment they are
to share as a married couple. In the story as Charlotte tells it, one

feels a sense of liberation and excitement as her mother leaves the suffocating environment of her childhood.

September
What always seems miraculous is when aesthetic necessities yield an insight which otherwise I would have missed. I repeat a word in a paragraph for instance and when I find what I think is a similar word, a simple replacement, a whole new meaning is revealed.

But a painting follows which shows Franziska sitting alone, in a vacant apartment. One thinks then of this vital young woman who just days before, working long hours in the wards of a hospital, was situated at the heart of public life, sitting now by herself with nothing much to do.

September
Of course, one must be willing to break the aesthetic and find a new form. A form which appears to be merely graceful or beautiful can be a kind of censoring mold, a habitual pattern which stifles knowledge of thought and feeling.

But Charlotte's father returns soon from the war, and the house takes on life. Charlotte is born. There are family dinners. Celebrations. Holidays. Despite the fact that the family is Jewish, there are Christmas trees. Presents. And at the heart of it, in Charlotte's telling, an intimate relationship between Charlotte and her mother.

September
It is perhaps five years ago now—I was already writing this book— when I began to see that my own despair had become a habit, an old pattern I had inherited from my childhood.

In the portraits Charlotte draws of her mother throughout this work, one senses a woman with great vitality and an independent spirit. But there is no place for her to live out these traits. And as she begins to long for death, these qualities fire her self-destruction.

September
To continue in that old form would inevitably lead to a cul de sac. *A foregone conclusion.*

Before Franziska attempts suicide, she tells her daughter stories at night, creating a vivid fantasy of an afterlife, a heaven with glorious angels. One day she will go there, she tells her daughter, and she will be happy. *If you ever go there will you send me a letter telling me what it is like?* Charlotte asks. *Yes,* Franziska promises.

September
In my most despairing moments I found myself believing that I was somehow cursed to repeat over and over the painful episodes of my childhood for the rest of my life.

In this part of Charlotte's story I am reminded of the power of German idealism, the hypnotic notion of a state of perfection that transcends any possible earthly existence.

September
In truth I did repeat those episodes many times.

The world has lost its meaning for Franziska and bit by bit she withdraws from life. Those around her are unable to diagnose her trouble. And she herself does not say what is the matter. She makes one suicide attempt and is rescued. But when she is left alone for a few moments, she jumps out a window to her death.

September
But who is to say which came first, the belief or the events?

Why did Franziska end her life? Charlotte has no simple answer. Instead, cast in a certain irony, she depicts the explanations
she was given by others, and she presents her own memories, the
experience of a child who has lost her mother. No one tells her
that her mother committed suicide. Wishing to protect her, con-
soling adults tell her that her mother has died of influenza. She
depicts herself as not fully touched by the tragedy, waiting daily
for her mother's letter from heaven.

September
The stories we tell ourselves, particularly the silent or barely audible
ones, are very powerful. They become invisible enclosures. Rooms with no
air. One must open the window to see further, the door to possibility.

Charlotte is met with two silences. Her mother's silence and
the silence of her family. A gloom descends. One can feel the
child's utter loneliness in the way she has painted herself. Clearly
she knows something which has never been spoken. And she is
isolated in this knowledge, even from herself.

September
I read this in a review of a book on the Civil War in the New York
Times. *Walt Whitman writes, "The real war will never get in the*
books."

In one frame she pictures herself as a child running terrified
through the upstairs hallway to the bathroom. She is frightened by
the sense of something lurking there that has a mysterious connection with her mother. A red-limbed skeleton looms over her.

September
My daughter is just now reading Whitman for a class in college.

I am reminded of the long hallway in my grandmother's
house. The walls were covered with an orange-pink paper, em-

bossed as if it were silk, and the lamp was red glass. The hallway seemed endlessly long. I would run to the end of it whenever I was hurt and weep. In my memory this hallway is like an elongated uterine cave, a safe place, yet pulsing with unmanageable sorrow.

September
Among the poems he wrote on the war, "The Wound Dresser," so simple, straightforward:

> *From the stump of the arm, the amputated hand,*
> *I undo the clotted lint, remove the slough, wash off the*
> *   matter and blood. . . .*

What I remember is an overwhelming loneliness, yet I was not lonely for lack of company. There were my friends in the neighborhood and my grandparents. And the visits of my father. I was rarely alone. But I was in mourning. I was very young, but I had witnessed the disintegration of my family, and I had no language for that grief. No one would speak of it with me.

September
He catches it so well, that awful moment of suspended knowledge, when one cannot bear to know.

Recently I dreamed I was in my grandmother's house. I had inherited it, and I was changing the architecture.

September

> *His eyes are closed, his face is pale, he dares not look*
> *   on the bloody stump,*
> *And has not yet looked on it.*

A few years after her mother's death Charlotte's father falls in love with another woman. A famous opera singer, daughter of a rabbi. Charlotte is quickly infatuated with her father's new wife, called Paulinka in her story, who is beautiful, charming and accomplished. She has found a mother again, and at the same time a woman whose very nature opens up worlds for her. Those wider worlds that exist outside the private world of the home.

September
A few years ago one could easily have written, "the real Walt Whitman will never get in the books." That he was gay, a nurse during the Civil War, tender, almost motherly with wounded men, this was a buried story.

Had this opening existed for Charlotte's mother, would she have continued living? I know that my own mother felt confined in the smallness of domestic life. For a time she took courses in interior decorating. But she was discouraged by my father and her own parents in this. When I ask myself why she became an alcoholic, this is always among the answers.

September
My daughter learns in class that Whitman was homosexual. Buried stories coming to light. There is some hope in this.

Over time, as many women do, my mother became inseparable from her confinement. She was defined by all she could not do, and then never did and then feared doing. She lost the capacity to imagine any other life, until finally the life she had began to be her choice, as she remained inside her house, unemployed and unengaged in public life, private and shy in her manner. At last, it seemed as if this choice *were* she. Herself then interior, indecipherable, uncommunicative, forever turned away, a person inaccessible behind her private doors.

October

Last night I watched the celebration of the reunification of Germany. The ceremonies began at midnight in Berlin, in time for the evening news here. Fireworks in the sky over the Brandenburg Gate.

If there is a complaint from someone in this condition it is rarely articulated except paradoxically as if it were an extension of the condition itself. Madness. An addiction to pills. Hours of watching television. Drinking. Suicide. But of course, one says, this could have been predicted. This was in her. This is who she was.

October

The crowds in front of the old Reichstag sang the national anthem. The former words, "Deutschland, Deutschland über alles," now forbidden, replaced by new words, translated as, "Unity and justice and freedom for the German Fatherland."

In the ensuing part of her story Charlotte pictures herself as she attempts to escape the predictable female role. *Perhaps I could learn to draw, that might be just the thing.* The words accompany a painting of herself as a girl, bent over a desk, intently moving her brush.

October

The unification of Germany is only the latest in a whole series of events which were once thought to be impossible. Yet they are still singing "Fatherland."

But just as Charlotte discovers this new possibility within herself, events in the public world are taking an ominous shape. In one of the paintings that tell her story a red flag bearing a swastika is raised over a mass of uniformed soldiers, arranged in identical, neat lines. And in the corner of the frame a copy of *Der Stürmer* reads, *The Jew has betrayed and deceived you.*

October

Some things change and some do not. In Prague a playwright who has written Kafkaesque plays making fun of government bureaucracy has become head of state. Yet judging from letters he wrote in prison, his attitudes toward women are traditional.

Charlotte's father, a prominent surgeon, is expelled from the university where he teaches, despite the fact that his knowledge of new surgical methods could save many lives. Now he will only be allowed to work at the Jewish hospital. And her stepmother, a famous performer who has escaped Hitler's campaign to return women to the kitchen, does not escape anti-Semitism. She is assaulted by young storm troopers who shout from the audience, *Out—get out—out—get out.*

October

It is difficult to say how things will turn out. But one thing is certain. The old opposition between East and West, the polarity through which the world was once explained, has broken down.

Charlotte pleads to go to art school, but her stepmother, wishing something practical for her, enrolls her in a school of fashion design. What is she thinking? She is an artist herself. But the times have changed. Women cannot rely on men to support them. And there is a depression.

October

No one knows quite what to expect.

I remember my father's attempt to convince me that I should go to secretarial school instead of college. It was assumed that I would need a way to earn a living. And how else could a woman earn a living except as a secretary? But to me even the thought of secretarial school made me bitter. I was determined not to submit to this plan.

October
Last spring Veronica, just returned from Berlin, told me that all over
the city, and particularly along the Kurfürstendamm, you could hear the
sound of stone being chipped away.

Was there anything more behind Paulinka's choice for Charlotte? Could it be that she felt competitive with her young step-
daughter? Or was it some richer mix of emotions, including that
odd dissociation that so many successful women have toward
young women trying to escape the common female fate?

October
For several months now I have saved a photograph of the half-fallen
wall because it reminds me of a day I spent there two years ago, when the
wall seemed like it would be a permanent landmark.

Charlotte persists in the direction of what she wants. She fails
in the school of design and the school of fine arts has turned down
her application. But she takes drawing lessons. Her teacher will
not let her rest until she succeeds in completing a realistic rendering of a cactus, which includes every stalk. And so finally she
passes the entrance requirements of the school she wants to attend.

October
I stood on the steps of the Gropius Museum with Hella as we looked
into the windows of offices just across the wall. We were on our way to the
old Gestapo headquarters, which had just recently been excavated.

It was in this period of her life, while she was longing and
preparing to be an artist, that she met Alfred Wolfsohn. He was a
music teacher with radical and new ideas about the process of
creation. Because he was Jewish, during the Third Reich it was
difficult for him to find work. He was introduced to Charlotte's
stepmother by an old friend of hers who was attempting to help
Jewish artists in such circumstances. Paulinka, moved by his stories

of suffering in the First World War, and perhaps also because she was drawn to him, hired him to give her lessons.

October

The wall seemed so strange, a barrier rising up suddenly in the midst of a neighborhood, the buildings on the other side so close we could see in the windows.

Wolfsohn's new theories about art were inspired by his experiences as a stretcher-bearer in the war. He came out of the war shell-shocked, and he had lost much of his memory. What he could not forget, however, were the voices of the men who lay wounded and dying on the battlefield. In particular one voice returned to haunt him, a voice he heard for two days crying out for help. He could not crawl to him. He had had to ignore this plea, to save his own life.

October

Hella, the friend of a friend, part of a group working for peace, was shepherding me through the city. In the old Gestapo building, now a kind of museum, we watched films of a man being beaten. And she wept. I realized then her pain was double; she suffered both as a witness to this brutality, and as a German.

Survival when others have perished brings its own suffering. The question inevitably poses itself, *Why was I chosen to live?* In the wake of this question, it is a comfort to discover something unique one might give to the world.

October

That story C. told me, when she was visiting from Germany. How after several years of a seemingly contented life, married with children, she hit a wall within herself, and could not continue. She left her marriage and eventually began a search into her past.

Wolfsohn felt that to heal himself he had to explore his own voice. In the cries of the dying he had heard a range of the human voice beyond all conventional expectation. Men with untrained voices cried out in the highest soprano notes, a pitch believed to belong only to women. He studied with a series of voice teachers until finally one of them allowed him to express his feelings with his singing. But no teacher was willing to explore with him the extremities of the human capacity which he had found on the battlefield. He believed this larger capacity would reflect the fullest dimensions of the human soul.

October

She had always known her father had been in the Gestapo, but now the meaning of that became clearer to her. It was hard to reconcile this with her memory of him—he was the more affectionate parent, full of life, playful—until, one day a memory returned of how he beat her as a child. She had forgotten this side of her father.

Over time Wolfsohn developed his own method of teaching voice. What was it like to study with him? His methods are still being taught at the Roy Hart Theatre in the South of France. A few years ago I visited this theatre, which is mostly a school. I wanted to meet Marita Guenther. She is the senior teacher there; she studied with Wolfsohn for years. And she became his lover.

October

First cold day. The last of our Indian summer this week. Different layers of distrust peeling away. I can feel how most of my life my whole psyche has been organized around fear.

The morning we met it was pouring rain, then hailing, and then the sun came out, bright, even hot. *Isn't it beautiful?* Marita said, throwing open the windows of the room so we could see the weather directly. Her voice, even speaking, was so rich and vibrant it bordered on music. *We have everything here,* she said, mean-

ing the weather in the region in France known as the *Cévennes,*
I'm so glad you are seeing all the possibilities.

October
     Nan and I move in and out of an extraordinary and sometimes
frightening trust.

How did she come to know Alfred Wolfsohn? She herself was
German, raised in Leipzig, and Wolfsohn was a second cousin of
her mother, but she never met him in Germany. She only came to
know him after the war, in England, where he took refuge and
where she emigrated when the danger was past. Wolfsohn was
Jewish, but her situation was more ambiguous. Her grandmother
on her mother's side was Jewish. Therefore, according to Nazi
logic, her papers were stamped *25% J.*

October
     Is it because we both suffered such severities in childhood that we can
be so close? There are also, of course, those hellish moments when we
evoke each other's nightmare—mine of being locked out, hers of being
locked in.

Like me, Marita was raised by her mother's parents. She remembers one day when, after her grandmother's death, her uncle
came to visit. He was an actor, who was considered by the Nazis
half Jewish, and so he was being denied parts in the theatre. She
overheard him arguing with her grandfather in the next room
about all the atrocities, including his own unemployment. But her
grandfather was a Bismarckian who still believed in empire and
emperors. *Don't talk like that,* he told his son. *These are the rumors of*
warmongers.

October
     Now I can see how deeply history is implicated in the pattern of self-
destruction in my family.

Was Marita's grandfather aware that the Nazis were accusing the Jews of being warmongers? Later, she did learn that her own father was anti-Semitic. She had discovered the terrors of history within her own family. It is not surprising then that in 1949, when she was twenty-one years old, she left her family and country both.

October

A history which no one in the family questioned. We were as if victims of an impersonal force, beyond and above us.

On an earlier trip to Europe, in Germany, I was told another story about a man who had one Jewish grandparent, a grandfather. He himself was allowed to be in the army and he had a record of heroic action. He thought this might allow him to save his grandfather. He went to the Gestapo to plead for his grandfather's life but was literally thrown into the street. Years later he became a serious alcoholic and then he committed suicide. The woman who told me this was his good friend, the daughter of a Nazi general and, later, an active member of the generation of conscience in Germany that tried to bring the events of the holocaust to public light.

October

This joke told in a cabaret in the new Germany, "A wonderful future lies behind us."

I myself have an ambiguous status. Perhaps my great-grandmother was Jewish. This cannot be known. But stronger than any such possibility is the reality I experienced as a girl, adopted into a Jewish family. This bonded me to the particular history of a people. Yet I am not Jewish. I have another history too. I belong either no place, or in two places at once. Thus I have come to understand both the freedom and the strange vulnerability of exile.

October
It is so satisfying to put into words what has not been expressed
before, whether it is comedy or tragedy, a small or a large meaning.

Marita knew no one in England. But before she emigrated her
mother gave her the name of her cousin. He was in London, and
she was in the countryside working as an *au pair,* with too few
days off to visit him and almost no money. Still, after she arrived
she sent him a letter. It would be comforting to have even the
most minimal contact with anyone who knew something of her
history.

October
What then distinguishes this process of writing from Himmler's fanat-
ical record keeping?

Weeks went by with no response and she finally assumed he
had no interest in meeting her. But he was away, and now, as she
reconstructs it, she believes he was in Amsterdam, visiting Charlotte's father and stepmother, who had just returned from Villefranche where they found Charlotte's work, *Life or Theatre?*

October
What seems clear to me is that Himmler used his records not to reflect
but to replace experience.

Wolfsohn wrote her immediately upon his return and they
were able, over time, to arrange a visit. The man she met capti-
vated her. He seemed to call up in her, as he had in Charlotte, the
depths of herself and her own longings. He convinced her to take
a voice lesson. And this first lesson changed her life.

October
I wanted to add this to the fourth chapter. But it proved impossible.
As Reichsführer SS, head of the secret police, Himmler organized a crude

information retrieval system. Index cards stored on an enclosed mecha-
nized wheel could be brought to hand by pushing a series of buttons.

Marita spoke to me of this experience in the way that a religious pilgrim speaks of revelation. There is no language adequate
to what she experienced. Except the image of a vein of gold
inside her, and somehow within her voice. I have had such experiences. One comes upon a new body within the familiar body.
And yet this new body, strange as it is, seems to be the rightful
body, a body that opens out further and further to worlds one has
dreamed or imagined at the fringes of reason might exist, a territory at once expansive and unknown and yet near, close as a lover,
ready, willing.

October
It is perhaps a choice each of us makes over and over, even many times
throughout one day, whether to use knowledge as power or intimacy.

So powerful was the knowledge she drew from Wolfsohn's
lessons that from that hour forward her life began to move in a
different direction. It was not easy to follow the path that opened
up for her. Risking unemployment and poverty in this still strange
country, she moved to London. Eventually she found work as an
usher in a movie theatre. And every hour not at work was spent
studying with Wolfsohn.

October
All along as I write, I have Charlotte's images in my mind. It is not
simply the recognizable shapes, faces, moments that move me. I am im-
mersed in the colors she used, and the vitality of her compositions become
part of the atmosphere of my body.

The hours were long and tiring, but she had something to
sustain her that she had not had before. Within her own throat,
tongue, mouth, ears, and indeed all her flesh and bones she had

found a medium resonant with her deepest being, even that which in herself was not yet fully formed.

November
More astonishing to me than any technological achievement is the simple fact that a human hand holding a pencil or a brush can render in a few lines or washes of color a state of feeling, an insight, layers of history.

Twice I observed Marita giving a lesson. The approach is simple. Why is this so often the case when the effects are powerful? The singer is asked to make sounds. Nothing must be held back. Nothing censored. The whole body is engaged. In the beginning the aim is not control but instead an exploration of every possibility, even if the sounds are unpleasant. So the sounds the singer makes are unconventional, even ugly. They are not on any scale. They transgress.

November
I am thinking about smart bombs.

By this process the voice is liberated from the boundaries of culture. It makes a terrible sense that Wolfsohn should have discovered this method in the midst of a war that seemed to be tearing civilization to pieces. And he was no bystander to that disintegration. The destruction that occurred among nations continued after the war in his own mind. He had lost part of his memory. It happened after he was discovered under a pile of bodies.

November
I find the idea of a smart bomb intriguing. If it is true that social institutions like the military can make wishes, would this represent a wish for a more refined, subtle intelligence, the intelligence that we are after all born with, and then over time relinquish?

What was it like for Wolfsohn to lose part of his memory? I have some idea from the illness which, though it is in my immune system, also affects my mind at times. It is as if pieces of oneself were missing. The forgotten word, the incident, the name is present just enough to feel its absence. One has a sense of being that cannot be put into words, and so that part of the self exists in a neighboring world, close yet inaccessible.

November

I remember the stunning moment when, in our small seminar on nuclear technology, Emilio Segré, who was speaking to us that day, pulled a small tube, less than half a meter long, from his jacket pocket. This was the first particle accelerator. In that moment one could see so dramatically that the most important ingredient in atomic research is the human mind.

One can imagine why he would not be able to remember. He had lost consciousness. He was in a coma. But even in a coma, some part of him would have taken in all he felt and heard. Did the stretcher-bearers who carried him discuss his death? Did he struggle as in nightmares one struggles to call out when no voice comes? Did he wake at once or in fitful starts, taking in the rancid smell of rotting flesh, the feeling of cold limbs, his eye perhaps open on a gaping wound, a mutilation? To be taken for dead and wake among the dead; such an experience requires a second birth.

November

What an irony that nuclear weapons, which spring from such creative insights, should reduce the warrior to a technician.

But this birth is not into a new body. It is into an older body, the body of origin, body of birth, the body before it has been socialized out of its own knowledge of itself. In this sense Wolfsohn's insights were not isolated. He was part of a larger movement trying to regain this body. A movement that included

Isadora Duncan, Wilhelm Reich, Ida Rolf, Elsa Gindler, Gerda Alexander, Ilsa Middendorf, and later Moishe Feldenkrais, Emilie Conrad Da'Oud. Like Wolfsohn, many of these pioneers came to discover this original body when they faced a physical crisis. Elsa Gindler was told she was dying of tuberculosis; Ida Rolf nearly died of pneumonia. Feldenkrais was told he would be disabled for the rest of his life.

November
Yesterday, driving over the bridge, I was exhilarated.

Among these practitioners, many believed the body holds memories of hidden traumas. As the body is healed those memories come to the surface. Then earlier and forgotten feelings must be expressed. Stories told.

November
How frightening, when I could not drive my car, when I could scarcely walk across a room! It brought back to me the feeling of being a small child, and the trauma of abandonment.

It is a method used now to heal the survivors of sexual abuse and torture. The survivor tells the story of suffering over and over to a listener who will hear and respond to all that happened. The compassion of the listener is crucial. Is this because part of the trauma is the cruelty and coldness of the perpetrator? The survivor has been humiliated and blamed as well as physically wounded. The one who listens provides an accepting field for the story. An essential dimension. Moment by moment we help each other to see.

November
I put my hand to my face. My skin is soft in the way it used to be. The touch, pleasure. It is a feeling I could never have described when it

was gone, but nevertheless I longed for it. The body remembers who we are supposed to be. And in this there is grief.

When Marita teaches voice she is entirely present to her students. She goes with them into the treacherous regions. She does not reject the difficulties but encourages her students to explore these while she accompanies them. If the voice is cracking the singer does not go around that crack so much as enter it. The world inside that opening, a world that in all probability has been avoided for years, is rich with meaning. But it is also dense with troubling memory, sharp and disturbing emotion, and even the painful sensation of a prisoner, long held in darkness, waking into light.

November
More troops have been sent to the gulf. I find it hard to take in. Is this because I am feeling so much joy in my own life?

It was just this understanding that inside the cracks in the conventional surface a wider and healing awareness might be found which was to have a profound influence on Charlotte's life. Much as I sat in the corner of a studio watching as Marita gave a lesson, Charlotte depicts herself as a young girl standing near a door secretly ajar; listening to Alfred Wolfsohn give her stepmother lessons.

November
Thinking of this is like one of those paintings in which the light is very intense and the shadows very dark.

Charlotte's relationship to Wolfsohn is not unequivocal. In her story she depicts him as trying to seduce her stepmother, and she pictures her stepmother responding. She herself adores her stepmother almost like a lover. She is jealous of other suitors, even friends. But this time her jealousy extends in two directions. With the passion of a lover, she wants her stepmother's exclusive love, but she also wants to be her stepmother. That is, she wants to be an artist. Does Wolfsohn possess the power to confer this fate upon her?

November
Much joy in my life now. And intimations of another way of being.

Charlotte meets frequently with Wolfsohn and she shows him her work. He is the first person who takes her seriously. He encourages her by asking her to illustrate his manuscript as a birthday present to him. But this guardian who bears her into the world of art has two faces. Making love to her stepmother, he also seduces Charlotte. Then we discover he is also engaged to another woman!

November
I can see in myself the glimmering of a possibility. To shed the fear I have carried around for so long.

Was this part of the story true? Marita told me she believed Charlotte's paintings. She had never met her, of course. By the time Alfred Wolfsohn came into Marita's life, Charlotte had already died in Auschwitz. But years later, after Wolfsohn's death, a team of filmmakers and writers approached Marita wanting to know all she could remember of Wolfsohn, and what he might have told her about Charlotte. She traveled with them to Amsterdam, where Charlotte's work had been preserved, and spent hours studying each painting. Charlotte's stepmother, who was also interviewed by the filmmakers, claimed the story was not true. *It was fictional, wasn't it?* The names were altered. She said she was never Wolfsohn's lover and doubted that Charlotte could have been. My own inclination, like Marita's, is to believe Charlotte's story; though in the end, as a work of art, what matters is its verisimilitude. Certainly it is a story that is resonant with other lives. It is one I myself recognize.

November
That fear of rejection. Of being left out in the cold. Is it possible that could leave me?

The memory is painful because within it is a kind of humiliation I like to believe I have put far behind me. I am a young woman. I have written a play. The director I show it to was once a lover. Now, without reading it, he takes the play in one hand and with his other hand leads me into the bedroom. I comply. I go with him.

November
I read in the papers today that Samuel Kramer died. He was the great Sumerian scholar who a few years ago, together with the storyteller Diane Wolkstein, wrote a modern rendition of the ancient Inanna myth. The goddess who descends to the underworld and has everything taken from her.

A woman who becomes an artist is a kind of thief. Like the Jewish artist who is seen by the anti–Semite as stealing culture, she breaks the trance of domination by the very practice of her art. It follows then that a young woman who tries to become an artist would also become the object of a sexual conquest.

Charlotte's story is not, however, a simple story of victimization. The violator is also the teacher, the enabler. What he has taught survives and perhaps can even be freed of all traces of the spell of violation. The teacher himself, also, is more than just a violator. He is attractive precisely because he has pulled himself halfway out of delusion. He is only partly submerged in the old order of domination. His insights have come to him through a crack in the veneer of civilization, which was also a crack in his own soul. He had the courage to look in this direction.

November
I saw Diane perform this text in New York a few years ago. It was a
harrowing time for me. A long relationship ending, my daughter in a crisis
of adolescence, and the old demons of my childhood returned.

Charlotte has painted a picture of Wolfsohn looking at one of
her paintings. Here she writes, *In this moment he almost becomes a*
delicate young girl himself. Later she depicts him in one of his many
philosophical moods as he dreams of moving beyond the boundaries of gender. Hoping for a time when men and women will
become a single being, he envisions the heroine of a new age as a
young girl who will face her own depths.

November
It was an astonishing performance, and I felt myself becoming Inanna,
slipping into the underworld, my flesh stripped from my bones, left hang-
ing in a terror of suspension.

But under this idealized vision is a darker image. He does not
really accept young girls as they are. Sitting across from Charlotte
at a café table, he tells her to try to control her face. He does not
like to see what she is feeling all of the time. Does she mirror back
to him too much of his own vulnerability, his volatile moods, his
sense of insecurity as a Jew in Nazi Germany, an artist with unconventional ideas? Though, according to Charlotte, he becomes
her lover, he treats her publicly like a bothersome child. When she
brings him the illustrations she has worked so hard to render for
his birthday, he leaves hurriedly without even bothering to look
at what she has given him. He may wish to incorporate the feminine into himself, but he also rejects this capacity.

November
According to Kramer's obituary, his work began when he went on an
archaeological expedition to the ruins of Ur, Kish, and Uruk, the ancient

walled city that was home to Gilgamesh. These sites are all in the country that is now called Iraq.

I am thinking now of my own generation, coming of age in the decade of the sixties. It was fashionable then in the alternative culture for men to wear long hair, feathers and beads and even, at times, caftan-like gowns. In this way a certain androgynous appearance was achieved. But this union was accomplished more in the manner of an empire annexing a colony than that of an equal union. Women did not have respect in this milieu. Rather the evocation of the feminine as a primordial power of nature had been claimed as part of the masculine signature.

November
The history of warfare and poetry have been intertwined for centuries.
The Iliad. *The* Aeneid. *Samurai poetry.* El Cid. Gilgamesh.

Charlotte's story begins in a period between the two great wars. A menacing public history has been unfolding at the edge of her private story. Until, finally, members of Himmler's Gestapo show up at Charlotte's front door searching for her father, whom they take away to a concentration camp.

November
From a recent translation of Gilgamesh, *this beginning: "The one who saw the abyss . . . who saw things secret, opened the place hidden." That was when the journey of the warrior was symbolic of a soul journey.*

Charlotte is trapped as if by a vise, one arm of which is the torment of her private life and the other the danger of the public world. Wolfsohn has become a permanent resident in her family's apartment. She pictures herself at the doorway not wishing to enter. Inside, her sometime lover alternately grabs at her and shunts her aside whenever her stepmother and his beloved appears. She longs to go out to a café, but Jews are forbidden these public spaces.

November
Over Thanksgiving the President and his wife travel to the Persian Gulf. They sit with soldiers on top of tanks eating Thanksgiving dinner.

Although Charlotte's stepmother does succeed in using her influence to win the release of her husband, Berlin has become very dangerous for anyone who is Jewish. The decision is made to send Charlotte to live with her grandparents, who are living in exile in Villefranche, near Nice, in the South of France, as guests of a wealthy American woman.

November
I read that the troops have been carefully instructed about how they must treat Bush. Those allowed to eat with the President and his wife have been carefully selected.

In the beginning it seems to Charlotte that she has finally found a safe haven. High on a cliff the silvery leaves of a pepper tree are blowing in the wind. Beneath her the Mediterranean Sea seems to reflect her dreams on its blue surface. As she paints, looking into the waves, she asks, *What makes you shape and reshape yourself so brightly from so much pain and suffering? Who gave you the right?*

November
The President's wife wears battle fatigues.

It may be that her grandparents are sometimes less than understanding. *Are you here in the world only to paint?* her grandfather asks, and suggests she ought to work as a housemaid. On the other hand, her grandmother, who wishes to protect her from that fate, wants her to meet a young man. But despite these pressures, she is in a place where she can do her work, and she is coming into her own.

November
I can easily imagine Barbara Bush as a field commander, raising binoculars to her eyes, as she calmly surveys the field.

Yet the troubles of the world have not disappeared. Charlotte and her grandparents listen nightly to the radio. They can hear Hitler's speeches. They can hear the progress of the violence as it closes in around them. The harrowing sorrow of her grandmother, cast for some time into a fragile abeyance, returns to center stage along with news of the raging war. She sinks further and further into a depression. Fearing she will go mad, she tries to hang herself.

November
No doubt the allure of crossing over the line into masculine territory made uniforms attractive to me as a child. Did my father feel more manly in his blue firefighter's uniform?

How is it that in the past I did not put together the two histories which I lived through to make one history? Now I can see clearly that my mother's alcoholism and the small suicides of omission practiced by my father are part of the history of the Second World War and the Cold War that followed. That terrible stunning violence and then the silencing pall which proceeded from it did not stop at the doorsteps of our homes. Everyone became less visible, less.

November
One day public opinion polls announce that the only reason Americans would support a war would be to prevent Iraq from having nuclear weapons. And the next day Bush announces this as the principal reason for going to war.

It is now that Charlotte finally learns the truth about her family history. Struck by the pain and panic of his wife's attempt at suicide, her grandfather blurts out the real story. *Your mother,* he tells her, *and your aunt Charlotte, and your grandmother's brother, and your great-grandmother and your cousins all committed suicide.*

December
Very little rain still. The days are very short now. Red sunsets made more brilliant by pollution, yet still so beautiful.

Charlotte's mother was just one in a chain reaction of deaths within her family. In her work in progress about Charlotte's life and work, Mary Felstiner points out that the suicide rate in Germany was high. And rising among upper-middle-class women, and among Jews. The first one to die in this manner was Charlotte's grandmother's brother. Why? He had shown signs of madness. Unmotivated laughter. Depression. So the family kept him isolated until he recovered. Then his mother pushed him into an unhappy marriage with a wealthy woman.

December
Long conversation with my sister. She is exploring the possibility that our father abused her. This would explain so much in her life.

Were there other hidden causes behind this death? What if his marriage was unhappy for another reason? Not only because he did not like his wife, but that he did not want to be married to a woman at all. I am thinking of the film *Anders als die Andern (Different from the Others)* produced in Germany in 1919. The movie begins as the hero reads about the suicides of three men, each for no apparent reason. But the hero of this film feels he knows the cause. They are victims of society's repression of homosexuals. By the end of the film, the hero himself commits suicide, stricken by the same prejudice.

December
The thought of this creates such disturbing emotions in me. I have no
memory nor even a vague sense of having been molested by my father.
And yet I felt he was in love with me in some way that embarrassed him.

Neither is it apparent if perhaps Charlotte's aunt, the first
Charlotte, felt the sting of anti-Semitism more than Franziska,
Charlotte's mother, who was fair in coloring and perhaps less
subject to bigotry. Or was it possible that the family internalized
some of this attitude, and showed a subtle form of favor to one
daughter? I know I received a certain special attention as a child
because I was blond.

If my sister was abused, was I a witness to this? How I wish I knew
the truth now. Terrible conflict. My father's love sustained me as a child.

How deeply prejudice of any kind etches its way into being
until the presence need hardly be named. What is left is an amorphous feeling of inferiority whose origin can no longer be traced.
The distinction between privately and publicly inflicted wounds
can hardly be made. They are blended in one life, one psyche, one
body into the same pattern of pain, which can even seem, after a
time, to be self-inflicted.

December
A conference about the Hanford Experiment. In 1949, the govern-
ment released large amounts of radiation into the air. A secret experiment,
meant to determine the size of the Soviet nuclear arsenal. In an airport
hotel I sit at a round table with survivors and listen as they tell stories of
exposure and illness.

Charlotte pictures herself as a girl in a moment of despair
standing by the window of her home in Berlin as she contem-
plates jumping. Wolfsohn has failed to acknowledge her birthday
gift, and he has rejected her. First she throws her money out of

the window. Then she thinks of throwing herself out too. But she tells herself that the fellow is not worth it. And besides, someday he will tell her that he likes her paintings. This is reason enough to go on living.

December

Across the table from me sits a woman who clearly had not connected her own illness with the experiment before this moment. She grows more pale with each story, and finally hides her face in her hands and weeps.

Now, once again it is her work that will save her. First she uses Wolfsohn's teachings in an attempt to give her grandmother hope. For a moment, her grandmother springs to a new vitality. But it does not last. The moment she is left alone she jumps to her death. Now, alone with her grandfather, who is bitter and selfish, mourning her grandmother's death, exiled and in danger from an advancing hostile army, confronted with a terrible family secret, she must act to save herself.

December

The symptoms the survivors describe are all so familiar to me. The coldness. Legs suddenly weak, almost as if paralyzed. The nervous system off balance. Numbness. Loss of memory.

Her life is in danger from two directions. From her own hand as directed by her family history, and from the hands of others, as directed by our shared history.

December

As disturbing as they are, there is a strange comfort for me in hearing the stories of these survivors. To hear the inner life, the suffering of the body, spoken.

Since just before the war the South of France had become a refuge for those fleeing the Gestapo. The control of France near

the Italian border passed from the Vichy to the Italian government. For many reasons, including their resistance to German
domination, the Italians refused to carry out the German order to
deport Jews. Because of this Villefranche was safe. But this was
just a temporary safety. Near the end of the war, the Italians
signed a separate armistice with the Allies, and because of this
their armies were soon in retreat from the Germans. Now the area
where Charlotte was exiled fell under German occupation. The
Gestapo began a ruthless search of the area. Driven by revenge,
they searched every hotel and boarding room, arresting all and
beating anyone who even looked Jewish.

December
I think of the years of atmosphere testing, and my own illness. Radia-
tion damages the immunity of the cell.

Sometime in the midst of this terrible history Charlotte and
her grandfather were arrested. They were taken to Gurs, a labor
camp in France. But the miraculous took place. Because he was ill
Charlotte's grandfather was judged unfit for work. He was sent
home, and Charlotte too was released so that she could care for
him.

December
That dream I had. A child threatened by a murderer on the loose.
Finally a man in a uniform arrives. He is a fireman like my father. I am
relieved because he is here to rescue the child. But then I see he is the
murderer.

The chronology of her narration is unclear. The original order of the paintings has been lost. I do not know if it was before or
after their arrest that Charlotte said to her grandfather, *You know*
. . . I have the feeling the whole world has to be put together again. To
which her grandfather bitterly responds, *Oh, go ahead and kill*

yourself and put an end to all this babble. In another frame they are on a crowded train. Is this the train they rode to the camp? Here, Charlotte confesses that she would rather be crowded uncomfortably among strangers than shut up in a room alone with her grandfather.

December

I had this dream years ago and I have never forgotten it.

After some time, her grandfather will die. She will meet another refugee from Germany. Become pregnant with his child. Marry him. And then she will be arrested again, and this time deported to Auschwitz, where she too will die. Most of her great work, *Life or Theatre?* will be completed between these two arrests.

December

A card from Israel, from Shirley, arrives. Camel saddled in gold moving among palm trees. She has reservations to fly here at the end of January but is not certain she wants to leave Israel during the crisis. "Wish we weren't so anxious here," she writes, "it casts a pall over everything."

In the epilogue to her story Charlotte writes, *She found herself facing the question of whether to commit suicide or to undertake something wildly eccentric.* She chooses the second course. It is a decision I understand, yet perhaps the courage is not so obvious. She is moving against the direction of history. It is like taking a train off the tracks on which it has traveled for so many years that the sound of its whistle, the color of the engine, the steam curling in the air over it, have literally shaped your days ever since you can remember. You have timed your waking with this train. You have learned at what hour you must return home. You have sat down to meals with its music in your ears. You have ridden it so often your feet can move by themselves through the station without a conscious thought. Once the train has changed its path the landscape, which you can hardly separate from your own body, will seem fractured, torn, wrong.

December
She sends a poem with her note. In it are these words: "The dead are so light."

To make such a change requires more than blunt bravery. Something, some new knowledge, must replace what is lost. She recalls her teacher and his admonition to her that, in order to go out of oneself, one must go deep into oneself. Now when Wolfsohn returns to her in her dream, he reminds her of the painting she did as a girl called *Death and the Maiden*. And from this she realizes she need not commit suicide. For she can make another kind of descent, into the depths, and return, resurrected.

December
Is it true that there may actually be a war? I can't help feeling it is all shadow boxing. Powerful men making threats they will not carry out. Is this wishful thinking?

Before she begins her work she draws a picture of Wolfsohn and then tears it to pieces. Only after this can she hear his teachings in her dream. She offers no explanation of this destruction. But I am imagining that she has destroyed her seducer, and her compliant love for him. This destruction makes it possible for her to use what he has taught her now about art and salvation.

December
The polls still show a majority against the war. And then there is the hope Congress will slow the machinery down, and give the economic sanctions time to work.

Now with *dream-awakened eyes* she sees all the beauty around her. The blue sea and the warm sun. And she knows what her work is. She will remove herself from ordinary life, so that she can create her world *as new out of the depths*. She will paint and write the story of her life.

December
Most of the hostages have been released. But Iraq has not withdrawn from Kuwait. Debate in Congress over whether or not the international boycott is working.

It was from the publisher of Charlotte's book *Life or Theatre?* that Marita learned Charlotte sang as she painted. The concierge of a hotel in Villefranche wrote this to him. Charlotte had rented a room at this hotel where she might work in peace, free from her grandfather's demands. The concierge hardly even saw Charlotte, who was adamant that she did not want to be disturbed. But every day she would leave a bowl of soup outside Charlotte's door. And that was when she could hear her singing.

December
The beginnings of a peace movement. It is déjà vu. It's been twenty years since the war in Vietnam. I can measure my life this way. World War II. Korea. Vietnam. And throughout, the Cold War.

Charlotte was working at a furious pace. The work accelerates as it nears the end, the drawings becoming more simple, brush strokes hurried. She must have known she did not have much time.

December
Long discussions about the deeper reasons for the war. Oil. The banking interests of wealthy Kuwaitis in the United States. The armaments industry.

Looking back, I want to call to her, to alarm her about the ensuing danger. But of course she knew. Why else would she so carefully pack up her paintings in a suitcase and take them to her friend, the doctor in Villefranche, to be hidden.

December
And it is perhaps also a fear of what the Buddhists call emptiness. The void left by the end of the Cold War. We have no crisis to define us any more.

The doctor in Villefranche urged her not to try to marry her lover, that it was too dangerous. He advised her to flee with the other refugees into the mountains behind Nice, to hide with the others in one of the small villages near the Italian border. Some of the refugees who hid there did survive.

December
Hussein is making the demand that the territories occupied by Israel after the Six-Day War be returned to the Palestinians.

It is so easy now, in the safety of my study, to think about ways she might have escaped. I have a book which tells me in black and white which route of escape was successful. But nothing was so clear at that moment in history. Any decision might be the wrong decision.

December
I have finally found a book of poems by Mahmoud Darweesh, the Palestinian poet Shirley told me about.

Perhaps if she had dropped her brushes a few pages earlier. Perhaps if she had made what now seems so clear was the right decision, and escaped into the mountains. Yet, as I place myself in her shoes, I can feel the passion of her work. It is a work that will not be interrupted.

December
Shirley told me he is very close to Arafat and has written some of the famous statements of the PLO.

I am imagining her state of mind as she worked. The story of her mother's suicide is still ringing in her ears. It is as if a mirror has shattered. None of the fragments of who she is or who her mother was will come together. And who is her father now, this father who has lied to her? She dips her brush into cerulean blue and strokes a river into place, the river where the first Charlotte drowned.

December
They read their poems together from the same platform at a conference in Rotterdam.

Bit by bit she reconstructs her world. The line of her father's mouth the day he returned from the concentration camp. Paulinka's strange smile as she gazed at Wolfsohn. Her own sadness folded into the contours of the house of her childhood. Each image is like a tiny flame and she is drawn into this light which, if once it was like the dying embers at the site of a conflagration, is now the first sign of new life.

December
Before the reading, at their first meeting, Darweesh greeted her in Hebrew.

As slowly the mirror reassembles, the clarity of her vision sharpens. Hasty thoughts thrown to cover the gaping place where something she seems to have always known yet had no words for pulling her down into a spiral, throwing the composition into chaos, disperse now and the pattern of meaning becomes clear. The atmosphere of the room, her paint, the canvas, brush are charged with excitement, and this, despite all that goes on around her, borders on joy.

December
That haunting image from the First World War. German and English soldiers meeting between the trenches to celebrate Christmas.

The colors she used are still vibrant. You can go to see her work today in the Jewish Museum of Amsterdam. The ocean so blue near Nice. The air filled with the most brilliant light. *The war raged on,* she wrote, *and there I sat by the sea and saw deeply into people's hearts.*

December
The sense of absurdity which descended between the wars. One can well understand it. The fashionable debauchery of that time, which Hemingway records in The Sun Also Rises. *My mother grew up in this atmosphere. Adulated her parents. Said when they would dress up to go out drinking they looked like movie stars. Her alcoholism part of the history of war.*

After she liberated herself from her private history, what would this young, newly delivered life become? There was not enough time to know. Except to say that in the end what one might call a private history is not so private after all. Though I was born in another country, Charlotte's story reaches as if into the recesses of my own secrets. And I am wondering now, do any of us have enough time?

December
As with any of the stories in the book, I have had to read and write and tell Charlotte's story many times. Only by doing this does it become mine.

I would like to end the book here but I cannot. It is fitting that I treat Charlotte's story as a war story. She died in the holocaust. Now, nuclear holocaust makes us all targets of war. But there is also the soldier's story.

December
It is a delicate balance, telling someone else's story, entering another life, identifying, feeling as this other might have felt, and yet remaining aware that a boundary exists over which one cannot step.

Soldiers continue to wage war in the old way. Yes, the technologies are increasingly sophisticated. But still there are those who place their bodies in the way of weapons and aim their own weapons at others. And what is even more true is that the idea of the soldier remains as a fixture of all our thought, so that in some way each of us is both civilian and soldier. In the full understanding of ourselves, the story of the soldier is also our own.

December
Writing about one's own life, it is only when one writes about the most intimate and seemingly idiosyncratic details that one touches others.

What I wanted above all in this last chapter was to render a portrait of the war story, and to do this by portraying the storyteller. And so I thought of Ernest Hemingway.

December
Is this because it is private and hidden feelings one longs to hear expressed?

In the beginning I did not know that Hemingway's real experience in warfare had been exaggerated as part of his public image. He served in the ambulance corps in Italy near the end of the First World War. He was under fire in that war only once and then just for a few minutes before he was wounded in the leg; he spent the remainder of the war in a hospital.

December
I like the feeling of intimacy in a journal. Pajamas. Unmade bed. Breakfast dishes. Body smells.

Yet, even so, it was not so much the documentation of the experience of the soldier I wanted as the creation of the myth. And for this Hemingway was perfect. He created a legend in which he performed the principal and heroic role.

December
The starched uniform of the soldier a counterbalance to the terrible intimacy of ruptured flesh.

Hemingway's literary style became the voice for the Lost Generation, a term which described the generation that had come of age during the Great War and been embittered by it. But as I came of age, his voice embodied the masculine ideal. Laconic. Tough. Tight-jawed. Humphrey Bogart was the perfect actor to play one of his heroes in *To Have and Have Not.*

December
*Hemingway's great influence on our generation. The language. That story David Lueck told me (cut from the fifth chapter). How as a boy he hung a map of the battlefields of World War II in his room. (His hero, Douglas MacArthur.) Before he was twenty-one, he was fighting in Korea, and, while he was there, reading—*A Farewell to Arms.

Hemingway was the paradigmatic American writer, fishing in the waters off Havana, or, his beret pulled slightly lower on one side, cigarette in his mouth, typing his latest account of a bullfight or recreating the landscape of a battlefield from memory.

January 1991
In one way it seems strange to be going on vacation now. In midwinter, mid-crisis, to a warm, lush island in the Pacific Ocean.

There were many coincidental connections between Charlotte's and Hemingway's story.

January
Looking at the surface of the sea, one would never guess at all that lies underneath.

January
Continually, a sweet scent in the air. Shedding clothes, tensions, fears. Everything sways here like the ocean. So evident, a maternal feel to the earth. My body bellying out, because of age, health returning. I like the feel of it. Breast heavy.

January
Reading Hemingway in the midst of all this. Detect a sharply divided response to pleasure in him.

January
A beauty that tears one open.

January
We watch the news. Every day brings us closer to the deadline for an invasion.

January
Feeling close to the origin of existence here. Mud on the slope, palm fronds on the path smeared with it, lizards, ancient land animals, creatures in the sea looking like pure protoplasm, earliest ancestors.

January

So much childbirth in Hemingway's stories. Especially in his war stories.

January

Eating breakfast in our room, we watch the Senate debate on television. Senator from New Jersey offers an eloquent argument for extending the period of economic sanctions. Meeting violence without violence!

January

The vote taken while we slept, we wake to find that Congress has given the President the right to declare war immediately after the fifteenth.

January

A turtle swims to shore just a few yards from us. I've never seen one so close. But it moves too slowly. A man on the beach tells us all the turtles on this beach have some kind of tumor.

January

On the news channel they show men training with live ammunition in the desert at night, the landscape lit with greenish floodlights and shell bursts. It looks like the moon.

January

Going home now, I don't want to lose this feeling of ease in my body, as if the sea and land have come into me.

January

The day of the deadline. Picking us up, my daughter says she wants to leave the airport as soon as possible. Everyone is anxious now about terrorism. Suddenly it occurs to me even she could be a casualty.

January

It is so difficult to believe. We are at war. The phone rings as I am unpacking. Joanna says fire has been exchanged. I run upstairs to the *television. A reporter is quietly describing bombs as they are being dropped in Baghdad. I sit stunned on the edge of the bed. Everything in my life has suddenly stopped.*

January

A feeling of horror spreads through my body, a cold and shivering sickness.

January

Scud missiles falling on Israel. So far none of them chemical. I think of Shirley. Then I remember what she told me. Her fear Israel would use nuclear weapons, and now I am terrified too. They are wearing gas masks in Israel. And I am holding my breath here.

January

Looking out the window. Sunlight. That warmth in midwinter we often have here. But my eyes will not take in the light. I am thinking, "This could be the end, the last of it."

January

All day on the news they repeat the same stories. What is it they are not telling us? They claim they are only bombing military targets in Iraq. But that is always the claim.

January

A reporter in Iraq hears children screaming from the bomb shelters, the ceaseless noise and terror of it all having shattered them.

January

I wake and just as I have for the last several days turn on the television for news. But there are only game shows and cartoons. What is happening? I feel betrayed. Something I need to know is being kept from me.

January

I am thinking of Käthe Kollwitz. Her summer house in the Harz Mountains was so close to Dora where the V-2 rockets were produced, and she knew nothing of that.

January

Like a lie between two lovers that sours everything, a lie told by the government sours society. It must be repeated by so many. Some are implicated, some knowing but not knowing. Perception itself begins to disintegrate.

January

The degradation of lies. The staleness of it. Fetid. Against this just the sensation of air rushing over skin, into the lungs. A bath.

January

Included among "military" targets in Iraq: telephone and communications offices, gas companies, bridges inside cities, factories of all kinds.

January

A diagram of a bunker built under Saddam Hussein's presidential palace. In antiquity a city was defended at its perimeter. Now the defenders go underground or into the air to continue waging war while cities above and beneath them are destroyed.

January

Planes equipped with computer images which flash over the windows directing vector, guns, bombs. The pilot sees colored arrows, coordinates, maps. What is outside the window hardly concerns him any more.

January

A man over the radio suggests that if there were one death for every sortie there could be 44,000. But does every sortie drop bombs on civilians? I try to add up the numbers but these are hopeless calculations.

January

We take a day out from the war. I stay in bed with a sore throat, aching muscles. We make love. Is it still possible to do such a thing? To feel pleasure? Tenderness?

January

Words an extension of the body. Like hands or feet. Used for so many purposes. To escape or come near. As weapons. Identification. This is who I am. I am my story.

January

They are calling the bombings "surgical strikes." Image of a doctor wearing a white mask leaning with his scalpel drawn over Baghdad. I think of the margins of the Bayeux tapestry into which women embroidered broken bits of bodies injured in the Norman conquest.

January

I can feel myself holding back, falling into silence. As if trying to mute my own intelligence. I want to retrieve that small animal inside, the howling, the whimpering.

February

Fresh-faced young men. Malleable. Not knowing yet who they are. But still caught in the old story which just now begins to define them.

February

Code name "Desert Storm." As if it were all a secret. How would you translate "Desert Storm"? A storm in the deserted place at the core of the self?

February

That story I read in the Bay Guardian about an attempted murder. One man meets another man on the weekend, sleeps with him, then *suddenly finds himself being stabbed. Says he will not forget the look in his assailant's face at that moment. As if he weren't there. Vacant.*

February

Struggling against despair.

February

For just a moment as the Cold War began to break apart it seemed to me a door opened. But the door is closing now. It is terrible to witness.

February

If I tell myself this is the way it has always been and always will be, I escape the pain of it.

February

Everything terrible in my childhood repeated itself at least once until it created a pattern that was seared into memory, and response.

February

Can the words here reflect the mood? Even more unfinished. Ragged. In a certain way, torn.

February

In the afternoon, resting, we read to each other from a novel I read as a child; it gave me comfort then, to know I was not alone in the turbulence of my life. What are they reading now in Iraq? Mesopotamia. Cradle of civilization. Sumer. Birthplace of writing.

February

How to tell a story without fashioning it along the prefabricated lines? As a nation, we are immersed in an old story and cannot see what is happening. Once again we picture ourselves as the liberating army. And this layered over a still older story. Man as warrior. The archetypal glory of the hero.

February

Today is the first day since the war began that I read the book review page in the Times. In this memoir Charles Scribner, Jr., refers to Hemingway's great insecurity about his masculinity. Gender enmeshed in the predictable narration of our destruction. Bush worrying about the "wimp factor." Trying to show his strength.

February

Suddenly I understand the news clipping Nan gave me several days ago. Pilots preparing to drop bombs in the gulf war were actually watching pornographic films just before they left in sorties.

February

It has existed for a long time, an objectified relationship with women, as part of the training by which young men offer themselves to kill or be killed. It is in the Iliad. Achilles's anger. The reason he absented himself from the first days of battle. Because Agamemnon stole his possession, a woman he had captured in an earlier battle and kept as his prize.

February

What David Lueck told me happened in Korea. About how he and the ambulance driver picked up two young Korean women, prostitutes, and brought them to the front. They were hungry. The men lined up to go into the back of the ambulance with them. Years later, he was sickened by his participation. Even that night, he crept back to give them winter jackets. "Softheartedness," he said, "not a trait men in combat wish to admit having."

February

Today in the papers they talk about an arsenal of weapons possessed by both the U.S. and Iraq which will create the effect of nuclear weapons without radiation. A burned-out crater in place of a small village.

February

Smart bombs are aimed at Baghdad, but Basra, which is a military headquarters and closer to the sea, gets ordinary bombs. Meaning they cannot be aimed, meaning there can be no attempt to avoid dropping them on civilians.

Basra, fabled site of the Garden of Eden.

February

Dream. I am a refugee during the Second World War, a Jew, trying to escape the holocaust. I have a little dog called Bifra. I leave it behind and it falls into the hands of a Polish man who is a Nazi collaborator. He names the dog Bisra. Then I awake with the word BASRA on my lips.

February

Massive bombing of the trenches where Iraqi soldiers are holed up in bunkers. Now the soldiers have become like civilians, huddled in the ground, frightened, with utterly no way to defend themselves.

February

Faced with the hopelessness of these circumstances, I can feel within me the temptation to insulate myself as my father did. To pretend nothing touches me and fabricate an expression of cheerfulness. Or to become cynical, like my mother when she drank.

February

Despite the war, I feel I must get back to work. I'm glad to have this daily task now. To struggle with the shapes of sentences. Perhaps from a web of language, language is the only way out.

February

I am trying to continue where I left off in the text. But perhaps this will never be possible. In a book review today I read that any sight, *any sentence, any event to which one is exposed leaves a permanent impression. The brain is changed forever. Of course Whitman knew this when he wrote, "A boy went out one day and all he beheld he became."*

It fascinates me that the lives of Charlotte and Hemingway touch in so many ways. Like Hemingway, Charlotte's teacher and lover had been in the ambulance corps in the First World War, where both men were wounded. Both men used their experiences in the war in their work. Did Hemingway, like Wolfsohn, suffer from a kind of shell shock? The question is controversial. If Hemingway was traumatized, it was a subtle trauma, one inflicted not by war alone, I suspect, and at the same time one he shared with many other men.

February
Article in the Times *about new methods of treating post-traumatic stress disorder.*

And there were other connections. Charlotte's mother had been a nurse during the First World War and met her husband, Charlotte's father, in a German army hospital. Hemingway fell in love with a nurse after he was wounded, and he fashioned his novel *A Farewell to Arms* around that experience. Charlotte created her work in a part of the world familiar to Hemingway. He vacationed and even wrote there.

February
Shell shock has this in common with rape and sexual abuse: it is not only the body that is wounded.

Both Charlotte and Hemingway mingled private and public worlds in their work. Still, for each the balance was different. Charlotte is centered in the private world and leans out. Hemingway leans inward, never reaching the center. He chases after an ineluctable female presence, but returns inevitably to the masculine provinces: warfare, hunting, fishing. He is known by his last name. She by her first.

February
The world as one has known it has collapsed. Nothing can be trusted any longer. Did my father do this to my sister?

Then there is the question of suicide. It haunted them both. But Charlotte confronted this fear directly. And she did not die by her own hand. Hemingway was often aware of suicide in the wings. As Charlotte's mother had killed herself, so had his father. He himself was subject to fits of despair throughout his life. Finally he was given the same treatment suffered by German soldiers who had been victims of shell shock, electroshock therapy. It was after this, feeling that the fineness of his mind had been destroyed, that he took his own life.

February
It is as if the war narrows the scope of imagination.

Born in 1899, Ernest Hemingway was part of a generation whose lives were shaped by two World Wars. He was a contemporary of Himmler, Fermi and General Douglas MacArthur. He belonged to a prosperous middle-class family and grew up in comfortable circumstances in the safe but somewhat narrow environment of Oak Park, Illinois, a suburb of Chicago. His father was a doctor. His mother, who had inherited money of her own, was an educated woman who had been trained as an opera singer. She had a short career on the stage until, the story goes, she found the stage lights burned her sensitive eyes. She was a feminist, and took a strong interest in the cultural life of the city, to which she purposefully exposed all of her children.

February
I wanted so much to believe that the breakdown of the Cold War was also the beginning of a shift into a new way of thinking and being. Or perhaps an ancient one, still able to imagine peace.

Ernest was his mother's favorite child. She doted on him, keeping him in a close, affectionate relationship, and even slept in the same bed with him until he was five years old. He returned her affection. But as he grew older he rebelled. She dominated the family, including his father, and later he would imply that this was the reason he grew to hate her.

February
Archaeologists express concern over the ancient sites in Iraq which could be bombed. Remains of Neanderthal culture. Evidence of the first agriculture. The first villages and towns.

Making fun of his mother's zealous care for him, when he is a young man he will call her *Mrs. Heminstein*. Intertwined as this name is with his attempt to free himself from the influence of his mother, this is also an early sign of Hemingway's anti-Semitism. Did he know, or just sense intuitively, that misogyny and anti-Semitism are similarly interwoven in history?

February
A report that Iraqi airplanes have been seen parked at the archaeological site of the ancient city of Ur. This was one of the oldest cities of Mesopotamia, dating from 3000 B.C.

Like many boys of this generation, including Heinrich Himmler and my grandfather, Ernest was dressed in ruffles and lace. As one of his biographers, Kenneth Lynn, perceptively observes, Grace was particularly keen on picturing her son as feminine. One photograph of him taken at the age of two in which he wears a flowered hat is labeled "Summer Girl," in her handwriting. As he grew older, she would often dress Ernest and his older sister in identical clothing as if they were twins of the same sex, either as boys or as girls. I do not see this as a simple perversity. It seems possible that Grace might project her wishes for a wider range of being on her children, making them act out changes of gender she wanted for herself.

February
Among the structures of ancient Ur was a large ziggurat, a calendrical tower, built, according to its modern discoverers, to observe the heavens. Ziggurat means "hill of heaven."

As much as Ernest tried to move away from the influence of his mother, he also wanted to get closer to his father. Of course, like many men, his father was not as present in the home as Grace, and he was more remote in his moods. He was also given to depression. Ernest loved to go with him when he went hunting or fishing. The family had a second home in the woods at Lake Walloon, and there Ernest would also accompany his father when he ministered care to a local Native American tribe. As a boy he witnessed emergency surgeries, bone settings, childbirth. Clarence was proud of his son because he was not squeamish when he looked at the preserved organs the doctor kept in glass jars in his study.

February
In a book on architecture I read that calendric structures reveal rhythmic patterns reflecting calendric changes: the waning and waxing of the moon, the rise and fall of tides, menstrual cycles.

As he moved into manhood, Hemingway began to hate what he saw as his father's cowardice and submission to his mother. In an early story he depicts his father backing down in a fight, admonished by his mother to keep the peace.

February
A bunker in Baghdad bombed. Filled with civilians. A man weeping in front of the bunker. So many in his family dead. All his children. It is unimaginable. Yet I am implicated in these deaths.

One might be tempted to look at Hemingway's childhood as the sole explanation for the obsession with masculine heroism that became the subject of much of his work. But psychoanalysis itself employs too narrow a lens to explain any life. When the perspective is widened one sees that his childhood was not so much unique as it was a variation on a theme. No wonder the legend Hemingway made of himself became so popular: both his real story and the mythology he created mirrored the world to which he belonged.

February
Day by day the stories issuing from the Pentagon about the bombing of the bunker change. First they say there were no civilians there. Then that the military officials were hiding among the civilians. Then that they were misinformed.

My grandparents were both born in the state where Hemingway was raised. They were at the southern end of the state, in an area more rural than the suburbs of Chicago. But even in 1949, after my parents divorced, when I visited Chicago with my grandparents, the city still seemed to smell of the slaughterhouses.

February
Sacrament of language, binding thread of words. One wants to trust others. Yet when a lie is told the body is cast into a state of profound disturbance. One must choose then between oneself and society.

Like Grace, my grandmother dreamed of becoming an artist. She wanted to be an actress. Extraordinary as it was for a woman of her generation, she studied drama for two years at the University of Illinois. The story goes that a traveling theatre asked her to join. But her father would not allow this. She shared Grace Hemingway's hunger for culture and the finer things of life. In the early days of television we watched plays by Thornton Wilder, ballet, and Liberace playing Chopin or Rachmaninoff was one of her favorites. During breakfast she read to us from the *Reader's Digest*. My grandfather was hardly interested. He liked to read mysteries or westerns. In the early days of television, we watched Wild Bill Hickok together as he rode into the scrub brush of the Southern California hills. My grandfather's fishing tackle in its khaki case sat in a privileged position in our basement. Though their easy chairs rested just a few yards apart in our living room, my grandparents lived as if in separate worlds. But when Hemingway's late story "The Old Man and the Sea" arrived at our house under the covers of the *Saturday Evening Post* both my grandparents read it.

February

In the back of the house the plum tree blossoming again.

I have a strong feeling of familiarity for Grace and Clarence Hemingway. A marriage conventional and proper on the surface concealing gaping holes of dissatisfaction. My grandfather the wage earner respectably dressed in his three-piece suits. My grandmother his wife keeping house, putting up preserves, baking cakes on holidays, roast beef every Sunday for a meal eaten early on the Limoges spread over a linen cloth.

February

Sunday. Time out from the war. Nan and I go to the park. Photographs of the space program in the Science Museum. Huge machines making it possible to view stars as they never have been viewed before.

But this was just the surface. The appearance everyone worked so hard to create. Just beneath that appearance was something else. I can remember my grandmother standing beside the washing machine that in those days had a hand-fed wringer. This was a task she hated more than all her other domestic tasks, most of which she performed with only an unspoken resentment, one that had settled permanently into the features of her face. As she handed the wash to my grandfather so that he could hang it on the line in the backyard, she was openly complaining.

February
But now, in many places on the planet, without sophisticated machinery, we can hardly see the stars at all any more.

As I helped my grandfather with his tasks, I thought of him not so much as a parent but as an older sibling, who, like me, might easily incur my grandmother's wrath. It was she who ruled our household. Every family has its own explanation for its patterns. Charlotte's grandmother believed Charlotte and her father had failed Franziska and that is why she committed suicide. In my family my grandmother's resentful rule over my grandfather was explained by his behavior earlier in their marriage, when he was a womanizer and drank too much. Now she was getting back at him.

February
Don calls. We haven't spoken in weeks. So good to hear his voice, sounding as shaken as I am.

There was an incipient bitterness between them, however, that smelled of old scores unsettled. It stretched way back to before their marriage when my grandmother, shunted off to the family in Virginia, bore him an illegitimate and stillborn child.

February
Now it comes out that forty percent of the "smart" laser-guided bombs are missing their targets by thousands of feet.

But this historical argument missed a reality which existed daily before our eyes, though we never spoke of it, and that was the deterioration of my grandfather. He had collapsed. He was like some star whose flame, moving out toward the periphery, had left nothing at the center.

February
Slowly, year after year, decade by decade, we grow used to the unspeakable.

At the end of a story Hemingway wrote about a son's disillusionment with his father, the young hero says of him, *Seems like when they get started they don't leave a guy nothing.* It is a theme that will repeat itself throughout his work. A man shorn of all that has meaning for him, losing even his self-respect, left with nothing.

February
One cries out, but it is as if in a dream where the voice is silent. It is a terrible feeling to witness this destruction, which is also on the most fundamental level a self-destruction.

I can remember my grandfather sitting in his chair staring into space. This was not the meditative mood of reflection. His silence made me uneasy. I sensed in his stillness a fundamental failure of being.

February
It is no wonder this war evokes childhood memories. What I felt as I witnessed my mother's drinking; what she must have felt witnessing her father's alcoholism.

Though I sympathized with my grandfather in his submission, in my heart I was glad my grandmother held the seat of power in our family. She was present, in this world, aware, despite her resentment, of the needs of a child to eat regularly and sleep between clean sheets. And though my grandfather often seemed more lenient, his anger was volatile like a child's rage, and in some strange way it partook of the emptiness that had settled so deeply in him.

February
What one sees as a child. My grandmother's reigning unhappiness colored the atmosphere; it was the air we breathed. But we never spoke of it.

Clarence Hemingway suffered from serious bouts of depression. He was alternately vacant to his family and autocratic, finding fault with everything, impossible to please. Growing up, Ernest fell under the shadow of his moods, and this angered him. When was it he began to blame his mother for his father's transgressions?

February
A chain reaction of silences. The lack of intimacy between my grandmother and grandfather. Did any secrets pass between them?

Tracing the complicated circuitry of gender in our lives, there is also this. My grandmother's manner of authority, the qualities which made her able to dominate other people's lives, were said to have come from her father. Was the same true for Grace Hemingway? Her father, Ernest, after whom Hemingway was named, was the head of the Hemingway household until his death, when Ernest was five years old. Then Grace took over the helm from her father.

February
Those tender stories lovers tell each other at night before sleep,
mingling histories, dreams; another way of making love.

Both of Hemingway's grandfathers had fought in the Civil
War. Anson Hemingway, his father's father, commanded black
troops in the infantry. It was this grandfather who took Ernest at
the age of eleven to join the crowds greeting Theodore Roosevelt
as he rode into the Oak Park railroad station. Teddy Roosevelt
was the young Hemingway's hero. He read Roosevelt's *African
Game Trails*. And he wore his khaki uniform, fashioned after
Roosevelt's safari clothes, whenever his father took him to the
Hall of African Mammals at the Field Museum of Natural History
in Chicago.

February
*How isolated we were then, my family. All of us! My loneliness not
just from that divorce, but from the greater separation which preceded it.
Secrets dividing us.*

Ernest was not alone in his worship. Teddy Roosevelt, or
T.R. as he was affectionately known, became a symbol at the turn
of the century for the revival of certain *rough and ready* masculine
virtues, now nearly vestigial. He was the big game hunter, the
cowboy, the statesman who spoke softly and carried a big stick.
He openly celebrated war. *No triumph of peace could be quite so great,*
he said. Peace, or the absence of war, brought its own problems,
among them, he warned, the greatest danger being *effeminate ten-
dencies in young men.*

February
We hope against hope for a peace settlement.

As a child Ernest boasted to his parents that he was *afraid of
nothing*. But there were two sides to his fantasy life. At one mo-

ment he would sidle up to his mother, asking her to play *Kitty* with him and stroke him and purr. Then, switching to a different mode, he would swagger his way through stories he made up in which he was the brave and vanquishing hero.

February
Bush has rejected the Soviet peace proposal. He makes the startling demand that Iraqi troops withdraw before a cease-fire.

I can remember myself at the age of ten staring into the mirror as I buttoned my collar, tried on one of my grandfather's ties and combed my hair back in the style of a man. I liked to imagine myself as Kit Carson, dressed in buckskin, forging through the wilderness. To swing to the other side of the divide between the sexes was a way for me to escape the confining world of domesticity so filled with my grandmother's resentments.

February
Sense of foreboding all day. Difficult to work. Nan calls. Iraqi troops are in retreat, and they are being bombed and fired on while they withdraw!

Could it be that part of the sting for a man who is called effeminate is the implicit threat of being reduced to the small world assigned to women? By 1917, leaving his mother and sister behind, Hemingway had moved into the wider world of men. He was nineteen and just graduated from high school when he went to work as a reporter at the *Kansas City Star*. Three weeks after he arrived, he joined the National Guard. Congress had declared war on Germany that spring. He wrote his family that he planned to enlist later in an active unit. His longing to go to war grew more intense that fall when he went to hear Billy Sunday, the famous Chicago evangelist, urging young men to do their patriotic duty.

February
Allied troops in Iraq. And still the war doesn't end. The rumor is that the coalition wants Saddam Hussein dead. He has become like the Antichrist, the symbol of all evil.

On the surface one might find a contradiction here: a religious man exhorting men to war. But this is a traditional transposition of values, part of a shared history that goes back at least until 1096, when joining the First Crusade became a way not only of testing manly virtue but of expiating sin.

February
Finally a cease-fire. Papers, television proclaiming a great victory. It is as if no one died. The suffering of "the enemy" still invisible.

One thinks then of King Richard in battle with the Turks, his body, according to Bulfinch, *as if it were made of brass impenetrable to any weapon.* As the legend goes, surrounded by Turkish warriors, he cut down men and horses alike, *cleaving them to the middle.* One of the strongest Turkish warriors, an officer of distinction, lost his head, his shoulder and his right arm to a single blow of Richard's sword. The king emerged safely from battle *stuck all over with javelins like a deer pierced by the hunters.*

March
I remember that sculpture of St. Sebastian I saw three years ago hanging on the wall of a church in the Black Forest. He was wounded from the arrows. His golden loincloth looked like a skirt. I noticed this because of the sway of his hip, and his face, so feminine.

That Richard is likened to a deer must have had overtones of an earlier time in the eleventh century. According to the Celtic religion, the deer was a divine messenger. And then there are the wounds themselves, similar to the wounds of any soldier, which seem to manifest what has always been so, as if in warfare an inner condition had moved to the surface, even through mutilation making a man seem more whole.

March
I was very ill that day but somehow managed to go out to see the pictures made of flowers by the village women adorning all the paths, celebrating the resurrection of Christ. They do this every year at Easter.

To his friends and family Hemingway boasted of plans to enlist as a Marine or an aviator. But he knew this was impossible: his eyes were bad. He could stay in the National Guard, but the likelihood of being called up before the war's end was small. Then, in February of the next year, representatives of the Italian Red Cross appeared in Kansas City to recruit ambulance drivers.

March
One image in particular struck me, an image of a whip supposed to have been used to flagellate Christ, pincers, and a ball and chain, carried out in petals of spring blossoms.

On June 2, 1918, Hemingway arrived in Paris with one week to spend before he would be dispatched to Milan for his assignment. According to a letter he wrote, on the first day of his leave he was picked up on the street by a woman who took him to a mansion near the outskirts of the city where, he said, using the chaste language of his upbringing, *a very beautiful thing happened to me.* The woman he met that day told him that under no circumstances would she be able to see him again. But he spent the rest of his stay in Paris looking for her. At the end of his leave, he finally found her as, along with many other soldiers, he watched through a slit in a wall while she made love to a man dressed as a military officer. Was this story, which he wrote in a letter to a friend at home, fact or fiction? This was a theme—an unsuccessful search for a lost woman, a woman lost to him—that would be repeated more than once in his fiction.

March
Reading a book of pre-Islamic Bedouin poetry. The traditional theme describes the loss of a woman, the beloved, followed by a quest for her, and ending with the acceptance of a world deprived of her.

If the story is true he would not have been the first young soldier initiated at one and the same time into the mysteries of sex and violence. Yet if the story were exaggerated, this embellishment would also be part of an old tradition by which stories of military and sexual conquest are both aggrandized. But he was soon to have another intimate contact with the female body. At the end of his week in Paris, he boarded a train for Milan where just after his arrival an official of the Red Cross called him to a munitions plant which had exploded just outside the city. There were many dead and he was shocked to find women among the bodies. It was the presence of the long hair, he said.

March
A photograph of the United States ambassador to the UN speaking with an elderly woman in Kuwait. She is wearing a veil. And his face looks like a mask.

But he is also shocked by the presence of short hair among these women. It is strange how such a detail alerts the mind. His mother was a feminist. There is even subtle evidence that for a period she may have been in love with another woman. But short hair, at that time, would have been such an outward sign of deviation from the expected.

March
Joanna and I take a walk together. She is trying to decide whether or not to go to Chernobyl. A descent, like Inanna's descent. We are both concerned about her health.

From Milan he was dispatched to Section IV at Schio, near Lake Garda, where he drove an ambulance every other day, ferrying the wounded from the battlefront to an emergency care station. But he was disappointed. He found the work dull. There was nothing to do but look at the scenery, he said. He wanted to see action. He wrote a letter to a girlfriend at home implying he was closer to the battle and under heavy fire. Was this the first lie he was to tell about his experience in the war?

March
In the Times *an article saying it will take two years to put out the burning oil wells in Kuwait. The skies are black there.*

His hope for seeing action finally came when his commanding officers asked for volunteers to move closer to the line of fire at Fossalta where they were needed to distribute cigarettes, water and chocolate. Everyone volunteered, but Hemingway was among the chosen. Then, after less than a week in Fossalta, on June 7, he learned from the soldiers at the front that heavy shelling was expected soon all along the line.

March
I dream I am back in that house where as a child I was so often frightened. Is this because I am about to visit my mother after so long?

It must have been because of what the soldiers told him that he went out near midnight, carrying his rifle and rucksack over his shoulder, and bicycled to the trenches. He was determined to get closer to the action, and so he advanced to a listening post, one hundred and fifty yards nearer the Austrian lines.

March

Los Angeles. Dinner with Jesse and Rachel. Talk about the war. Rachel is against it. Jesse for it. She is afraid for Israel and sees Hussein as a kind of Hitler.

Does he run over the field? This is after all what he has been waiting for since the war started, ever since he was a small boy in his khaki uniform, to enter battle, to be baptized in this element, to become what he is supposed to become and at the same time to take into himself what has forever been promised him, the fiery center of his sex, himself.

March

I keep thinking about our talk with Jesse. As much as I dislike Hussein's dictatorship, I do not think he is like Hitler. Still I am troubled by our talk. The implications.

Is it perhaps a certain rapture that he feels now along with his fear as the shells crack and brighten the air and the machine guns rattle? He is as close as he will ever be to the heart of the matter. His blood rushes, the saliva in his mouth goes dry, and if his head is lighter than usual, still every muscle, every nerve seems vital in a new way, as if he had been reborn into this moment.

March

How can one be a pacifist in the face of such evil?

Later, much later, when Hemingway writes a version of this story, the first sensation he describes himself feeling is the wetness of blood filling his boots. A shell had exploded. The soldier in front of him was dead. And another with both legs blown off, also dead. But a third, near him, with a wound in his chest, was still alive.

March

And yet I can no longer accept violence as a solution. It is a feeling I have in my body, as if in the cells themselves.

It is here that the narrative breaks down. We know he was wounded by shrapnel in over two hundred places in his leg. But did he, despite these wounds, rise to lift the body of the other wounded man? And was he then struck by two machine gun bullets which wounded him again in the knee and the foot? The truth cannot be determined. Evidence exists that, as is so often the case with heroic deeds, the story strayed from the truth, giving the hero capacities which on closer examination are not only improbable but superhuman. Yet it is perhaps necessary, the enlargement, the careful whisking away of certain details, the flattering light casting one act into an unnatural brilliance, another unseen into the shadows. What goes on in battle is in the end just the raw material for the eventual achievement of glory.

March

At the museum here, as part of an exhibit about the Third Reich's condemnation of modern art, films of book burnings are shown. Among the books burned, Hemingway's A Farewell to Arms. *Chronicle of the underside of World War I. The same war which created Hitler.*

So, it is part of the same tradition that the story told by both sides in a conflict is the same, except that the roles of the good and bad, avenger and criminal, savior and oppressor have been reversed. In the Arab version of King Richard's siege of Acre a different story is told. After seizing the city's ramparts, not wishing to be burdened with prisoners, Richard ordered that 2,700 Arab soldiers together with 300 women and children be assembled before the city wall. There they were roped together and delivered to the Frankish soldiers who attacked them with lances, sabers and stones until *all the wails were stilled.*

March
Seeing my mother today. It has been a long time and she is so much more ill.

What was it like for Hemingway to be wounded as he was? The rapture before the shell broke was one matter but this was another. The body near him irrevocably altered, legs blasted to nothingness, not neatly torn but ragged, blood smeared everywhere, mixed with the mud. Later the images will make him shudder.

March
Attached by a thin plastic tube to a machine that increases her oxygen, she is worn out easily by conversation.

I remember David Lueck telling me what he had witnessed in Korea. His voice so low it could hardly be heard in the recording I made, he spoke in the way I have heard women speak of rape or abuse, as if in the very telling something monstrously ugly is brought into being. The terror and brutality seemed to brand him, making him in his own mind irredeemably inseparable from the ugliness. Yet what he saw defied description. It was told more in the difficulty of telling than in the telling itself. He could name the mutilations, intestines falling out of the body, along with shit, blood, pus, but no one who had not been there could have any idea. It was only over time I began to grasp what he was saying to me. It was not just the physical fear he was feeling, it was the weight of something sordid.

March
I am grateful for this time with my mother. I was deprived of my father's death. It was so violent, so sudden.

How much more important then it becomes to reassemble the fragments of these memories into something better, something fine, something that restores the shaken center into glory.

March
I can see now how crucial to a life the ending is. Death the last part of the story.

A few years after the war, when he has moved to Paris and begun his first brilliant short stories, Hemingway will draw a portrait of a young veteran who makes up stories about the war. *Krebs found that to be listened to at all he had to lie, and after he had done this twice, he, too, had a reaction against the war and talking about it.* This could easily have been a self-portrait. His story to Chink Dorman-Smith, a soldier he met in a bar in Milan, and later his friend, that he had been wounded leading Arditi shock troopers on Monte Grappa. The story to the reporter told just after his ship docked in America that his body bore more scars from shrapnel than any other man who fought with the Allied forces. The story told to Oak Park High School students that he had fought with Arditi shock troops at Fossalta. The claim to the memorial committee of Oak Park that he had fought in three major battles on the Italian front. The story he told in the cafés of Paris, about being buried alive for four days at the front.

March
How deep the need is, to tell the story, to hear it to the end.

Who is it he wishes to impress with his lies? Is it his father, who meets him at the railroad station, the same father whose critical judgments had wounded him so many times? Or his mother, proud of his accomplishments, whom he soon tells after the war, . . . *the mother of a man that has died for his country should be the proudest woman in the world.* . . .

March
In wartime, one quick and senseless death after another. So many stories without endings.

General Douglas MacArthur was among those men who wished to impress his mother with his heroism. It was she who urged him on in his military career, lobbying in Washington during the First World War to have him made a general. And years after his mother's death when MacArthur hired women to spend the night with him it was not to make love but to stay up all night hearing him tell the stories of his victories.

March
Aftermath of childhood. Aftermath of war. That silence at the end. The action has already occurred. Nothing can be done.

But there is also another story, of the soldier who wants to impress his father, or who cannot. I am thinking of a story I heard about a young man who was called up to do duty in the Israeli Occupied Territories. The violence, the killing, and what he saw as an injustice disturbed him. Finally he broke down. He was discharged and sent to a clinic. His father would not visit him there. This man was so disappointed with his son that afterward he ceased to speak to him at all.

March
That moment at the end of Iphigenia. Aristotle called it recognition. All the frenzy is done. Agamemnon has already killed his daughter, and his armies are sailing toward Troy. How terrible to recognize this.

In a letter to Bill Horne, another veteran, Hemingway wrote of the 6,000,000,000 females and 8,000,000,000,000 males *crying out for secondhand thrills to be got from the front.* The storyteller is never far from his audience. He can feel from his listeners what they want to hear. And what they want to hear has also been a part of him. It has been what he himself wanted to believe. It was even a kind of reason for being. The myth around which he organized what he called himself. It was a story he himself had heard not so much from any one person but in the atmosphere, indistinguishable from the medium in which one day he came to consciousness, learned to look into a mirror, to see himself and speak finally the syllables of his own name.

April
I do not want to enclose the text in a definitive meaning. As they come to me I write ideas in my journal instead of the text.

There was another story of course but it came unbidden in the middle of the night when he woke from a nightmare believing that he was still on the battlefield, wounded, unable to flee. But it was only his wife, Hadley, who heard this story, when she would wake at night with him and comfort him.

April
The intuition of Cassandra. The feminine realm of thought holds the secrets of our culture, and hence can make startling predictions.

But the true story had even larger dimensions than this nightmare that frightened him at night. Reality lay under the cover of a denser pattern of lies that had invaded every aspect of his life. Concealing whoever he was a man he had invented, who claimed to have given boxing lessons, or contracted venereal disease, or traveled all over Spain with a cuadrilla of bullfighters. Trying to reconstruct the bare facts of his life, one discovers only a confusing landscape full of shrouding mists and quagmires. There is no solid ground.

April
Cassandra condemned by Apollo, the reasonable god, to be unheard because she would not yield to his sexual assault. The second assault: what one sees, erased.

Perhaps this is why he hung on to everything, not only manuscripts and letters as most writers do, but even boxing tickets, notes written on the backs of old letters, to-do lists. Could it be that, having surrounded himself with lies, he needed hard evidence of his actual existence?

April
Shirley visiting again from Israel. We have lunch. I make some comment about the cost of Patriot missiles being so high. She says she found out, facing the threat of Scud attacks, that for her survival comes first.

I can imagine Hemingway sitting surrounded as he is by all these papers that document his existence, as he begins to locate something of himself closer to the center. Does he discover this by accident or from the atmosphere of his exile? Perhaps he is writing with his ear, trying to get the words, the voice, the rhythms of the sentences to hold that electric quality of recognition he has heard all around him. He ventures then just over the line of expectation. *I knew that I was hit.* He is breaking a mold *and leaned over and put my hand on my knee.* Disturbing convention. *My knee wasn't there.* Moving nearer to the truth than any of the tales he has told before. What emerges is a different picture. *I wiped my hand on my shirt and,* not what he longed for as a small boy telling tales, *another floating light came very slowly down,* but somehow more alive, vibrant *and I looked at my leg and was very afraid.* Indefinably vivid, sharp with wit, and clarity, making him feel as he once wrote, *cool and clear inside himself.*

April
She was grateful for the Patriots. Her son-in-law and children came
from Tel Aviv to live with them. "I tried to keep a diary," she said, "but
family life took over."

It is not so much that the facts are unchanged. This is fiction.
Names are invented, settings shifted. He has to reconstruct
through research the famous retreat of the Italian army he describes so well. But he is telling another more crucial truth. How
the war was not heroic. How there was fear and failure, and a
flatness at the end, a sickness of heart because *the things that were*
glorious had no glory . . . and the sacrifices were like the stockyards of
Chicago.

April
I understand this so well. Pushed to the point of survival, the mind
closes down and imagination ceases. Freeing thought from fear and
anxiety. The work of a lifetime.

I had seen nothing sacred, Hemingway writes, and the atmosphere of Left Bank Paris mirrors his words. All around him a
debacle proceeds. It is not only the numbers of men mutilated
from the war who can be seen in the streets, the severed limbs,
missing eyes, jaws crushed, part of a nose or cheek blown away.
There is also *La Révolution Surréaliste* proclaiming, *We shall triumph*
over everything. And first of all we will destroy this civilization . . . in
which you are caught like fossils in shale. Syntax and consciousness
split open, revealing as in a ruptured body the inner workings
before found grotesque or obscene. André Breton and Paul Éluard
mount an attack on the immaculate conception. *Everything that has*
been so many times undone is coming apart once more. Nightmares and
dreams once in the background are thrust into the public discourse. An artist trying to draw the shattered countryside of the
battlefields tears his drawing to pieces in frustration. Then, looking at what he has discarded on the floor, he realizes this is the
image he wants: fragments of what has been destroyed are reas-

sembled to make a collage. The familiar objects of domestic life—bottle, guitar, plate set by an open window—fracture in a torn and unbalanced geometry. Nijinsky leaping into the air points his toes inward rather than out. How can one bother about the beauty of roses when one has seen what one has seen? Art itself is under suspicion. Perhaps there should be no more painters. No more writers. No more. No more nothing. NOTHING. NOTHING. NADA.

April

It is always so astonishing to hear a story in which, under threat of death, a woman or a man responds unexpectedly, and imaginatively.

If there is an atmosphere of debauchery in Hemingway's first novel *The Sun Also Rises*—nights spent in bars, days drinking in cafés, in and out of bed, lovers exchanged like dance partners—this is also an accurate reflection of the times. Of what is now called the Lost Generation. The old manly virtues have lost their élan. In place of rectitude and diligence there is decadence.

April

That other story Shirley told me on her last trip. The young Israeli soldier, a friend's son, sent to the Gaza Strip, who picked up the stones thrown at him by Arab children and began to juggle them. After that, instead of throwing stones, every day the children gathered to watch him juggle.

At the same time the demarcation between the genders has become unclear. The line is crossed, recrossed, crossed over again. Like the surrealists who search for a phantom feminine self, Hemingway's hero Jake Barnes, who has been castrated by the war, seeks after a woman who has a man's name, short hair and a masculine manner of independence. One of Hemingway's best friends, Gertrude Stein, is a lesbian. And there are gay men too among his friends all over Paris.

April
And then of course there was Charlotte. Her grace in that moment,
faced with imprisonment, death.

Still, this is not a rebellion Hemingway embraces without res-
ervation. The moment is more complicated. To speak of glory is
obscene. Yet at the end of more than one story he tells there is
that man who is left with nothing.

April

It is about seeing.

The war had disappointed him. If the pieces of what he came
to know as manhood did not coalesce for him before the war,
warfare and especially a wounding battle were supposed to draw
the scattered fragments into one whole. But war failed him. The
fragments never came together, and what happened to him in the
war was transformed into *a distaste for everything*. This cynicism was
inseparable from his style. It was there in the tone of voice. The
turn of phrase. The cadence of his speech. He captured it elegantly.

April
A tragedy occurs along the plot lines of the old story, with its predict-
able ending. And yet if the story is told differently, perhaps another ending
can be imagined.

This is a voice I know well. My mother, who was born in
1914 and became as hard a drinker as Hemingway ever was, knew
this voice too. It became hers too. Especially when she was drinking. Everything became funny to her but the humor was not light.
What was thought admirable was deflated, and as the night wore
on, all that she ridiculed included herself too, her own past and
her future, which she raged against and then wept over in the
enveloping depths of her morosity.

April
Ramsey Clark in the high school auditorium here, speaking about what he saw inside Iraq during the bombing. Whole neighborhoods destroyed, a mosque, buildings perilously near a hospital.

The voice of a world-weary cynicism was one Charlotte must have encountered in Berlin. Her own work is filled with the ironic tone of cabaret humor with its sexual innuendo, its stripping away of layers of fakery, pretension, fraudulence, sentimentality.

April
The worst story he told was about entering a hospital just after a young girl had her leg amputated. There was no anesthetic. She was in shock. Laughing hysterically, grinning, shaking.

As I write this I realize that, despite the fear I had of my mother's drunken moods, nevertheless a certain electricity sprang from the harsh honesty of her voice that I was drawn toward.

April
This story haunts me, makes me shudder, disturbs my sleep, and yet still I would rather know than not know.

Yet the honesty which made my mother at times the most vibrant member of our family lacked a dimension. It was not that brand of truth-telling which forges a bond between souls. Was the courage to speak out bought with a severance from others? What she said was not connected to any larger circle of meaning. Except insofar as this was part of a shared style of those times. The hard-bitten detective believing in nothing but holding on to a shred of dignity through biting one-line revelations. The reporter, winking at human foolishness, drunk at night, never shocked by anything, objective.

April
I wake from a dream. I am a city. My body, the streets, buildings. A missile enters. The city is shattered. My clothes torn off and scattered, as in a rape.

In his first formative years as a writer of fiction Hemingway was also a reporter and, like a good reporter, he was detached from what he witnessed, except when events fascinated him as a potential source of plot. In 1922 he covered the international Economic Conference of Genoa, among the most important meetings of the decade. Did he grasp the significance of what he saw? The Treaty of Versailles was in effect. Europe was recovering from war. Russia had just had a revolution. The Russian Commissar for Foreign Affairs, Georgi V. Chicherin, proposed that both the Soviet Union and the Western countries disarm. The proposal was rejected. In place of more pertinent news, he filed a story about the difficulty of gaining access to the Russian compound. His language was terse, cynical.

April
Long article in the Sunday Times *about the troubled reunification of Germany. The East Germans are now "the other," rejected, dispossessed, hated self of the nation.*

Thinking of the idea of "objectivity," I remember that satellite the Pentagon plans to use to record the process of conflagration in the event of a nuclear war. Computers will gather accurate information. It is designed in the belief that the side with the most data will have won the war. It is a bizarre fantasy. Perhaps a handful of human beings and animals linger on earth, slowly dying of radiation poisoning, exposure, starvation, while overhead a satellite circles the earth, producing, with delicate computers, a three-dimensional depiction of the destruction. What a sad but intriguing metaphor, a metal object moving through space, filled with inaccessible knowledge, carrying a self-portrait which simultaneously depicts a massive and suicidal outbreak of violence and, through its sheer technical brilliance, the greater boundaries of human intelligence.

April
It was on the last trip I made to Germany, three years ago, that I could feel so powerfully the angst of that nation. The heavy burden of that past. Anyone born there must confront it.

The detached posture of the reporter became part of Hemingway's fictional style. The voice that captured the attitude of a generation. Ridiculing glory, but still masculine, it is this voice that can at one and the same time express disillusionment and yet allow a civilization to continue on in the direction of still another war.

April
Are we creating the same burden for our grandchildren now?

Later in life, after a second war, Hemingway will begin to lose his magic as a writer. He becomes the object of his own creation. What he writes about his own life is in an odd way less true than his fictional accounts. Edmund Wilson will call it "fatuous, maudlin."

April
Slowly indications arise here and there in the back pages of the news that the Patriots were not as effective in stopping missiles as the Pentagon claimed.

The story goes that he sensed his own failure. I can imagine him as he sits writing once more. He is searching for that electric edge he felt so often in the past. That indefinable substance that would make the words crack. He is a fine imitator of his own style. But he knows the difference. In those earlier works there was a sharpness, like the sharpness of air let into a closed room. Perhaps he knows that in order to find what he wants he must sink into himself. It is there in the memory and the more real he makes it, the more alive it is, the more something real comes out of him and to the surface.

April

I am thinking again of Inanna and what she saw. The power from this, the underworld, the shadow land not beautiful at first sight but redemptive in the redeeming.

Yet the descent frightens him. If he is sinking with a long line of his vision into his own depths, as watery and lacking a foothold as they are, what might he find? There at the heart, in the place that defines him as a man, is he perhaps insubstantial? Not who he should be, the line hopelessly tangled, a creature undefined, between one state and another, monstrously unknowable. It is better not to look in that direction too long.

April

Telling Hemingway's story, I become fond of him. It is in the nature of the process. My thoughts centered on him. The attempt to see as he sees.

Does he recognize what is there in the shadows, spongy and swallowing, does he know this to be part of himself? If he can gain mastery. If he can possess it and kill it at once. Bring in the biggest fish. Shoot the animal there in the thicket. Jump into the ring, his cape flaring, his sword sunk into the neck of the bull breathing its breath close to his cheek.

April

The irony of Hemingway's obsession with bulls. The bull, according to Marija Gimbutas, an old matriarchal icon.

And is he then, with that scent, that brush, reminded of a different body? Watery itself and sinking. A surface without clear beginning or end. The soft of his skin the same as the smooth of the sheet. When he cups his hand over a woman's breast does this feeling return? Neither male nor female but of the inside coming and going, fluid, pliable, then active, suffused, tingling, hot and moving, then cold, wet, a sharpness, waves of it, a medium, chimerical, himself alive.

April
I read this account from a young man traveling in the Sudan. At the center of a circle of starving refugees women singing the songs they had once sung to their bulls and cows at home.

But this is a self he will not own. Is this why over and over again he tells two stories? A man left with nothing. A man losing a woman. The hero castrated in war who cannot join with his beloved. The hero escaping death in war, whose child dies, whose dying lover never awakens?

April
And that story Abigail's friend told me, whose mother was in Dresden when it was bombed. Taking refuge by a river, she found herself facing a lion escaped from the burning zoo, shivering and terrified like herself.

It was for the desire of a mythically beautiful woman that the city of Troy was besieged, its houses plundered, its walls destroyed, its women and children assaulted, raped, killed.

April
All official history accompanied by another history. That history which is told by word of mouth. The stories we pass between us.

And so begins a different descent. If at first there was an opening, a chink in the barricaded pose, the aperture does not open but closes. Perhaps if he could read again what he had written. Surmise the characters he so deftly drew of men who blamed others for their own failings, so that finally, unable to come to terms with or even see themselves, they were left with nothing, not even themselves.

April
The story I was told during the war by the daughter of a career military officer. How he raped her repeatedly when she was a child.

It is there so clearly in his first novel, *The Sun Also Rises*. The hero hating a friend because he is Jewish. Hating him for all the qualities he hates in himself. Yet not knowing this, ignorant of himself in his projection. Castrated by the war, miserable because he cannot make love to the woman he wants, he dogs his friend with a steady stream of invective. But it is as if Hemingway never read his own story. Outside the pages of his fiction, he remained an anti-Semite.

April
The second story from a Lebanese scholar just returned from an international women's conference where she heard from Philippine women about the countless U.S. servicemen who, stopping in the Philippines on their way home from the gulf, eagerly sought out child prostitutes.

A second world war is just over the horizon. This is not difficult to see. But what may be more difficult, perhaps even impossible at this moment, is to notice a certain resemblance between the enemies. Anti-Semitism can be found on both sides. And just as Hemingway with increasing bravado hurls himself into one more test of his manhood, a new movement celebrating masculine strength and courage is born just over the borders to the east.

April
That other quite wonderful side of my mother's honesty. I am so grateful for that time after she stopped drinking, when she was able to acknowledge what had happened between us.

The war will come and go, many will be dead afterward, among them Charlotte Salomon; arrested a second time and sent to Auschwitz, she perishes with the others. The carnage is shocking. And then the shock fades with memory. Now legends emerge. Stories with heroes.

April
Now it is my own life I must acknowledge.

Hemingway will continue to watch prizefights and bullfights. Guided by the same man who led Teddy Roosevelt through the veldt, he will go to Africa to shoot lions and tigers. But despite all his heroics, like his father he will continue to succumb to a terrible, inexplicable depression. Drinking no longer relieves his despair. He thinks of suicide.

April
Reading the autobiography of Fadwa Tuqan, the Palestinian poet: "Feelings of freedom, of breaking right away from the atmosphere of the ancient house choked with its prohibitions, endless commands and restraints, exhilarated me."

Finally he enters a hospital. And there the doctors treating him prescribe the same therapy that was administered to battle-fatigued soldiers who had lost their nerve during the First World War. He is given electroshock treatments. Once released, he does not feel like himself any longer. Something is missing. His mind does not work as well. He cannot use language with the same grace. A certain sharpness of focus has vanished. The brain perhaps irrevocably damaged. This is what pushes him finally to do it. He takes a loaded pistol and fires it into his own mouth.

April
The truth is, I must learn to listen to myself. I must learn not to abandon myself. "To stand by the truth," as Gandhi said.

I remember the story of his death. We spoke of it among ourselves. Did he die before or after Marilyn Monroe died? I cannot remember. Only that no one liked the manner of these deaths. Perhaps her death was more predictable, but then, one might have seen in him too a certain tendency in the same direction, except one did not like to think about it. He was a fixture of our time. An icon whose passing signaled a shifting of ground. Things change. They do not remain the same.

April
What is so astonishing about putting one's life into words, about telling a story, is that certain aspects of being are not only revealed but come to exist fully for the first time.

Of course this was a time of change. We were seeking transformation. Women wanted to remake the world and ourselves after another image. Equality. Justice. Peace. In the year of his death the word *feminism* was nearly but not yet pronounced. We were different than our parents, facing a future that we hoped would not repeat the old story.

April
I know now that beneath the old story of who I am a larger self exists, a self I am eager to explore.

Looking back on what has gone before, one cannot help but think that each event, each moment, could not have happened any other way. But this confuses an honest accounting of the past with another kind of denial. Each moment of life is filled with choices. Should I keep my hand moving over this page? Should I continue the narration as planned? As it has been written before?

Or am I free to imagine?

May

The necessity for patience, especially now. At the museum a troubled woman destroys a sand painting meticulously created over days by Tibetan monks. The monks are not disturbed. The work is a meditation. They simply begin again.

I am thinking of Hemingway the day he rode in the cockpit of an RAF bomber during the Second World War. He was reporting the progress of the bombardment of launch sites for the V-1 rocket on the coast of France. His biographers tell us that for several days before this flight he had the feeling he did not want to go on living. Now, I am imagining him as he watches this strange metallic birth, the falling slow, yet the movement of the plane so fast, as if inconsequential, the flak of fire missing the plane, the pilot quickly steering them back toward Dunsford, all over in a flash, exploding sites behind him, he and the pilot, the crew, even the higher command, become somewhat like missiles themselves, robots guided at a distance, going into space, headed toward their targets, which they find or do not find, blind, wounded or not wounded, surviving with little to tell (unless one makes up a story), with only the rush of blood, the fear, the heart beating fast, and then the return, automatic and dull, explosion mirroring explosion, but what after that is there? No answer comes to him.

May

How much time do we have? Joanna returned from Chernobyl. White face from all she has seen. Children unable to run, sick with radiation.

But now he will make no attempt to fill this silence. So as he climbs out of the cockpit the nothingness is all around him. He thinks of the battlefields of Piave. When he returned there were no signs of all that had transpired there. Except perhaps the grave-stones in some cemeteries, lined up in straight lines, all alike, and with the same silence, the same nothingness around them.

May

A child in the affected regions is told by his mother, "You are not supposed to touch the grass, you are not supposed to touch the soil, you are not supposed to touch the flowers, the vegetables," and so this child learns to hold back his hands, to ask, "Is this safe? Is this? Is this?"

It is no good continuing on as he has before. It has all gone flat for him. It being all he thought he had. It being what promised to rescue him from his fall. But in the stillness that he allows himself to hear now there is a hint of some possibility. Some other possibility. He knows the feeling when the words wring out of empti-ness what has not been said before. If he sticks to it this time, riding it all the way, riding it to wherever it will go, he has the feeling it will take him back to something, something he can almost feel, almost grasp with his hands.

May

I am not so different in my history of abandonment from anyone else after all. We have all been split away from each other, the earth, ourselves.

Of course, he cannot do this alone. The atmosphere must allow it. Even for him to see, there must be others willing to look in that direction.

May

Jews, Christians, Muslims, sharing one origin. Warfare among the members of this human family who have been fragmented, scattered to the winds.

And Charlotte?

May
To a certain region of the mind, nothing is ever lost. Perhaps we imagine we forget. But this is not possible.

The colors she is using are so vibrant, I will carry these images with me for all of my life.

May
Infinitesimally small bits of an atom enter a body, leaving a record of this passage.

I am imagining her now. She is singing as swiftly she finishes her last painting. It is an afterthought. Where will it go in the series? She cannot say. The image is so simple. A woman fleeing.

May
Civilians hidden in bunkers underground, the words unspoken, fragments of an earlier civilization to be found in the earth, a hand over a mouth, submerged histories, that image at the margin of our vision, government secrets, camouflage.

As soon as it dries it goes into the suitcase with the rest. Quickly then, take them to the doctor, take the whole series to the doctor and ask him to keep them until the war is over. Until you are safe. Safe.

May
Stripped away. A hand in the earth touching a bit of clay. Perhaps three thousand years ago. Emerging, like the sight of two whales, breaching for a moment, out of the Pacific Ocean, a thought, maybe a memory.

Or perhaps you do not put it in the suitcase. Perhaps it is a self-portrait and you have painted it on your way to an escape.

Perhaps you even leave it, in a room somewhere, or it blows out a window, and it is as if it never existed. No one will ever see it.

May
    Everywhere one sees signs of something different, possible, another way of being. If . . .

Because maybe you have had a stroke of luck. Maybe among all these confusing choices, despite your concern for the child you carry, you have gone into the mountains. Why is it that it breaks my heart now to imagine you alive? You are in that pass that runs between France and Italy. You are staring into the face of those rocks. Looking at the lines etched there. Beautiful as your drawings are beautiful. You think perhaps if you had time you might even be able to read them. They are like whispers. Exquisite whispers. Barely audible. But still you are certain now you can hear them.

May
    On the television last night, a program about astronomy. They say we are all made from star dust.

And you have the sense now of belonging. Because in the new mold that comes over you, right along with your hunger, your cold, your weariness, you know your story is the story. It is all one story.

May
    And they say that what appeared to be a void between the stars is filled with star dust coalescing into new stars.

This is something you would like to paint, you say to yourself, the stones, the mountain pass, the people walking at night. If you survive. But of course you cannot do it alone. The decision is out of your hands. It is all the others now who must make choices.

Those peasants living near the village in Italy. That woman who convinces her husband to hide you in the cellar. The baker who knows why he brings extra bread to your house. And perhaps even, the one in a million, that very exceptional soldier. He was so young when he enlisted. Just sixteen. He had no idea. His ideas were so foolish. He senses this family at the edge of the village is hiding someone. But he has also figured out something else. Something inside him that is buried. And so in this instant he looks the other way. Where is he looking? Numb and exhausted though he is, he wants to know, he wants this that he cannot yet even put into words but still he senses is there, and it is this promise, this hope, that keep him going.

May
A new edition of The Arabian Nights *arrived in the mail yesterday. I open it. Read the beginning. Read about Sheherazade. How she tells stories to save herself, and the world she loves.*

And you, though you don't know him, though you will never even see him, will retain some sense of him as you begin, after the war, to put down on paper all this that you saw and heard.

ABOUT THE AUTHOR

A well-known and respected feminist writer, poet, essayist, lecturer, teacher, playwright, and filmmaker, Susan Griffin is the author of more than twenty books—including *Woman and Nature: The Roaring Inside Her* and *Pornography and Silence: Culture's Revenge Against Nature*—and is the recipient of numerous grants and awards. Griffin lives in Berkeley, California.